WELCOME

ABOVE *A map of the Iberian Peninsula at the time of the conflict, showing the major provinces and locations relevant to the account you're about to read.*

The road to Waterloo began in the dust of an Iberian summer.

The Peninsula War may have only been a small part of Napoléon Bonaparte's downfall, but the additional agony of what he called his 'Spanish ulcer' began when he was at the height of his powers and continued until the eve of his defeat. The battles of Spain, Portugal and southern France showed that he could be beaten and they tied down enormous numbers of men and materiel.

Perhaps most importantly, it transformed the British Army - both how we see it and how it sees itself. For decades, the British Army had marched almost exclusively to pacify the nation's colonial outposts or seize new ones - and tellingly, those among the redcoat ranks who had seen recent service had done so at the behest of the rapine East India Company. The Peninsula War showed that the British Army could be a force for good. Despite the cynical and self-serving origins of the conflict, Great Britain stepped up when nobody else could and freed Portugal and Spain from the grip of a foreign invader.

The experience recast the British Army on a model that for good or ill saw it through two world wars and into the present, of a highly mobile and adaptable force spearheaded by the quick-thinking and hard-fighting British soldier. The battle honours of the Peninsula War and Waterloo take pride of place on the faded banners of most regiments and define how they see themselves, whether as dashing light dragoons, stalwart line infantry or daring light infantry.

For many regiments, colourful names like 'Talavera', 'Salamanca', 'Corunna', 'Badajoz' and 'Vitoria' dominate a third of their honours, speaking of an epic undertaking that moulded those who experienced it. Names we might be familiar with from the growled dialogue of Sean Bean's Richard Sharpe in the TV series of the same name, but unlike so many others that adorn pennants and crests, these are often battles about which we know little.

Here we hope to change all that.

James Hoare
Editor

CONTENTS

RIGHT *A 1823 romantic bust of Field Marshal Arthur Wellesley, the Duke of Wellington.*

6   **The Origins of the Peninsula War**
Discover the role played by royal machinations, commercial blockades, and imperial over-confidence in the eruption of the Peninsula War.

14   **The British Army in the Peninsula War**
From gentleman officers to "scum of the earth", Baker rifles to Brown Bess muskets, and red-coated line infantry to green-jacketed skirmishers.

24   **The Vimeiro Campaign**
The first British offensive in Portugal and the first victory of the war, covering the Battle of Roliça, the Battle of Vimeiro, and the controversial Convention of Sintra.

30   **Moore's Campaign**
Emperor Napoléon I leads the re-conquest of Spain while Britain fights at the Battle of Sahagún, the Battle of Benavente and the desperate Battle of A Coruña.

36   **The Oporto Campaign**
Lieutenant General Arthur Wellesley returns to Portugal and drives Marshal Soult from the north of the country at the Battle of Grijó and the daring Second Battle of Oporto.

42   **The Talavera Campaign**
Wellesley advances into Spain for the first time and discovers that his Spanish allies leave a lot to be desired at the Battle of Alcántara and the Battle of Talavera.

50   **The Lines of Torres Vedras**
Taking no more chances, Wellesley - now Viscount Wellington - embarks upon an ambitious line of fortifications to protect Lisbon.

54   **Masséna's Campaign**
Marshal Masséna pushes into Portugal to test his mettle against Wellington at the Combat of Barquilla, the Combat on the Côa, the Siege of Almeida, the Battle of Buçaco, the Battle of Sobral, and the Battle of Sabugal.

62   **Beresford's Campaign**
With Portugal secured, Major General Beresford tries to drive the French from the Spanish border at the Battle of Campo Maior, the Second Siege of Badajoz, and the Battle of La Albuera.

The 88th (or Connaught Rangers), the shock troops of Major General Thomas Picton's 'Fighting 3rd' Division charge down the mountainside and into the French at the Battle of Buçaco (September 27, 1810)

68 The Almeida Campaign
Wellington regains control of the border in the northeast at the Siege of Almeida, the Battle of Fuentes de Oñoro, the Battle of El Bodón, and the Combat of El Carpio.

74 The Salamanca Campaign
The greatest confrontation of Wellington's career to date drives Joseph-Napoléon Bonaparte from Madrid. Covering the Second Siege of Ciudad Rodrigo, the Third Siege of Badajoz, the Raid on Almaraz, Siege of the Salamanca Forts, the Battle of Salamanca, Battle of García Hernández, and the Combat at Majahalonda.

84 The Pyrenees Campaign
Following the dismal Siege of Burgos, the Battle of Venta del Pozo and the Battle of Tordesillas, Wellington embarks on the final fight for Spain at the Battle of San Millan-Osma, the Battle of Vitoria, the Battle of Tolosa, the Siege of San Sebastián, and the Battle of the Pyrenees.

94 The Bayonne Campaign
With events turning rapidly against Emperor Napoléon I, Wellington drives the Peninsula War into France to deny Marshal Soult the opportunity to recover and regroup. The Battle of Bidassoa, the Battle of the Nivelle, the Battle of the Nive, the Battle of Orthez, the Battle of Tabes, Battle of Toulouse, and the senseless Battle of Bayonne maintain pressure on the dying First French Empire.

101 The Hundred Days
The most tumultuous period in a profoundly tumultuous era as Napoléon I escapes exile on the island of Elba and strikes at the Prussian and the British armies before they're able to gather strength.

106 The Battle of Waterloo
Wellington and his battle-hardened veterans of the Peninsula War take their place in history, defeating Napoléon I for the final time in the climatic battle that remade Europe for a new century.

EDITORIAL AND DESIGN TEAM
Author: James Hoare
Designer: Mike Carr
Managing Editor: Roger Mortimer

PRODUCTION AND MARKETING
Production Manager: Janet Watkins
Head Of Design: Steve Donovan
Head Of Advertising Sales: Brodie Baxter
Head Of Distance Selling: Martin Steele
Head Of Circulation: Ann Saundry
Head Of Finance: Nigel Cronin
Chief Digital Officer: Vicky Macey
Chief Customer Officer: Gaynor Hemingway-Gibbs

Chief Content & Commercial Officer: Mark Elliott
Group CEO: Adrian Cox

CONTACTS
Key Publishing Ltd
PO Box 100, Stamford
Lincolnshire, PE9 1XQ
E-mail: enquiries@keypublishing.com
www.keypublishing.com

Distribution: Seymour Distribution Ltd, 2 Poultry Avenue, London, EC1A 9PP.
Tel: 020 7429 4000.
Fax: 020 7429 4001

Printed by: Precision Colour Print, Telford, UK
Printed in England
ISBN: 9781913295011

The entire contents of this special edition is copyright © 2019. No part of it may be reproduced in any form or stored in any form of retrieval system without the prior permission of the publisher.

Published by Key Publishing Ltd.
www.britainatwar.com

The Road to Waterloo — THE ORIGINS OF THE PENINSULA WAR

The Ruin of SPAIN

The Origins of the Peninsula War

"The English are a nation of merchants," the Austrian Emperor Francis II famously observed in 1805. "To secure for themselves the commerce of the world, they are willing to set the continent in flames."

By 1806 the United Kingdom of Great Britain and Ireland and the French Empire of Napoléon Bonaparte were locked in an economic war of attrition. Through his carefully constructed network of alliances and conquests, the bulk of continental Europe marched to the beat of the Emperor's drum, but the oceans - the vital arteries of commerce - were firmly under the gunsights of the Royal Navy.

Defeat at the Battle of Trafalgar (October 21, 1805) cost the French navy 13 ships (as well as 11 belonging to its unreliable Spanish ally). This was the culmination of a disastrous naval campaign that had virtually destroyed France's ability to project power across the oceans, already weakened by the loss of Caribbean colonies to Great Britain and insurrection in Haiti.

Ships of the line having failed the Emperor, he declared on November 21, 1806 that "No vessel coming directly from England [sic], or from the English colonies, or having been there since the publication of the present decree, shall be received into any port."

Great Britain's commercial prowess could also be a weakness, and Emperor Napoléon I became fixated with the idea of bringing Britain to its knees through the 'Continental System', an economic blockade that closed Europe to trade with Britain and its colonies. Britain, in response, sealed off the oceans to France and its allies, disregarding international norms and seized cargos bound for the ports of the Continental System regardless of which flag they sailed under. Neutral states quickly found themselves forced to pick sides, lest the British impound their cargo at sea, or the French impound them in port, but some tried to tread a fine line between the two.

LEFT: *Francisco de Goya's harrowing 1814 painting 'The Third of May 1808' shows the execution of Spanish rebels by the occupying French. A departure from the realism prevalent in historical scenes, this is regarded by many art historians as the first piece of 'modern' art.*

Whilst Spain was part of the Continental System and a formal French ally, it was a fair-weather friend to Emperor Napoléon I. The Kingdom of Portugal was even more reluctant to act, like Spain it had an overseas empire in the Americas that would be placed at considerable risk by antagonising Britain, but unlike Spain, Portugal had been allied to England and then the United Kingdom since the Treaty of Windsor (May 9, 1386). With a view to rendering his blockade watertight, Emperor Napoléon I ordered 20,000 French troops under General Jean-Andoche Junot to assemble at Bayonne, at the northern tip of the Pyrenees Mountains - the natural border between France and Spain.

After being repeatedly warned that their support for the British violated Portuguese neutrality, France issued an ultimatum on July 1807: join the Continental System, declare war on Britain, arrest all British subjects and impound British goods or they would be forced to do so.

Napoleonic France was at the very peak of its territorial expansion and influence, with the Emperor having parachuted his immediate family into thrones across Europe to magnanimously remould the old order in the image of French 'liberty, egality and fraternity' at bayonet point. When the Emperor sneezed, Kings and Princes alike stood ready with a tissue, but all of that was soon to be undone by a six-year war for mastery of the Iberian Peninsula that demonstrated to a cowed continent that the unstoppable French military machine could be stopped in its tracks.

Why now, France had suddenly chronically over-extended itself is attributed in part to the departure of Napoléon I's wily foreign minister, the infamous Charles Maurice de Talleyrand-Périgord. If "war is the continuation of politics by other means" as the Prussian general Carl von Clausewitz famously proclaimed, then Talleyrand was every ▶▶▶

TOP: *Don João, Duke of Bragança, the Prince Regent of Portugal, painted sometime between 1802 and 1806 just prior to the beginning of the Peninsula War.*

ABOVE: *A sporting gun called a miquelet, inlaid with gold and believed to be a personal hunting piece belonging to the Duke of Bragança, who preferred idleness over affairs of state.*

LEFT: *Manuel de Godoy in 1790, shortly before his appointment as Prime Minister. Godoy rose through the ranks thanks to the patronage of the Spanish Queen, Maria Luisa, and was granted the title 'Prince of Peace', establishing him as a potential heir to King Carlos IV.*

The Road to Waterloo
THE ORIGINS OF THE PENINSULA WAR

ABOVE: *A British cartoon of the ghosts of the Spanish Kings pouring scorn on Prince Fernando, Queen Maria Luisa (with Manuel de Godoy burying his head in her lap) and King Carlos IV. Napcléon Bonaparte and John Bull look on.*

bit the master strategist as his patron. His resignation in 1807 was to prove fatal for a regime that had accrued so many enemies as France had in so short a time.

A land of liars and scoundrels

A land untouched by the 18th century Enlightenment, Portugal was a holdout of absolute monarchy and the baroque politics of Lisbon's royal court had long been an object of intense frustration to the French. Marshal Jean Lannes, the short-lived French ambassador to Portugal and close confidant of Emperor Napoléon I, wrote within weeks of his appointment in 1801 that the Portuguese foreign minister was "an English pawn and a lying scoundrel" and that the Prince Regent was "a total non-entity - all he wants to do is hunt, then sing and have people tell him how good he is."

The weak and indecisive Don João, Duke of Braganza, who ruled on behalf of his increasingly unstable mother, Dona Maria I, made a desperate attempt to do the impossible: appease both major powers whilst filling the nation's coffers. Increasingly isolated from political reality by a clique of advisors, he fancied himself a master statesman, but to Britain and France, his vacillating was painfully obvious.

He even suggested to King George III that he make a show of declaring war on Britain while remaining covertly true to their alliance. On the other hand, he made repeated concessions to France and Spain - allowing Spanish ships to sail under Portuguese flags and refusing to sign a formal contract to supply Britain's Mediterranean fleet. They did nothing, however, when it was a private matter between Portuguese subjects and the Admiralty. In short, Portugal twisted in the wind, appearing to cater to all concerns whilst satisfying none.

London's interpretation of the dark clouds gathering over Iberia was much clearer headed than the view from Lisbon. With its army and navy in a miserable

The Portuguese royal family embark for Brazil from the port of Lisbon, depriving the French the use of their fleet.

Manuel de Godoy is seized by the Spanish royal guard as King Carlos VI attempts to placate the Mutiny of Aranjuez (March 17-19, 1808).

> "A British flotilla was dispatched to sit menacingly off the mouth of the River Targus as a platform for military action. With the flotilla was a force of 10,000 troops to be landed to either help the Portuguese defend themselves or to capture their fleet."

condition, there was no reasonable expectation of Portugal being able to offer much resistance and for Britain, the paramount concern was to deny the French use of the sizable Portuguese fleet.

A British flotilla was dispatched to sit menacingly off the mouth of the River Tagus as a platform for military action. With the flotilla was a force of 10,000 troops to be landed to either help the Portuguese defend themselves or to capture their fleet. The latter had to be undertaken swiftly to prevent the Portuguese from offering any resistance, and the true nature of their mission kept in strictest secrecy.

With France also preparing to resume hostilities against the great land armies of the Kingdom of Prussia and the Russian Empire, Portugal remained convinced that they could simply ride out the French threats. Lieutenant-General James St Clair-Erskine, 2nd Earl of Rosslyn, who had been sent specifically to rouse the Portuguese government from its self-obsessed lethargy was forced to admit on September 2, 1806: "I am sorry to say that I cannot see the least grounds to expect vigorous efforts from this nation in its own defence."

The operetta in Spain

Britain's plans to make war either alongside Portugal or against Portugal wasn't the only act of political cynicism unfolding. Discussions between France and the Kingdom of Spain had resulted in the secret Treaty of Fontainebleau (October 1807), which committed both powers to an invasion of Portugal and the partition of the country into three parts.

The very northern tip around Porto was to be designated the Kingdom of Northern Lusitania and gifted to Charles Louis, the infant King of Etruria (Tuscany) and grandson of the Spanish king, in exchange for Tuscany becoming part of the French Empire's Italian possessions. The south of Portugal would be ruled by the Spanish Prime Minister, Manuel de Godoy, as Prince of Algarves and the central belt around Lisbon would be administered directly by France.

King Carlos IV of Spain had reacted with fraternal horror to the French Revolution, but a series of defeats had forced him to terms with the regime that had beheaded his distant kin - both France and Spain were ruled by different branches of the House of Bourbon. Although Spain had seen some measure of reform in comparison to Portugal - accelerated by fears of Madame Guillotine strolling through its own plazas - the nation's conservative forces remained deeply entrenched. This, after all, was the land of the Inquisition.

Although a Franco-Spanish alliance against Britain was in many respects the natural order of things, a nation of cardinals and counts had

THE ROAD TO WATERLOO 9

The Road to Waterloo

THE ORIGINS OF THE PENINSULA WAR

An 1808 portrait of Joseph-Napoléon Bonaparte in the robes of King of Spain. For most of his 'reign', his authority stretched no further than Madrid.

plenty to be wary of in the ambitious and expansionist Napoléon I. Don Carlos IV entrusted Manuel de Godoy - young, handsome and rumoured to be the lover of the Queen Consort, Dona Maria Luisa - to guide him through these troubled times, but Godoy was as much a political liability as he was a firm hand on the political levers.

Once wealthy beyond all imagination, in a matter of decades the glittering Spanish Empire, which stretched from South America to the Philippines, had become an enormous drain on the state rather than the source of its wealth. The cost of its security had grown so great that the responsibility

RIGHT: *All the gear but no idea. An ornate 1809 halberd produced for King Joseph-Napoléon of Spain's royal guard.*

had been placed in the hands of the locally-raised militia, while the Spanish army and navy limped on in desperate need of investment and reform.

In Spain proper, taxes and tithes were collected on feudal lines that saw enormous funds gathered by the landowning aristocracy and the local church from the poor, agricultural peasants, and that money was only used to improve infrastructure or the local economy if it was guaranteed to generate more revenue in return.

Only the fraternal dependence on the French Bourbons had helped maintain the illusion of Spanish potency and following a disastrous attempt to roll back the French Revolution, this had been replaced by a dependence on the Napoleonic regime instead. Godoy was no fool, he wrote to the Queen in 1801: "In so far as France is concerned, the only thing that France can be counted on for is that the French will never be friends of anything other than their own interests." He simply had little room to manoeuvre when it came to resisting those interests.

Blamed for the loss of Spanish ships and prestige at the Battle of Trafalgar and seen to embody Spain's disastrous pro-French foreign policy, Godoy was distrusted by the aristocracy and clergy, who focused their hopes on the Crown Prince, Don Fernando. Vain and easily led, the colonial administrator Ramón García de León y Pizarro was moved to comment of Don Fernando: "His head was so weak that he always moved in the opposite direction to that of sense and reason."

The Prince of Asturias - as the Spanish heir is usually known - resented Godoy's influence, and in turn, Godoy sought to oust the Prince from the succession. Emperor Napoléon I was perfectly happy to exploit the discord between the two, allowing the arrogant Prime Minister and the boorish Crown Prince to fall over themselves seeking French favour. The former acquiesced to the transit of French soldiers through Spain towards the Portuguese border - and mobilised 25,500 Spanish troops under French command - and the latter sought the Emperor's blessing for his conspiracies.

Emperor Napoléon I was not blind to Spain's wavering commitments, nor its depreciating value as a military ally. It's argued that he had no intention of partitioning Portugal (he made no plans for it, beyond the terms of Fontainebleau) and serving it up to the Spanish King's proxies and instead the movement of troops across the jagged Pyrenees had a dual purpose: Spain too was firmly in the Emperor's sights and as they marched, French military engineers made detailed sketches of the Spanish fortifications.

The invasion of Iberia

On October 12, 1807, the fiery General Jean-Andoche Junot - nicknamed 'The Tempest' - ordered his army to begin crossing the Bidasoa River into Spain. By November 30, Lisbon had fallen. Taken by surprise and stymied by indecision, Don João, Duke of Bragança chose appeasement rather than resistance. He declared war on Great Britain on October 20, rounded up the nation's British population by November 8, refused to mobilise the militia, and dispatched emissary after emissary to prostrate themselves before the French marshal.

Only when Admiral Sir William Sidney Smith of the Royal Navy came ashore with a French newspaper, its headline boasting of the overthrow of the House of Bragança, did Don João realise there was no hope of negotiation. Accepting the protection of the British fleet, the royal family fled for Brazil long before French columns entered the capital, having finally overcome the only real resistance offered by Portugal - torrential rain and provincial roads.

The sight of French columns marching across the Spanish countryside, and the treatment of the Spanish crown as a junior partner in its own affairs, rankled with the Spanish aristocracy. In turn, this fuelled the resentment that pooled around the feet of the unruly Don Fernando, Prince of Asturias, and he was happy to use it to his own advantage.

On October 27, Don Fernando was arrested for treason, accused of plotting to overthrow his father and murder his mother and Godoy. The grand soap opera of the House of Bourbon helped disguise French ambitions, with each party convinced the continuing build-up of foreign troops was an endorsement of their rival positions. They saw nothing untoward in France asking permission to transit an extra 40,000 men after they had already entered the country.

In January 1808, Emperor Napoléon I finally intervened directly and secured the Prince's freedom and by March, some 100,000 French troops were garrisoned in Spain. The total collapse of Portugal with little more than token bloodshed left the Emperor firmly convinced that Spain would roll over before him like a beaten dog.

On February 16, the invasion began with a diversion so far-fetched that it would have been dismissed in fiction: the French troops at Pamplona staged a snowball fight. As the Spanish garrison watched, they suddenly rushed the gates, taking the town and the fortress which was the first strategic waypoint on the road to Madrid. The citadels of San Sebastián, Barcelona and Burgos were also occupied, effectively moving the French frontier down from the Pyrenees and into the Spanish interior.

The Spanish royal family began a flight to the south. With the bitterest irony, they planned to follow in the footsteps of the Braganza neighbours they had betrayed by taking up residence in their American colonies. On March 17, they stopped overnight at Aranjuez - 30 miles south of Madrid - where an angry mob overran the King's guards, believing - thanks to

"On October 12, 1807, the fiery General Jean-Andoche Junot - nicknamed 'The Tempest' - ordered his army to begin crossing the Bidasoa River into Spain. By November 30, Lisbon had fallen."

ABOVE LEFT: *'The Corsican Spider in his Web!' The captive nations of Europe lay at Napoleon's mercy as he attempts to bite down on Spain, by the British cartoonist Thomas Rowlandson.*

THE ROAD TO WATERLOO 11

The Road to Waterloo

THE ORIGINS OF THE PENINSULA WAR

THE SLEEP OF REASON PRODUCES MONSTERS: FRANCISCO DE GOYA'S WAR

An 1825 portrait of the troubled Francisco de Goya by Vicente López Portaña.

Francisco de Goya's direction of travel was symptomatic of where the nation's educated classes found themselves. No friend to the powerful conservative forces that guided Spain - in 1813 some of his racier life studies had been seized by the Inquisition for obscenity - and a supporter of the French Revolution, the events of the Dos de Mayo Uprising plunged him into a deep depression.

Once a court painter, his art style now took on a nightmarish and confrontational quality as he sought to depict the horrific events he had witnessed and the feelings they inspired. His health had long been in decline, possibly of poisoning from grinding his own lead whites, and a set of 1797 etchings with the caption "The sleep of reason produces monsters" alludes to his deepening inner turmoil.

Goya spent the Peninsula War keeping a studiously low profile, but once the French occupation lifted, he engaged in some of his most celebrated projects, the so-called 'black paintings'. This began with the painting 'Dos de Mayo', depicting the French North African auxiliaries charging the crowds, and 'El Tres de Mayo', depicting the summary executions, and a series of 82 prints entitled 'Los Desastres de la Guerra' ('The Disasters of the War'), showing distressing scenes of privation and cruelty from the conflict.

One of Goya's 82 prints showing nightmarish scenes from the Peninsula War depicts a woman with a baby under one arm and a spear under the other killing a French soldier.

---

the propaganda of the Crown Prince - that Godoy had sold the country to France.

The mob forced Don Carlos IV to dismiss the minister, briefly imprisoning him at the castle of Villaviciosa de Odón, but when this failed to quell the violence, the King abdicated and escaped with his life. The newly proclaimed King Fernando VII entered Madrid on March 24 to the adulation of the crowds, but the saviour of Spain had a significant problem: he pinned his hopes on Emperor Napoléon I.

In the absence of the King, the French army under Marshal Joachim-Napoléon Murat - the Emperor's flamboyant brother-in-law - had occupied Madrid and it was instantly obvious where the power lay. Now safe from the crowds, Don Carlos IV recanted his abdication and forced Don Fernando to petition the Emperor for his 'paternal protection'. In response, he was told: "When you are king in your turn, you will know how sacred are the rights of thrones. Every advance made towards a foreign sovereign by a hereditary prince is criminal."

Just like that, the final stage of Emperor Napoléon I's trap was sprung. After subtly encouraging the Crown Prince for months, he had manoeuvred him into a position where he appeared a ruthless usurper. The Emperor concluded menacing: "A few murders may be committed on my isolated soldiers, but the ruin of Spain will be the result."

Murat convinced Don Fernando of the need to present his case to the Emperor in person, and the Spanish Bourbons - Don Carlos IV, Dona Maria Luisa and Don Fernando - were summoned to Bayonne. They must have surely known that the best the victor could expect was to rule on as a puppet of France, but in that, they wouldn't have been alone among Europe's monarchs. Yet still, they went.

The King, Queen and their Prime Minister were sent into exile, and the usurper was placed under luxurious house arrest at Château de Valençay in the heart of France. The Spanish crown was given to the Emperor's eldest brother, Joseph-Napoléon Bonaparte, who had successfully brought the sledgehammer of the French Enlightenment to the moribund old order over his energetic two years as King of Naples and Sicily.

"Death to the French!"

The Spanish people showed a shrewdness that had so far deserted their rulers. Although some Spanish intellectuals - such as the artist Francisco de Goya - hoped that the end of the old regime might accelerate the country's unfinished reforms, the departure of the Bourbons and the imposition of a foreign ruler provoked widespread nationalist revolt.

Fuelled by rumours of a French coup, crowds of Spaniards prowled the streets of Madrid and the air thick with anticipation.

Credit for instigating the Dos de Mayo (Second of May) Uprising is long attributed to a locksmith who witnessed the carriages spirit the royal family from the city and cried out "Treason! They have taken our King away from us and they want to take all members of the royal family. Death to the French!"

The mob stormed the palace, overrunning the French sentries and only vicious police action by the French garrison brought Madrid back under control. The Spanish soldiers in the city remained confined to their garrisons, ensure what steps to take and indeed whose side they were supposed to be on, having been assured until this point that the French were their allies.

The next morning Marshal Joachim-Napoléon Murat proclaimed: "The population of Madrid, led astray, has given itself to revolt and murder. French blood has flowed. It demands vengeance. All those arrested in the uprising, arms in hand, will be shot." Public meetings were prohibited, and craftsmen found in the streets with the tools of their trade - knives, hammers, even scissors - were arrested. An estimated 400 of the previous day's malcontents faced los fusilamientos - death by firing squad.

The damage had been done. Murat had restored order, but the repression that followed the Dos de Mayo Uprising plunged vast swathes of the country into open revolt, its character defined in part by two of the words it gifted to the English language: 'junta' and 'guerrilla'.

In Spain's provinces where regional identities blazed far more fiercely than national ones - particularly Asturias, Galicia and Catalonia - patriotic clergy, magistrates, army officers and aristocrats formed 'juntas' - meaning 'councils' - and seized control. They answered - in theory at least - to a Supreme Junta, which exercised power on behalf of the King, whoever he might end up being. The Spanish army, scattered around the country, was now in arms and the juntas ordered the people to rise up as an irregular guerrilla force, the Corso Terrestre ('Land Corsairs'), which harassed the French supply lines, raided their depots, slaughtered their patrols, and ensured that the only parts of Spain in which Murat could claim dominance were those directly under the boots of a French grenadier.

"Each day saw the murder of several Frenchmen, and I travelled over this assassins' countryside as warily as if it was a volcano," recalled General Guillaume-Mathieu Dumas. Just as suppressing an uprising had instigated a war, the act of tightening control over the European continent had resulted in the exact reverse. Spain and Portugal had been invaded, but they hadn't been conquered, and the French Empire was vulnerable.

> "Credit for instigating the Dos de Mayo (Second of May) Uprising is long attributed to a locksmith who witnessed the carriages spirit the royal family from the city and cried out "Treason! They have taken our King away from us and they want to take all members of the royal family. Death to the French!""

'The Second of May 1808', also known as 'The Charge of the Mamelukes' was painted in 1814 by Goya as a companion piece to 'The Third of May 1808' and shows the North African cavalry of the French Imperial Guard riding down the protestors.

THE ROAD TO WATERLOO 13

The Road to Waterloo   THE BRITISH ARMY

Over the Hills AND FAR AWAY

The British Army in the Peninsula War

ended Marshal Joachim-Napoléon Murat's hope of a swift victory and forced the increasingly harassed and overstretched occupiers to withdraw to the River Ebro, turning the kingdom of Joseph-Napoléon Bonaparte - or King José I, to give him his Spanish name - into a rump state barely more than a month into its existence.

France's formerly cowed northern rivals, Prussia and Russia, looked on with growing interest, but it was Great Britain that was keenest to exploit the Emperor's weaknesses, even if it made brothers-

LEFT *HRH Prince Frederick, Duke of York and Albany, the discredited commander-in-chief of the British Army at the start of the Peninsula War.*

The dance of the Generals

This was scarcely the only small irony of the British expedition. The formidable Rock of Gibraltar, which had been a British possession for almost a century had been considerably reinforced over the preceding months of the invasion threat - under the reasonable assumption that there would be a Franco-Spanish campaign to reclaim it - and now held a garrison of some 5,000 men under the acting governor, Lieutenant-General Sir Hew Whitefoord Dalrymple. They too could now be diverted to aid the men they had expected to be fighting tooth and nail to hold onto the British Empire's vital Mediterranean depot.

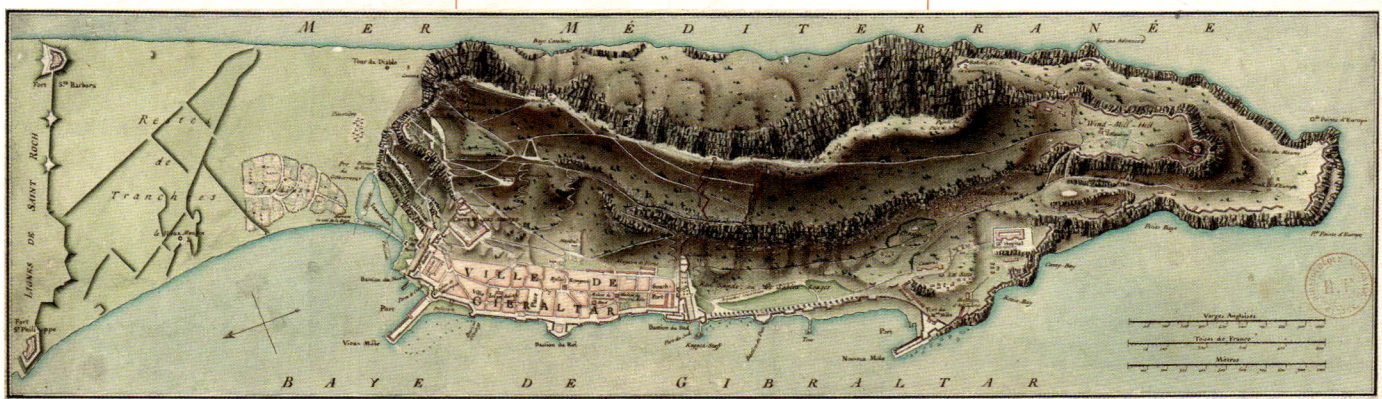

The widespread popular revolt in Spain struck the edifice of Napoleonic France like a sledgehammer to reveal the first crack in what had been decades of expansion.

Against all expectations (even their own expectations), the forces of the juntas secured several totemic victories, although these must be carefully qualified. The attacks on Zaragoza (June 15 - August 14, 1808), Gerona (June 20-21, 1808), and Valencia (June 26, 1808) were all conducted by complacent French commanders who expected the Spanish - who they viewed as backward, cowardly and borderline subhuman - to crumble in the face of blazing blue ranks of professional infantry. In defiance of their bigotry, the smaller numbers of defenders - mixtures of the Spanish regular army, local militia and enthusiastic volunteers, under leaders of variable ability - held onto the Medieval fortifications until the enemy was forced to withdraw

Finally, Spanish victory in the field at the Battle of Bailén (July 16-19, 1808) effectively

LEFT *'Halt of Troops' by John Augustus Atkinson, showing a British Army bagged train resting in the field, 1808.*

in-arms out of yesterday's bitter foes. In addition to London's existing aims of crowbarring open the Continental System, they could now increase their commercial footprint into Spanish-held South America, trade and treaties having long proven more effective instruments of British foreign policy than grapeshot alone.

This, of course, meant a large-scale continental land campaign - the sort that Britain had traditionally been wary of and preferred to outsource to the likes of Austria or Prussia - not just a naval one. Freeing Spain and Portugal from the insidious influence of Emperor Napoleon I would require more than prowling the Caribbean and, as the civil servant and satirist Richard Brinsley Sheridan later put it, "filching sugar islands."

As recently as 1807 Britain had embarked on an unsuccessful filching expedition against Spanish possessions in what is now Argentina and Uruguay, and an army of some 16,000 soldiers had been gathered in County Cork, Ireland, earmarked for an operation against Venezuela. Instead, they would now be diverted to liberate Venezuela's colonial overlords, such are the ironies of early 19th-century realpolitik.

ABOVE *A 1799 French military map by Jean-Denis Barbié du Bocage showing the formidable fortifications of the British garrison at Gibraltar.*

The Cork detachment had been placed under the command of a man on the cusp of becoming a military legend, the recently promoted Lieutenant-General Sir Arthur Wellesley, not yet Duke of Wellington. Extremely well-connected, he had acquitted himself valiantly in India and had the patronage of Robert Stewart, Viscount Castlereagh, the Secretary of State for War and the Colonies, and George Canning, Secretary of State for Foreign Affairs.

Castlereagh and Canning supplied Wellesley with new orders and astonishing freedom of action, not so much 'mission creep' as a 'mission stampede'. He was instructed to set sail for the Peninsula - not even the country is specified, let alone the region ▶

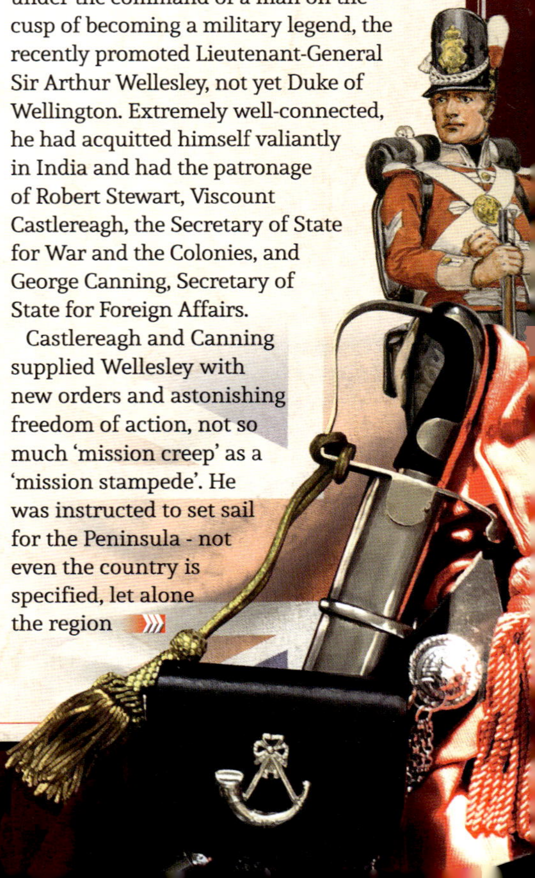

The Road to Waterloo
THE BRITISH ARMY

INFANTRY FORMATIONS

1. THE LINE
Although less manoeuvrable than the column, the principle aim of the line was to present the maximum number of muskets towards the enemy. Infantry regiments formed into a line, usually two ranks deep - although they could be formed three and four deep when greater depth was required to withstand an oncoming bayonet charge.

Firing was either from flanks to centre (which created a ripple of fire outwards in); from centre to flanks (in which the fire rippled outwards); or by grand divisions (in which each 'division' of four companies fired in turn to create a devastating mass volley).

2. THE COLUMN
The standard formation for movement as it was easier to control, and other formations could be more quickly reached from a column position. The company lined up in two ranks, either in 'close order' (one pace from the man in front and behind) or 'open order' (two paces), and proceeded at 'ordinary time' (75 paces a minute, which gave the column an average speed of two-and-a-half miles per hour), 'quick march' (108 paces), or 'wheeling step' (120 paces).

Each company then lined up behind the other and the standard distance between companies was equal to the frontage of that company, which was called 'open column'. So, if the face of a company was 20 yards, there would be 20 yards between them and the company behind, from that you can work 'half distance' and 'quarter distance'. The latter two were the preferred for most situations.

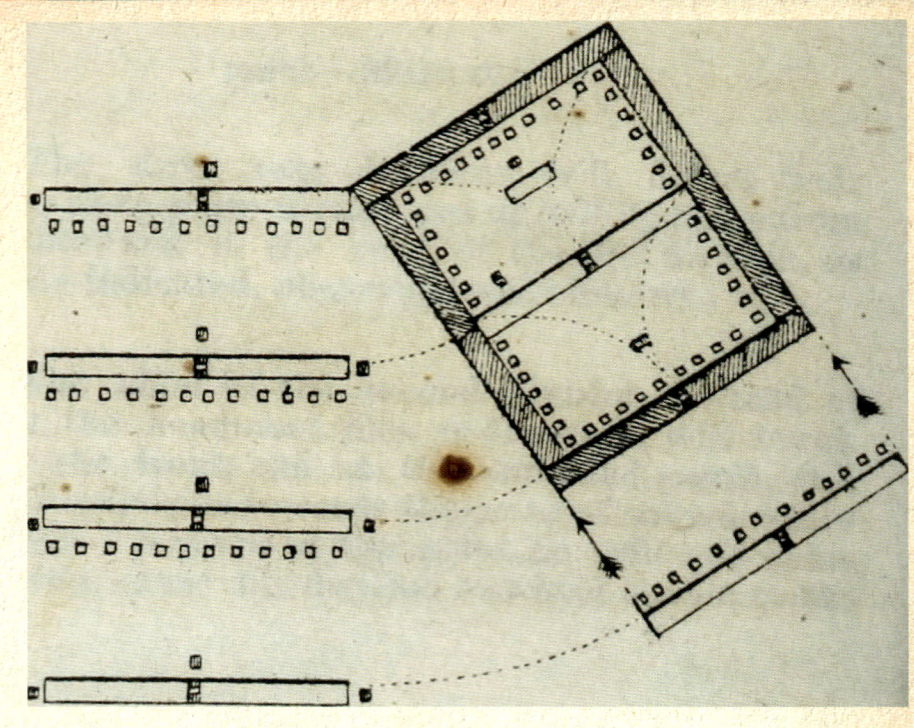

An illustration in the American Civil War drill manual Rifle and Infantry Tactics (1863), showing how a column can wheel to form a square.

3. THE SQUARE
More often an oblong than a square, the standard response to an enemy cavalry charge was to form into a hollow square formation. Forming a square was often the difference between life and death and as a result it had the most recognisable drum beat - a continuous, ominous roll that left no room for miscommunication.

The men formed up four to six ranks deep, with the first two ranks kneeling to present bayonets, and creating a fearsome wall of fire and blades that would deter any head-on charge. The officers, the regimental colours and the wounded usually took their place in the hollow centre, and the process was so well drilled that a battalion (or multiple battalions) was capable of marching in a square without losing formation.

A broken line or group of skirmishers who risked being overwhelmed could form a 'rallying square', an ad hoc knot of troops who formed into the same kneeling and standing configuration, and were often capable of seeing off a force of greater numbers.

- with an aim of forcing "the entire and absolute evacuation of the Peninsula, by the troops of France."

Wellesley and his army of Cork set sail on July 12, before the political fallout caught up with the two ministers and promptly set off after his protegee. At the time of Wellesley's command being approved, the estimate of the French forces occupying Portugal was put at 5,000 men, but a more recent report had updated this to 20,000, causing Horse Guards - the traditional headquarters of the British Army - to wake up with a start.

For many of the ageing generals warming the leather-backed armchairs in Horse Guards, the consensus was that Wellesley was a purely political appointment and too junior to be entrusted with such a crucial endeavour. *The Daily Advertiser* opined "we have every reason for fearing that this important command, on which will depend the fate of Spain, of Britain, and indeed the whole Civilised World, is at the moment, the subject of a dirty intrigue in the Cabinet."

At the very top of the British Army, connections, money and ability gave way to the issue of seniority. Above the rank of lieutenant-colonel, the business of purchasing commissions was replaced by the relentless advance of time and promotions were dished out based on how long ago they had obtained the rank of lieutenant-colonel - in instances where two generals of equivalent rank were present, the one whose commission was obtained earliest would take command.

What this meant was that once officers had survived the 'active' stage of their careers, they were destined to crawl further and further up the chain of command through no other virtue than simply living long enough. In 1808, the British Army had 130 lieutenant-generals and only three of them were more junior than Wellesley, so

Castlereagh and Canning were determined to do all they could to keep Wellesley isolated from challengers. That Wellesley was one of only a handful of generals with recent experience of not only battle, but of winning battles, was immaterial.

The British Army's commander-in-chief, Field Marshal HRH Prince Frederick, Duke of York and Albany, had ambitions to lead the army in Portugal and Spain himself but his uninspiring campaign in the Low Countries had cost him the confidence of Parliament and invited the ridicule of the public. For evidence of the latter, all that needs to be said is that Prince Frederick is the leading contender as the subject for the nursery rhyme 'The Grand Old Duke of York' which ensures his reputation for indecision and futility is cherished by each generation anew. However, as the second son of King George III, it was important not to put his nose out of joint - and to his credit, the Duke of York and Albany had proven himself more valuable as a military reformer than a field commander.

Fortunately, the size of the expeditionary force and its piecemeal composition was deemed to be beneath the dignity (such as it was) of the Duke of York and Albany, and with the same reasoning, Castlereagh was able to artfully fend off General John Pitt, 2nd Earl Chatham, the son of one past Prime Minister and the brother of its most recent prior incumbent. Sir John Moore, who had been dispatched on a disastrous expedition to Sweden with 10,000 men, was returning and having been denied the opportunity to shed French blood in Northern Europe, he was an obvious contender.

Canning, however, couldn't stand the man but could see him off by finding someone more senior who was more obviously suited to the Iberian theatre. Eventually, the competing interests of government and jealously guarded military tradition settled on Dalrymple in Gibraltar. Overall, he was 13th in the order of seniority and although had spent only one year out of his 45 year military career actually in the field, he was already deeply immersed in the bewildering political sensitivities of the Peninsula.

Castlereagh and Canning, meanwhile, were happy with Dalrymple as he would be an absentee landlord to Wellesley for much of the near future, unable to leave his garrison until he had been properly relieved, and distracted with trying to negotiate the transfer of British soldiers to help bolster the Spanish garrison at Cádiz.

What's more, Dalrymple had been given the political nightmare of Prince Leopold of Salerno to deal with. The son of the deposed Bourbon King of Naples (although still King of Sicily) and grandson of King Charles III of Spain, Prince Leopold had chosen this moment to attempt to establish himself as a potential figurehead for Spanish resistance. It's easy to understand Emperor Napoléon I's pathological hatred of the extended Bourbon dynasty: he'd booted the Spanish branch out of Spain and the Italian branch out of Naples, only for one of the latter's lesser princelings to pop up in Gibraltar making mischief on behalf of the former.

While Dalrymple focused on the sensitive business of trying to fob off the Prince of Salerno (the trust of the juntas was precarious enough without being seen to meddle in the Spanish succession), General Sir Harry Burrard, 1st Baronet was appointed his deputy and set off in pursuit of Wellesley to temporarily take over command in the field.

Coats of red and green

The opening for a land war in Iberia didn't exactly play to Britain's strengths. The British Army was small, but a number of recent reforms had done an enormous amount to make them fit for the rapidly changing 19th century battlefield.

In 1808, the infantry - the home of the vast majority of the fighting men in the conflict - consisted of three regiments of Foot Guards and 101 regiments of line infantry (or foot). A sense of regimental identity was still in the process of being fostered and from 1782 most had taken on a county affiliation or other affectation. Although this was too recent to have affected the composition of the regiment, the events of the Peninsula War would help to form a rich internal mythology for each regiment that bound them together and still serves as part of the binding lineage of the modern British Army.

Most regiments consisted of either one or two battalions, although Foot Guards could have as many as three and the 60th (Royal American) Regiment of Foot

BELOW *A regiment of regular infantry demonstrate volley fire in a line three-deep by John Augustus Atkinson, 1808.*

THE ROAD TO WATERLOO 17

The Road to Waterloo — THE BRITISH ARMY

had, thanks to its convoluted history, seven. A regiment's 1st battalion was typically reinforced if depleted by men from the 2nd battalion, which generally left the latter under strength if they happened to be deployed at the same time. Drafts of recruits from depot companies were a routine occurrence, but not always a welcome one as blooding new soldiers took time.

The typical battalion was 1,000 strong and was commanded by a regimental colonel or lieutenant-colonel and the soldier himself belonged to one of ten companies. Eight of these were 'centre' companies - so called because of where they typically marched in the line - and the remaining two were 'flank' companies. One grenadier company (usually the taller, more physically strong men who could hold the flank steady in close quarter fighting), and the other were a light company.

RIGHT AND BELOW RIGHT
Riflemen of the 5/60th (Royal American) Regiment of Foot and the 95th Rifles, both in their signature dark green jackets. Watercolour by the Victorian military artist Charles Lyall, 1890. The red facings of the 60th reflect their 'Royal' status.

The light company were often detached from the battalion to act as scouts, or as a screen for the line - flushing out the enemy, drawing their fire, and reconnoitring the road ahead. Light companies were a sign of things to come for the British Army, although it would be another half century at least before technology existed to effectively transform every soldier of the line in a light infantryman. Although light companies were armed with the hardy Brown Bess musket like their brothers in the line, specialist light infantry regiments had also begun to emerge over recent decades and were armed with the smoothbore Baker rifle.

Inspired by the sometimes bruising encounters they had endured with irregulars in the American Revolutionary Wars (1775–83) and with French chasseurs (meaning 'hunters') on the continent, light scouting companies had been formed temporarily to fight out of formation as 'skirmishers', although mercenaries from the German states most often served in this role, thanks to their long tradition of jägers.

Companies of jägers (again, meaning 'hunters'), had first been formed in the 17th century by Britain's traditional supplier of hired help, the militaristic German principality of Hesse-Kassel, who recruited gamekeepers and foresters, and armed them with more accurate smoothbore rifles. An elite corps, the jägers were some of the first modern infantry to be valued for their skills and their company commanders were encouraged to make use of much greater freedom of movement than the typical line officer, who kept his men in strict formation.

The 5th Battalion of the 60th (Royal American) were formed in December 1797 in Barbados from those jägers and other German, Swiss or Dutch freebooters who remained in British service at the close of the American Revolutionary Wars. They were the first British Army battalion to be entirely equipped with rifles and the first to wear dark green, rather than red. Whilst line infantry took their orders from drum beats, light infantry relied upon complex bugle calls that could cut through the chaos of battle and reach the isolated skirmishers, leading to the bugle cap badge of the 5/60th and later light infantry regiments.

It was also the first time that foreign officers had been commissioned into the British Army and in 1808, as in 1797, the 5/60th (Royal American) were commanded by Lieutenant-Colonel Francis de Rottenberg, Baron de Rottenberg, a native of Danzig (now Gdańsk, Poland) in the Kingdom of Prussia and veteran of the French army of the Bourbons. He had literally authored the book on the subject, *Regulations for the Exercise of Riflemen and Light Infantry and Their Conduct in the Field* (1803).

Along with *Instructions Concerning the Duties of Light Infantry in the Field* by another Prussian-born French exile to the British Army, General Francis Jarry, *Regulations...* became the foundation text for several freshly raised light infantry regiments, including the 95th Rifles - the subject of Bernard Cornwell's *Sharpe* series of novels. During the Peninsula War, each brigade usually had a company of the 95th or 5/60th Regiment attached, ensuring they were always where the fighting was thickest.

Rifleman Benjamin Harris, whose memoir *The Recollections of Rifleman Harris* (1848) is one of the few accounts from a private soldier in the Peninsula War and was used as a source by Cornwell, described them as a "reckless and devil-may-care a set of men as ever I beheld, either before or since."

18 THE ROAD TO WATERLOO

THE RISE OF WELLESLEY

A slovenly young man from a distinguished Anglo-Irish family, Arthur Wellesley was plucked from idleness by his older brother, Richard, who pulled a few social strings and had him commissioned into the 73rd Regiment of Foot to serve as aide-de-camp to the Lord Lieutenant of Ireland. Subsidised by his brother, he rose to Major by 1793, purchasing command of that regiment, the 33rd (or the 1st Yorkshire West Riding) Regiment of Foot later the same year, and entered Parliament courtesy of a rotten borough with only a handful of eligible voters.

He first experienced war in the miserable Flanders Campaign of 1794 and the chaos of the command and control left a powerful impact on him. He later wrote: "At least I learned what not to do, and that is always a valuable lesson"

In 1795 he followed his regiment to India in time for the Fourth Anglo-Mysore War (1798-9) where his brother had been appointed Governor-General. His boldness and gallantry during the Battle of Mallavelly (March 27, 1799) against the French-backed army defiant Tipu Sultan earned him the respect of his peers, although his appointment as governor of the newly-conquered province of Mysore was nothing short of nepotism.

In an inhospitable environment which presented numerous challenges to logistics and moral, he learnt the importance of leading by personality, of planning, of drill, and of discipline, curtailing drunkenness with floggings and even demonstrative hangings. Wellesley returned from India in 1805, having risen to the rank of major-general and been awarded a knighthood for his role in suppressing an 1800 uprising by the insurgent Dhondia Wagh and leading the British to victory in the Second Anglo-Maratha War (1803-5).

Wellesley was haughty, arrogant, and often obnoxious - hardly qualities in short supply in the army's upper echelons - but his redeeming quality was that unlike many of his contemporaries, his shyness prevented him flaunting these uglier angles of his nature. That he repeatedly lent on influential allies to further his career is undeniable, but nor can it be denied that he repeatedly showed himself deserving of their support.

Lieutenant Colonel Wellesley, aged 26 in the uniform of the 33rd (or the 1st Yorkshire West Riding) Regiment of Foot, circa 1795 by John Hopper.

Horse Guards and Horse Artillery

Cavalry was divided into light and heavy regiments, with the heavy cavalry consisting of the Life Guards, the Royal Horse Guards, seven numbered regiments of the Royal Dragoon Guards, and five regiments of Dragoons (confusingly numbered 1-4 and 6, there was no 5th Dragoons). The only distinction between Dragoons and Royal Dragoon Guards was that 'Guards' designated those regiments who had been titled 'Horse' before the cavalry reforms of 1746. Unlike French dragoons and cuirassiers, British heavy cavalry weren't substantially 'heavier' and would have been classed as medium cavalry in Emperor Napoléon I's army - the mounts being only marginally bigger in the main and their principal differences being their swords and sidearms.

The light cavalry used the 1796 Pattern Light Cavalry Sabre, which was a curved slashing weapon, but were also equipped with shorter barrelled variants of the standard infantry musket, called carbines, as well as a flintlock pistols (there was no standardised supplier). Heavy cavalry were usually armed only with a sword - the heavier, straighter 1796 Pattern Heavy Cavalry Sword - and a pistol, although Royal Dragoon Guards also carried a carbine. Difficult to wield due to its length and weight, the effects of the heavier blade in the hands of a well-trained cavalryman (or indeed the fictional Richard Sharpe) could be devastating.

The numbering of the 19 light cavalry regiments picked up with the 7th Light Dragoons and the majority were styled as such, with a handful being designated as Hussars and accordingly uniformed in the rakish

The Road to Waterloo — THE BRITISH ARMY

A recruiting party wows the rustics with tales of daring and courage in this hand-coloured 1797 print by Isaac Cruikshank.

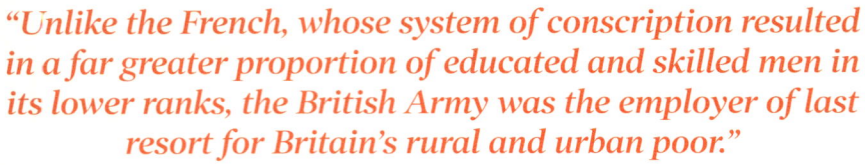

> "Unlike the French, whose system of conscription resulted in a far greater proportion of educated and skilled men in its lower ranks, the British Army was the employer of last resort for Britain's rural and urban poor."

over-the-shoulder fur coat, complicated Hungarian-style saddle, curved sabre and other cosmetic affectations. Though as increasingly versatile as their light counterparts, the heavy cavalry were the shock troops of the Napoleonic battlefield, while the light cavalry was used for scouting and running down retreating foes.

Cavalry regiments were formed of five squadrons of two troops each, with one squadron permanently stationed at the home depot. Each troop consisted of 90 men and was designated A Troop, B Troop, C Troop and so on, while the squadrons were numbered with the 1st Squadron typically led by the regiment's lieutenant-colonel and the next squadron by the next most senior officer.

Artillery was not a function of Horse Guards and the British Army upper echelons, but of the vast and bureaucratic Board of Ordnance. The Royal Regiment of Artillery was divided into 'foot' and 'horse' batteries, although that is ever so slightly misleading as in both cases the guns themselves were pulled by horses - the difference was that 'horse artillery' were pulled by a train of six horses, which allowed the crews to hitch a ride on the guns, while 'foot artillery' had to run alongside.

The scum and the gentlemen

Unlike the French, whose system of conscription resulted in a far greater proportion of educated and skilled men in its lower ranks, the British Army was the employer of last resort for Britain's rural and urban poor. Indeed, many did fit Wellesley's notorious claim that his army were "the scum of the earth" and there was no shortage of petty theft and alcoholism in the wake of the British Army, but for the most part the constant drilling, corporal punishment, and shared experience moulded them into what we would now describe as a 'band of brothers'.

Wellesley explained in 1831: "People talk of their enlisting from their fine military feeling – all stuff – no such thing. Some of our men enlist from having bastard children – some for minor offences – many more for drink; but you can hardly conceive such a set brought together, and it really is wonderful that we should have made them the fine fellows they are."

Recruits of Scottish or Irish origin tended to be of a higher quality than their English and Welsh counterparts but only because extreme poverty and the destruction of traditional industries in the face of dawning industrialisation drove many struggling artisans and skilled labourers to the colours. From the late 1770s, the ban on Roman Catholic recruitment had been lifted, increasing the flow of recruits from Ireland especially.

Terms of service were typically life, or until they were no longer capable of soldiering due to wounds or the ravages of alcoholism. The recruit usually received a lump sum, a 'bounty', for signing up for life, but in 1806 new short-service attestations were introduced with a view to attracting a better class of recruit -

LEFT *Three Light Dragoons negotiate with a farmer for his livestock in this 1796 mezzotint.*

The fashion of the day was for Hungarian-style Hussar regiments and John Mollo depicts a mixture of officers and private soldiers of the 7th, 10th and 15th Hussars circa 1808.

THE ROAD TO WATERLOO 21

The Road to Waterloo
THE BRITISH ARMY

FIREARMS OF THE BRITISH ARMY

ABOVE A shorter barrelled Brown Bess carbine, for use by light cavalry. ANTIQUE MILITARY RIFLES CC BY-SA 2.0

BROWN BESS MUSKET
The muzzle-loading smoothbore Land Pattern Musket was the standard infantry weapon of the British Army in the Peninsula. Heavy, inaccurate, and slow, it required as many as 20 consecutive movements to load, fire and reload.

The Brown Bess, as it was more commonly known, was loaded using a paper cartridge which was taken from a pouch on the soldier's hip. The top of the cartridge - containing the lead musket ball - would be bitten off and held between the teeth while some of the powder was sprinkled into the flash pan. The flash pan was covered with the frizzen to keep the powder in place and the hammer set to half cock. The rest of the powder from the cartridge was emptied into the barrel before the lead ball and the remainder of the paper cartridge were added and packed tight with a ramrod.

The hammer was taken back to full cock and when the trigger was pulled, the flint held in the jaws of the hammer hit the frizzen, creating the spark that ignited the powder in the barrel and firing the weapon.

Only really effective at 100 yards or less, and rendered inaccurate by the lack of rifling in the barrel and the irregular shape of the ball, muskets were designed to fire en masse where they could do the most damage through sheer odds. The rate of fire was estimated to be three to four shots a minute although the higher figure was the preserve of the best infantrymen.

BAKER RIFLE
Introduced in 1801, the Baker was the first British produced rifle - meaning its barrel was 'rifled', engraved with a spiral that 'spun' the ball and made it fly further and straighter. It was also the first rifle that wasn't too complex, fragile or expensive to be used in significant numbers by the British Army.

As it was shorter than a musket, the rifleman was usually issued with a longer sword bayonet to increase the effective reach of the rifle in close combat. Slower to load too, the balls had to fit the barrel tightly to be effective against the rifling. They were stored in greased leather and had to be driven into the barrel with force. The powder poured from a horn with a spring-loaded catch that automatically measured out the correct amount.

The estimated rate of fire was two shots a minute, but you at least had a chance of hitting something - with the effective range being 200 yards, and there is evidence of targets being hit as far as 600 yards away.

PAGET CARBINE
Taking its name from its principal patron - Major-General Henry Paget, Lord Paget - the Short Light Cavalry Carbine was designed to be more efficiently used by a man on horseback. Although its reduced 16-inch barrel cost the trooper vital range and accuracy, the swivel ramrod (which was attached to a hinge) wasn't easily lost in the heat of barrel, the curved sliding ring made it much easier to detach from the belt, and it was significantly lighter.

Introduced in 1808, just in time for the Peninsula War, the Paget carbine took a while to bed in. Captain Jonathan Leach of the 95th Rifles wrote: "This little pop-gun of a carbine was so inferior to that of the French that the enemy often dismounted and shot at our dragoons at a distance which rendered our short carbines almost useless."

BELOW A Paget Carbine, kindly provided by the Lincolnshire auctioneers Garth Vincent. GARTH VINCENT

---

seven years for the infantry, and ten for the cavalry and artillery.

Some effort was also made to induce militiamen - who were already familiar with drill and discipline - to join up, with mixed results. Non-commissioned officers were promoted from the ranks and usually rose no higher than sergeant-major. Literacy was a requirement above corporal, and although it was possible for a ranker to ascend to the ranks of a commissioned officer - they were a minority.

Rather than blue-blooded aristocrats (who when they did enlist, usually made a beeline for the Guards regiments), most officers were sons of gentry - lawyers, doctors, clergy and the like - who gravitated towards the British Army to maintain their status. Mirroring the composition of the ranks, the second and third sons of Anglo-Irish landowning families - like Wellesley himself - were more common than their English counterparts, due to the lack of opportunities for young men of some breeding but modest funds.

Officers could be promoted on merit, but the vast majority earned their commissions either through patronage - personal connections that saw a family member or close friend approach the regimental colonel on their behalf - or purchase. The market for rank placed a premium in the more established regiments with the noblest heritage and the fanciest tunics, while the cheapest were the newly established regiments of the line where there was less glory in the commission and far more positions available.

In 1794, Major-General James Craig wrote: "There is not a young man in the army that cares a farthing whether his commanding officer, his Brigadier, or the Commander-in-Chief himself approves his conduct or not. His promotion depends not on their smiles nor frowns - his friends can give him a thousand pounds with which he goes to the auction rooms in Charles Street and in a fortnight, he becomes a captain. Out of the 15 regiments of cavalry and 25 of infantry which we have here, 21 are literally commanded by boys or idiots."

The U.K.'s leading provider of

Battlefield Tours

with Specialist Guides from only £289pp

NEW 2020/21 BROCHURE OUT NOW!

LOW DEPOSIT
Secure your place from only
£50 pp
Call or visit our website for full details.

leger
HOLIDAYS

Over 80 escorted tours to choose from including WW1, WW2 and other conflicts.

Walk in the footsteps of heroes® on a Leger Battlefield Tour.

Thanks to our expert **Specialist Guides**, who accompany every tour, you'll embark on a fascinating journey of Remembrance and discovery.

Taking in a combination of battlefields, memorials and War Cemeteries you'll learn why battles were fought at particular locations and your guide will help you interpret the landscape and look for signs of the battle evident today.

A choice of local coach joining points across the UK, **many of which are FREE**, and the option to upgrade to **Silver Service coach** with extra legroom and rear lounge, or **Luxuria**, with extra wide seats and touch screen TVs.

Waterloo Re-Enactment Weekend
4 days from only £359

Walking the Waterloo Battlefields
5 days from only £539

All Quiet on the Western Front
4-5 days from only £319

D-Day Landings in Normandy
4 days from only £319

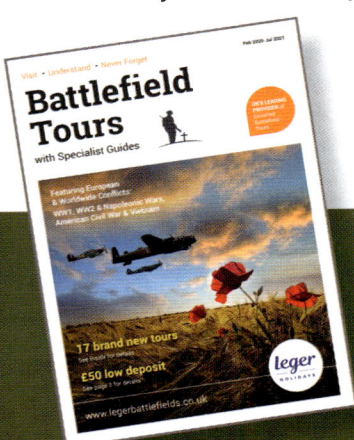

Call or visit our website today for a brochure!
01709 385 829
www.legerbattlefields.co.uk

ABTA No. V3582

The Road to Waterloo — THE VIMEIRO CAMPAIGN

HELL
by Another Road

The Vimeiro Campaign, August 1-30, 1808

While Portugal had done little to oppose the Franco-Spanish invasion, the hard months of occupation and the attendant collapse of the already precariously underdeveloped economy had finally pushed the population into unrest. This was particularly acute in those regions which had been occupied by the Spanish army and promptly abandoned in some disorder.

Between June 6 and 24 vast swathes of the country erupted into open insurrection, turning on French citizens and suspected collaborators. A protean new army was formed of veterans, volunteers and conscripted militia, which answered to a national junta in Oporto led by the unifying figure of Archbishop António de São José de Castro.

General Jean-Andoche Junot's army of occupation was suddenly in a precarious position. Virtually isolated from the French forces in Spain by hundreds of miles of hostile terrain, crawling with bands of murderous guerrillas, they were all but confined to Lisbon and a few towns where even there the atmosphere grew steadily more tense.

The French response was no less bloodthirsty than it had been in Spain. In accordance with the values of the day, civilians who took up arms outside of the uniformed context of an army or militia - as the Spanish and Portuguese did in the process of a guerrilla war - were an affront to the rules of civilised conflict and so the

BELOW *An 1812 print showing the British Army coming ashore at Mondego Bay at the start of the Peninsula War.*

24 THE ROAD TO WATERLOO

French response can be rationalised, but the sheer scale of that response cannot be excused. The towns of Leiria (July 5, 1808) and Evora (July 29, 1808) were quickly occupied and their defenders butchered as they surrendered.

Though Britain ached to take the fight directly to Spain, until the Spanish requested boots on the ground it was a diplomatic impossibility. Puffed up by their recent victories, the juntas were happier receiving supplies and arms than redcoats. Wellesley, who only became aware that he had been replaced when he arrived and found the news waiting for him, first contacted the junta of La Coruña in northern Spain.

Rebuffed, he then sailed for Portugal and the sheltered harbour of Mondego Bay where a student revolt had seized control of the fortress from the skeleton French defenders. The landing took place over a week from August 1, while Wellesley - already establishing himself as a man with a firm grasp of logistics - set about gathering wagons, mules and other pack animals, while the first British casualties occurred when redcoats drowned in the surf, their shore boats capsizing.

In his 1832 memoirs, Captain John Patterson of the 50th (or the West Kent) Regiment of Foot, wrote of the landing: "As soon as the Portuguese boats, crowded with our soldiers, reached the foaming and rapid surge, a desperate pull was made by all the rowers when, dashing over its surface, we were launched upon the sand in a most unceremonious manner, being pitched, or rather tumbled out, more like a cargo of fish than a boatload of gentleman warriors."

Shaken by the sea journey - a torturous experience for the early 19th-century provincial poor who made up the bulk of the British ranks - and disorientated by the scalding white sands beneath their feet and the relentless August sun, some men died of dehydration even before they reached the bivouacs.

With space on the troopships at a premium, cavalry and artillery were both critically underrepresented. The 15,000 men who sailed with Wellesley were accompanied by only 380 light cavalry (the 20th Light Dragoons) and a handful of guns, but almost immediately the local support they had been counting on left a lot to be desired. The nearby Porto junta had some 5,000 men under arms, but General Bernardim Freire de Andrade could barely feed his surly peasant militia, let alone control them. Indeed, in early 1809 he was murdered by his own men.

ABOVE *General Jean-Andoche Junot had risen through the ranks, like many senior officers in the more meritocratic army of Napoléon I. He is painted in the uniform of a sergeant (a rank he held in 1792) by the French artist Henri Félix Emmanuel Philippoteaux.*

Rather than offer support to Wellesley, Freire - who was already monopolising the local supplies - demanded the general furnish his army with bread. Eventually, they struck a compromise and three Porto battalions, a battalion of light infantry and 250 cavalry (2,000 men in all) were detached to serve under the command of Lieutenant-Colonel Nicholas Trant, a British staff officer formally commissioned into the Portuguese army for the purposes of propriety. The condition, of course, was that the British feed them.

The Battle of Roliça

Staying close to the coast so they could be supplied by the Royal Navy, Wellesley began to march his force south through the pine woods, the sun-bleached scrub, the tangled vineyards, and the olive groves. Meanwhile, General Junot detailed a garrison to remain at Lisbon and readied his remaining 13,000 men for action, sending a detachment on ahead under General Henri François Delaborde to delay the British advance.

Passing through the town of Leiria, the British saw the first evidence of French brutality in the face of Portuguese defiance. In his memoir, *Rough Sketches of the Life of an Old Soldier* (1831), Captain Jonathan Leach, 95th Rifles, wrote: "The walls of the convent into which I went with some other officers were covered with blood and brains in many places; damning proof of the scenes that had recently been acted there."

The first shots had already been fired. On August 15, the British advance guard of four

The Road to Waterloo

THE VIMEIRO CAMPAIGN

ABOVE The British advance towards the French-held ridge in this depiction of the Battle of Roliça by William Heath, 1814.

RIGHT The British begin a harrowing charge uphill into the French guns at Roliça in this illustration from Histoire du Consulat et de l'Empire (1865).

companies of 5/60th (Royal American) Regiment of Foot and 95th Rifles overran the French outpost at the Medieval walled town of Óbidos, dominated by a Moorish castle. Rifleman Benjamin Harris of the 95th, described this first encounter with the French. In their enthusiasm, the four companies of riflemen gave chase and collided with the advance guard of Delaborde's force as they approached from the south.

"The first man that was hit was Lieutenant Banbury; he fell pierced through the head with a musket ball, and died almost immediately," he wrote. "I thought I never heard such a tremendous noise as the firing made on this occasion, and the men on both sides of me, I could occasionally observe, were falling fast. Being overmatched, we retired to a rising ground, or hillock, in our rear and formed there all around its summit, standing three deep, the front-rank kneeling. In this position we remained all night, expecting the whole host upon us every moment."

With the skirmishers of the 5/60th and 95th holding high ground overlooking the road along which the French had fled, the rest of the army moved into Óbidos to spend the night. The headlong charge of the Rifles had taken them beyond the support of the rest of the 6th Brigade and they had paid the price, with some 39 dead and injured in the clash. It was a less than auspicious beginning.

At dawn on August 17, Wellesley advanced from Óbidos in a crescent formation - the left wing under Major-General Ronald Craufurd Ferguson and the Portuguese right-wing under Lieutenant-Colonel Trant angled forwards like horns to encircle the smaller French force of fewer than 5,000 men, which Delaborde had lined up along a

26 THE ROAD TO WATERLOO

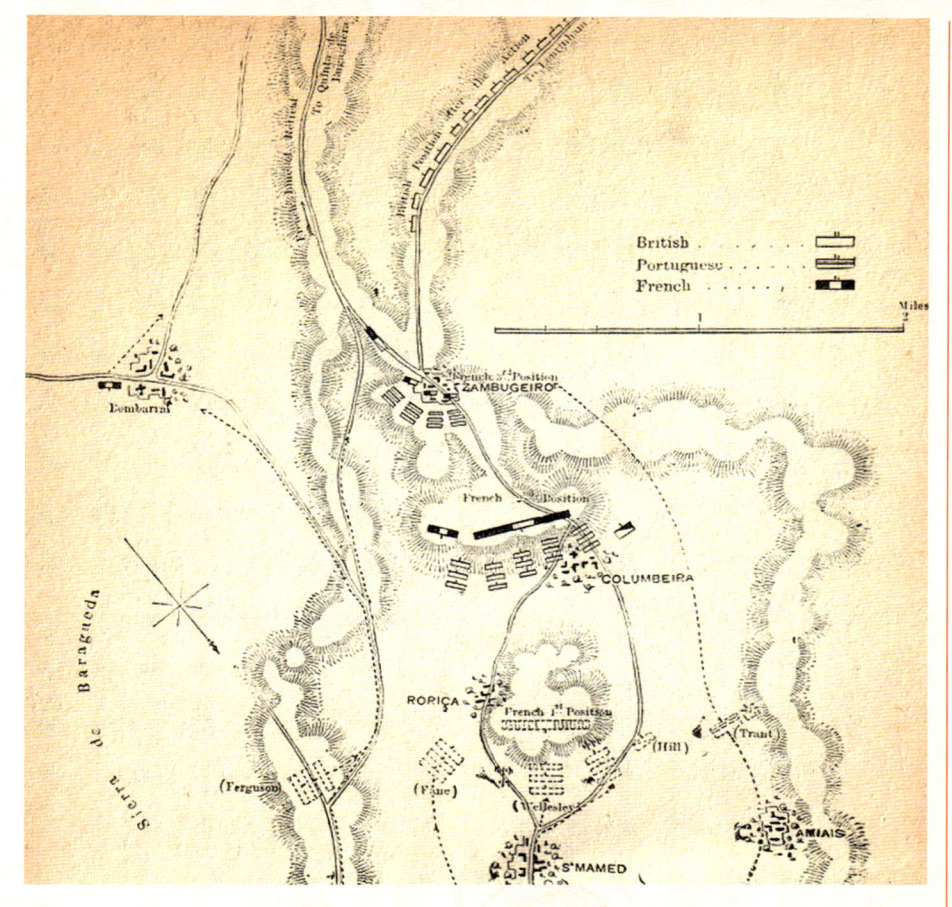

LEFT *A map showing the initial disposition of both armies and then their second position near the village of Columbeira, with the French having withdrawn to evade the pincer.*

BELOW *A more detailed illustration by William Heath, circa 1814, shows the view from the British lines at the Battle of Vimeiro.*

low ridge east of the village of Roliça. There the French were able to command the high ground and block the road to Lisbon and the protection of Junot.

In the centre of the crescent, Wellesley led the bulk of his force in full parade-ground pomp, trying to draw Delaborde's attention from the obvious pincer that was unfolding in plain sight. The manoeuvre was flawless, but so too was Delaborde's parry - using his own infantry as a screen he drew the army back to a steep hill two miles south of their starting position.

Increasingly struggling to keep pace, Captain Leach of the 95th, recalled: "Never before nor since do I remember to have felt more intense and suffocating heat than we experienced in climbing the mountains to the attack; every mouthful of air was such as inhaled when looking into an oven."

In the confusion of the battle and thinking that the pincer had snapped its claws shut around Delaborde's French, the gallant Lieutenant-Colonel the Honourable George Augustus Frederick Lake led the grenadier company of 29th (or the Worcestershire) Regiment of Foot into a suicidal charge up the steep slope without support. Advancing uphill with bayonets fixed into withering French fire, a ball struck Lake under the arm and punched clean through his body, knocking him from his horse. Sergeant-Major Richards darted forward to cover his commander, but the hail of volley tore him to shreds in turn.

Desperate to save Lake and his isolated company, Wellesley ordered a general attack and as one the rest of the force lurched uphill through the thick scrub. Rather than a pincer, it was now a desperate line charge. With their superior numbers, it was only a matter of time before the British left flank was able to push onto the hill and Delaborde ordered a deft withdrawal. The British had taken 487 casualties and the French an estimated 600.

Though the price paid in both men and morale was too steep too early, the sight of a French withdrawal was one seldom seen on the battlefields of Europe and Wellesley took the victory for what it was. With Junot ahead of them, he decided to withdraw to the coastal village of Vimeiro where Sir Henry Burrard was set to land with some 10,000 reinforcements.

The Battle of Vimeiro

Though outnumbered, General Junot wasn't prepared to give the British time to recover their breath. He saw an

> *"If you had to pick a site for a valiant last stand, you'd be pushed to find a better one than Vimeiro. On the morning of August 21, distant clouds of dust betrayed the approach of French columns."*

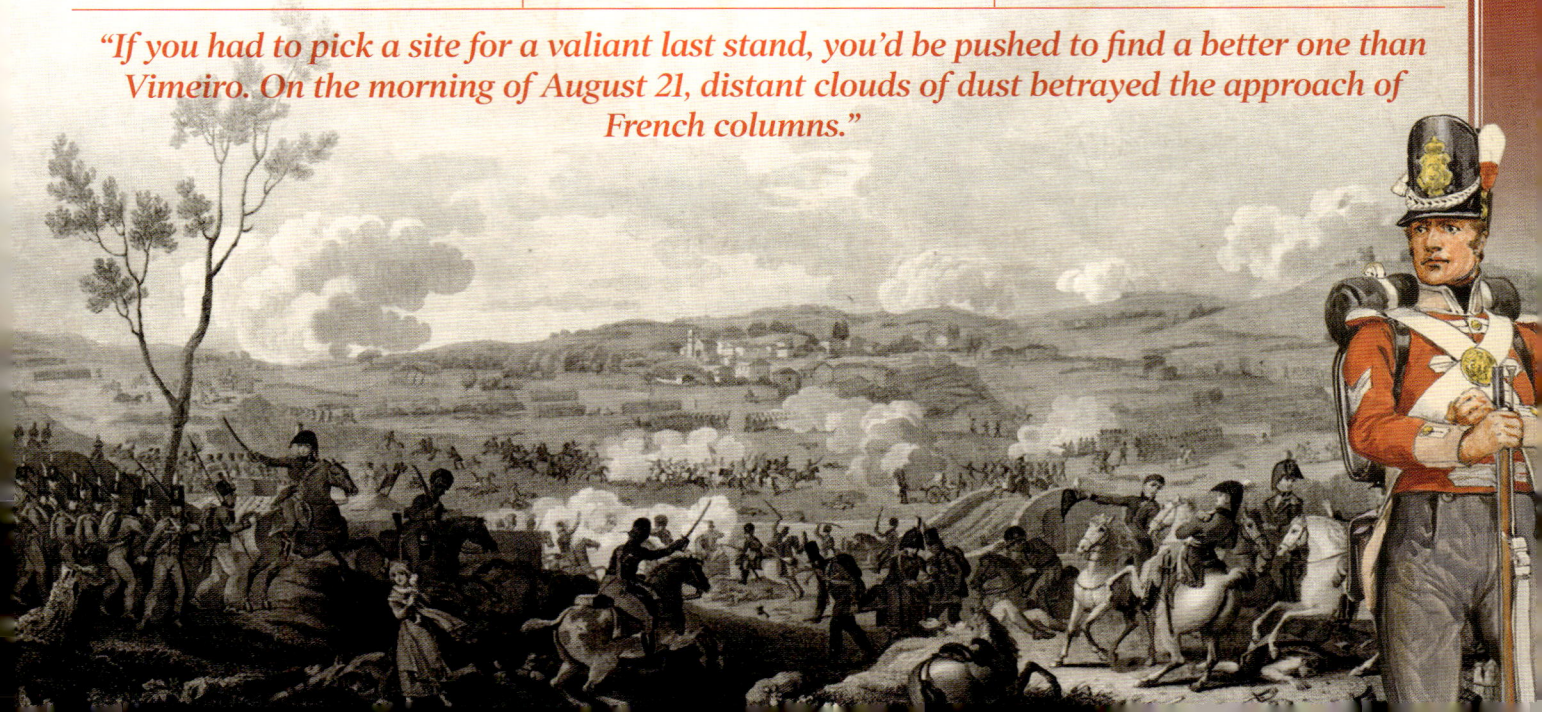

The Road to Waterloo

THE VIMEIRO CAMPAIGN

LEFT *A mezzotint of Charles Turner's portrait of Sir Hew Whitefoord Dalrymple, produced later in the general's life.*

> "We are going to Hell by another road," Wellesley wrote to his brother. "[Dalrymple] has no plan, or even an idea of a plan, nor do I believe he knows the meaning of the word plan."

opportunity to drive them into the sea and give Wellesley no option but to call for an evacuation and abandon Portugal altogether.

If you had to pick a site for a valiant last stand, you'd be pushed to find a better one than Vimeiro. On the morning of August 21, distant clouds of dust betrayed the approach of French columns. Wellesley deployed his men around the village in a manner that would soon become his signature formation, with the bulk of his infantry concealed by the crest of the hills, he used lines of skirmishers - the rifles and the light companies of the line infantry - to sow chaos and block the enemy's progress.

Two fresh infantry brigades had already been landed, bringing the number of defenders to around 18,000. On the easternmost ridge immediately north of Vimeiro, running north to south were five brigades (with Trant's Portuguese watching their northern flank). Two brigades held the hill directly east of the village, and a single brigade held the high ground to its immediate south.

The French formed into two divisions, one under General Delaborde and another under General Louis Henri Loison, while a reserve of infantry, cavalry and artillery was held in the rear. This was an army which for nearly a decade had known only victory and Junot ordered them into a full-frontal assault.

Relying so heavily on tightly packed volley fire against equally tightly packed foes, the columns of French infantry found themselves easy pickings for the more accurate and longer range Baker rifles, while the French musketry found disparate, scattered targets in skirmish lines almost impossible to dislodge. "As they came swarming upon us, they rained a perfect shower of balls, which we returned quite sharply," wrote Rifleman Harris of the 95th. "Whenever one of them was knocked over, our men called out 'There goes another one of Boney's invincibles.'"

As the French finally drove the skirmishers back, British infantry formed up into lines - the standard defensive formation - and cleared the crest of the hill. Captain Patterson wrote of the 50th, nicknamed 'the Black Cuffs' for their facings: "The 50th Regiment, commanded by Colonel George Townsend Walker, stood firm as a rock, while a strong division under General Delaborde continued to advance at a rapid step, from the deep woods in our front, covered by a legion of tirailleurs [French skirmishers], who quickened their pace as they neared our line.

"Walker now ordered his men to prepare for close attack, and he watched with eagle eye the favourable moment for pouncing on the enemy. When the latter, in a compact mass, arrived sufficiently up the hill, now bristling with bayonets, the Black Cuffs poured in a well-directed volley upon the dense array. Then, cheering loudly, and led on by its gallant chief, the whole regiment rushed forward to the charge, penetrated the formidable columns and carried all before it."

With the advance directly towards Vimeiro slowing to a crawl and two generals - Delaborde among them - wounded, Junot rolled the dice and gambled on splitting his smaller force in two, sending the right-wing up into the

BELOW RIGHT *General Junot's French Army undergo an orderly evacuation from Lisbon as per the contentious Convention of Sintra.*

28　THE ROAD TO WATERLOO

British left flank at the northern end of the ridge. There, the approach to Vimeiro was covered by a single isolated hill and pine, it was ideal for skirmishers. Like a nest of furious wasps, a small number of British sharpshooters were able to hold up the entire French flanking manoeuvre, until they finally broke through and flung themselves up the slope.

Again, the bulk of the redcoats were sheltered below the crest of the ridge and Major-General Ferguson held them low and steady until the French were at 100 yards when they revealed themselves with a thunder of short-range musketry. Writing in his 1819 memoir *Journal of a Soldier of the 71st, Or Glasgow Regiment, Highland Light Infantry: From 1806 to 1815*, Private Thomas Pococke recalled: "We gave them one volley and three cheers – three distinct cheers. Then all was death. They came upon us crying and shouting, to the very point of our bayonets. Our awful silence and determined advance they could not stand. They put about and fled without much resistance. At this charge, we took thirteen guns and one general."

Finally, with each French brigade broken in turn, Junot was forced to withdraw - having suffered 1,800 casualties to 135 British dead and 500 wounded. Captain Patterson described the scene: "As far as the eye could reach over the well-planted valley, and across the open country lying beyond the forest, the fugitives were running in wild disorder, their white sheepskin knapsacks discernible among woods far distant."

With so few cannon and horse, it was pragmatism that made Wellesley the 'soldier's general' rather than any innate faith in the humble redcoat. Burrard, who had come ashore during the battle and wisely held back rather than confuse the situation, formally took charge and denied Wellesley's urging to give chase and run down the remnants of the French army in Portugal. The cautious and conservative Burrard believed him too impetuous by half and Lieutenant-General Sir Hew Whitefoord Dalrymple, who arrived the following day, echoed his deputy's sentiments emphatically.

"We are going to Hell by another road," Wellesley wrote to his brother. "[Dalrymple] has no plan, or even an idea of a plan, nor do I believe he knows the meaning of the word plan."

The Convention of Sintra

General Junot was defeated, but thanks to the intervention from Burrard and Dalrymple he wasn't yet broken. As his demoralised army retreated to Lisbon, they were harassed en route by Portuguese guerrillas, but the French situation wasn't beyond hope and the army wasn't beyond recovery.

Junot quickly sought terms and Dalrymple was happy to oblige him, convinced that the French numbers in Lisbon were significantly higher than they were. The French garrison could retain its arms and artillery and was to be chauffeured to a French port by the Royal Navy - crucially, there were no guarantees that the army could not be used in the Iberian theatre again, a common clause in treaties of this sort. The Portuguese were furious to have been completely sidelined throughout the negotiations, especially as the French were being permitted to take local collaborators and their ill-gotten loot home with them.

In the defence of Dalrymple and Burrard, Britain had not known victory against a major power on a continental battlefield in well over half a century and it's only with hindsight that we know just how vulnerable Junot's forces were. Hindsight, unfortunately, travelled to London with news of the Convention of Sintra (August 30, 1808) as its companion, provoking outrage in Parliament and press alike.

Wellesley, who was himself extremely nonplussed by the terms of the French evacuation, took the opportunity presented by the death of his deputy in Ireland to return to Britain and get an early start in the blame-shifting. He wrote to his patron, Castlereagh to assure him "Although my name is affixed to this instrument, I beg that you will not believe that I negotiated it, that I approve of it, or that I had any hand in wording it."

It was a prescient move, Dalrymple - whose reports had been firmly pushing the responsibility onto Wellesley - and Burrard were recalled to London to explain themselves, and all three were to face an inquiry.

Although matters in the Peninsula were far from settled, their immediate aims had been achieved and Lisbon had been liberated. A regency council was formed to govern Portugal on behalf of the Prince Regent in Brazil and the highly-regarded Lieutenant-General Sir John Moore arrived to take command - until the reputations - and futures - of Wellesley, Dalrymple and Burrard were firmly resolved.

The Road to Waterloo — MOORE'S CAMPAIGN

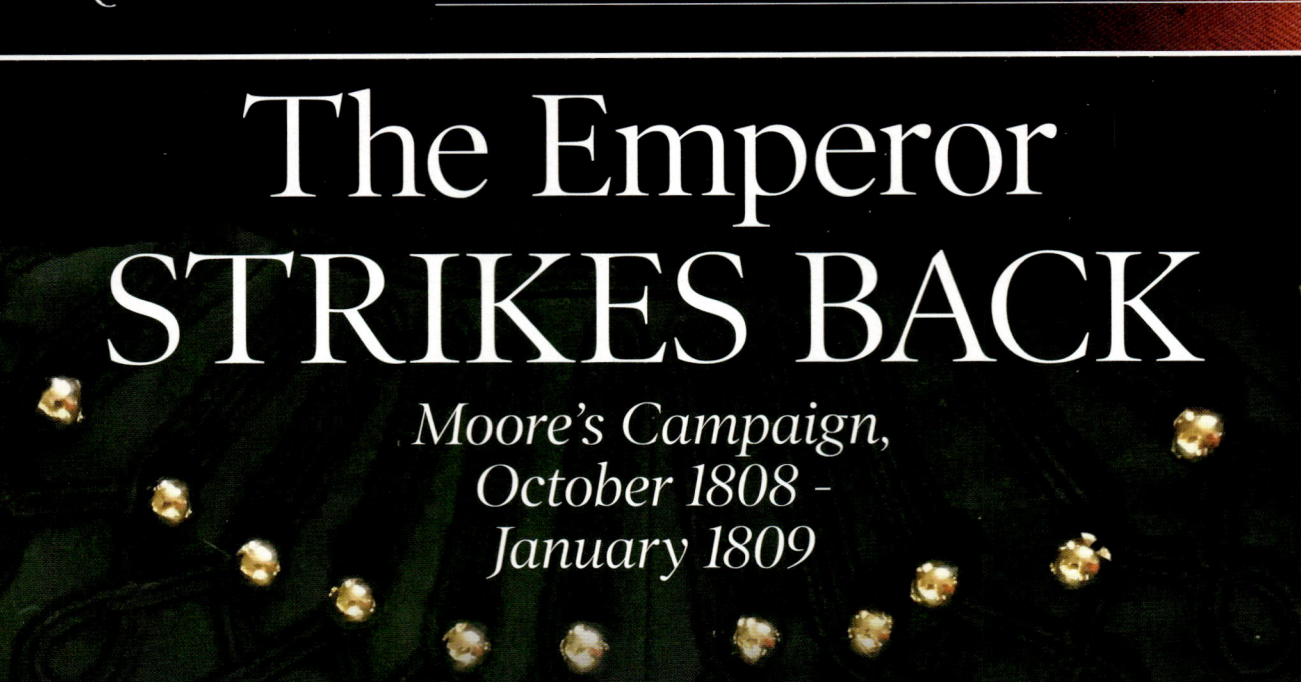

The Emperor STRIKES BACK

Moore's Campaign, October 1808 – January 1809

With the Convention of Cintra being treated as little more than a pause in the eventual hostilities, it's difficult to work out what its benefits had been to Great Britain. Now affairs were temporarily settled in Portugal, Spain found itself the almost exclusive target of the French military machine.

Convinced their war was all but won following the partial withdrawal of the

The same landed elite who held the reins of power under the Bourbon dynasty continued to abuse their ancient privileges. They spent vast sums of their tenants' rents on fantastically attired volunteer companies rather than a single coin from their own purse on the defence of the nation, while no sum was too high when it came to buying exemptions from conscription for their kin.

to an insurrection piecemeal, and with one of the greatest military minds in history at their helm, the victories came quickly. With his most capable (and a competitive) marshals in the field, the French drove into the heart of Old Castile at the Battle of Burgos (November 7, 1808), while the Battles of Tudela (November 23, 1808) and Cardedeu (December 16, 1808) opened up Barcelona. With the regular Spanish Army

ABOVE Lord Henry Paget depicted just prior to the Peninsula War as a dashing Lieutenant General of Cavalry.

ABOVE RIGHT The French Emperor Napoléon I accepts the surrender of Madrid at his camp, December 4, 1808. Painted in oil by Antoine-Jean Gros, 1810.

LEFT A portrait of Sir John Moore painted prior to the general's death by Thomas Lawrence.

French to the safety of the River Ebro, the juntas submitted to complacency. They were still predominantly regional in their interests with little meaningful coordination at a national level and few generals were prepared to put their men to the field beyond their own provincial boundaries.

When the French pulled back, they were largely left alone. The killing blow that the puppet ruler of a much-reduced Kingdom of Spain, King José I - aka Joseph-Napoléon Bonaparte - was expecting failed to materialise. It took over two weeks from the French leaving Madrid for a Spanish army to turn up and claim it, and the few lacklustre offensives on the Ebro were easily batted aside.

One of the most universally loathed facets of the old regime, not even a national emergency could make the peasants embrace conscription enthusiastically and entire communities refused to participate, while among those who did desertion was common.

The Eagle on The Pyrenees

Emperor Napoléon I, meanwhile, had taken the French defeat at the Battle of Bailén (July 16-19, 1808) - and his brother's headlong flight from Madrid - personally. Detaching a sizeable chunk of his battle-hardened Grand Armée from their vital work of menacing Central Europe, the Emperor resolved to lead the 130,000-strong invasion force across the Pyrenees himself and put the Spanish in their place.

Addressing his men, he declared: "I am here with the soldiers who conquered at Austerlitz, at Jena, at Eylau. Who can withstand them? Certainly not your wretched Spanish troops who do not know how to fight. I shall conquer Spain in two months and acquire the rights of a conqueror."

Fighting with a clear strategy and in concentrated strength, rather than reacting

shattered and in full retreat to lick its wounds at Zaragoza and Cuenca, it was left to guerrillas and hastily-assembled militia to hold the road to Madrid.

Back in September, Lieutenant General Sir John Moore had been ordered to concentrate his army along Portugal's northeastern border, abutting the provinces of Galicia and León, where he was to aid the Spanish in any manner they deemed fit. He had been reinforced by 12,000 fresh troops under Major General Sir David Baird, but they were landed at A Coruña in northern Spain, while the bulk of the original army was scattered around the country, particularly around Lisbon.

For most of October, the French campaign had left the west and north of Spain virtually unmolested, with the fiercest fighting in the centre of the

The Road to Waterloo — MOORE'S CAMPAIGN

country and in the stubbornly independent provinces of Aragon and Catalonia. Moore decided that he would rendezvous with Baird in the vicinity of Salamanca in Old Castile, taking advantage of the focus of French interest elsewhere to project his army deeper into Spain than had been ordered. If Moore had succeeded in seizing the initiative with this bold manoeuvre it would hardly have been a problem, but he made a decision that placed timing in other hands.

The withdrawal of the three lieutenant generals - Dalrymple, Burrard, and Wellesley - to answer for Cintra left the disposition of the army in a certain degree of chaos. Moore discovered local knowledge to be in perilously short supply and with winter rolling in, he opted to err on the side of extreme caution. With barely enough cavalry or artillery as it was, he had no desire to see half of it slide down an icy ravine.

Leaving 10,000 men to garrison Lisbon, Moore set off with the bulk of the infantry directly to Salamanca and sent the cavalry, artillery, and a wagon train on a circuitous 400-mile route to join the main Lisbon to Madrid highway. Moore arrived at Salamanca on November 3 and Major General Sir John Hope and the wagons finally joined him on December 3.

With the increasingly inclement weather, Baird landed at A Coruña later than expected on October 26 and discovered - as Wellesley had before him - that there was precious little comradely spirit from the locals to assemble a logistic train. He was forced to scrounge oxen and carts and a month later had made it only as far as Astorga, 165 miles from A Coruña and with another 120 miles to go before they reached Moore's rendezvous point.

Squandered opportunities

Moore had not only failed to seize the moment, but quite a lot of moments had come and gone whilst his army idled at Salamanca. The weather was worsening considerably and with it the news from the front.

He briefly considered a full retreat - dispatching orders to send Hope's wagon train back to Portugal - but it

ABOVE *A trooper of the 15th (or King's) Regiment of (Light) Dragoons (Hussars) with a Paget Carbine by military artist FW Scott.*

was the unexpectedly dogged defiance by Madrid's defenders that restored his confidence in the campaign, as did the news that General Pedro Caro y Sureda, 3rd Marquis of la Romana's Spanish Army of the Left was regrouping at León. He countermanded his original order to Hope and instead directed them further into Old Castile where they might be able to draw the French out and ease the pressure on Madrid.

Before they left Salamanca, news arrived that the Spanish capital had fallen. Moore, now committed, reasoned that a British offensive into the heart of Spain would keep the French Emperor from pushing on into Portugal. On December 11, a captured French courier revealed that the army of Marshal Jean-de-Dieu Soult - one of the greatest of Napoléon I's ambitious and energetic commanders - had moved west of the River Carrión and was now isolated from the rest of the French invasion force.

Moore marched north to catch up with Baird and La Romana, but while the latter remained as non-committal as expected, Baird's contingent brought the British strength up to 25,000 men. Still not enough to take on the entire Grand Armée, but enough to entrap Soult, who was still blissfully ignorant of the British presence.

On December 13, under the watchful eye of Emperor Napoléon I and his Imperial Guard, Madrid's leading lights obediently trooped into their churches to declare public oaths of fealty to King José I. The monarch's role was in name only whilst his domineering little brother remained in the country and the resulting Decrees of Chamartín were a radical reshaping of Spain.

With a few strokes of the pen, the feudal rights of Spain's landed gentry to raise taxes, military levies, and hold courts were abolished. Two-thirds of all religious organisations were shuttered and their properties auctioned off into private hands, and about 300-odd years later than it should have been, the Spanish Inquisition was abolished.

Browbeaten and humiliated by his brother, King José I fixed a benevolent smile and waved through the destruction of his realm's entire social fabric. Few peasants would have wept for the end of the Inquisition or for the curtailment of overweening aristocratic power, but the Roman Catholic Church was sacrosanct. All nightmares stoked from the pulpit had been made real and the demons of the Godless, classless, anarchic French Revolution stalked the land.

Now the field armies of the juntas were on the back foot, the Spanish guerrilla war began in earnest. Isolated patrols of French soldiers were butchered, and messengers intercepted, every movement of the French was watched, recorded and exploited.

The Battle of Sahagún

Moore set off to surprise Soult, entrusting the vanguard to his cavalry commander, the enthusiastic Lieutenant General Henry Bayley-Paget, Lord Paget. The 40-year-old veteran of many campaigns, Paget was described by his brother as "always at the head, and in the thick of everything that has been going on. He is, in this respect, quite a boy, and a Cornet instead of a Lieutenant General of Cavalry."

Soult had become aware that the enemy was moving towards him in some force. Although he failed to get any meaningful intelligence on their numbers and location, he moved his own cavalry screen further forward to the towns of Mayorga and Sahagún.

At the latter, General César Alexandre Debelle, commanding the 8th Dragoons and 1st Provisional Chasseurs, found his morning ablutions of December 21 rudely disturbed by the bold 10th and 15th Hussars - properly and cumbersomely titled 10th (or Prince of Wales's Own) Regiment of (Light) Dragoons (Hussars) and 15th (or King's) Regiment of (Light) Dragoons (Hussars) - supported by a detachment of horse artillery with four guns. The exchange entered the lore of the Peninsula War, with the stirring 'Sahagún Song':

"We saddled our horses, and away we did go
O'er rivers of ice and o'er mountains of snow,
To the town of Sahagún then our course we did steer,
'Twas the 15th Hussars, who had never known fear."

Numbering somewhere over 1,000 men, the 10th and 15th marched 12 miles through the frosty night, their baggage and ammunition wagons trailing behind so that they could ride fast and light. Paget's plan was for the 10th Hussars and the artillery to cross the Bridge of

LEFT 'Heroes of Corunna Bang Up to the Mark, or A New Way to Exercise Cavalry Horses' a mocking editorial cartoon unfairly suggesting that the cavalry were little more than coachmen for the retreating army. In truth they had fought the only successful offensive engagement of the campaign as well as several rearguard actions.

BELOW The miserable retreat to A Coruña through the snow-covered hills of Galicia. Sketched by the diplomat Robert Ker Porter and published in Letters from Portugal and Spain, Written During the March of the Troops Under Sir John Moore (1809).

> "Numbering somewhere over 1,000 men, the 10th and 15th marched 12 miles through the frosty night, their baggage and ammunition wagons trailing behind so that they could ride fast and light."

THE ROAD TO WATERLOO 33

The Road to Waterloo   MOORE'S CAMPAIGN

The view of the Battle of A Coruña from the French lines.

Sahagún and drive the startled French into the 15th Hussars waiting on the other side.

Arriving in thin mist and early morning light, the 10th Hussars galloped across the bridge to scatter a solitary picket, who sounded a bugle and put the camp to flight. The French, in their gleaming helmets and fierce horsehair plumes, attempted well-ordered retreat, skirting the flanks of the 15th to fight over the perilous ground of a frozen vineyard. Covered with roots and furrows that could bring down a horse more surely than a carbine, many of the French dismounted to give fire from the cover of a ditch.

Captain Alexander Gordon recalled: "The 15th then halted, wheeled into line, huzzaed, and advanced. The interval betwixt us was perhaps 400 yards, but it was so quickly passed that they had only time to fire a few shots before we came upon them, shouting: 'Emsdorff and victory!' The shock was terrible; horses and men were overthrown, and a shriek of terror, intermixed with oaths, groans, and prayers for mercy, issued from the whole extent of their front."

With many of the Frenchmen out of the saddle, the charge was devastating. The British counted only four of their own killed and 21 wounded, and those French who survived surrendered or fled. The losses taken by the 1st Provisional Chasseurs were so heavy that the regiment was later disbanded entirely.

The Battle of Benavente

Reaching Sahagún later that day, Moore

RIGHT *A mid-19th-century map, showing the wider Battle of A Coruña, with the top of the image being the east.*

ordered his army to rest and planned to march at sunset on December 23. The initiative was rapidly disappearing, not only did Soult now know where the British were but by the afternoon Napoléon I was turning north to cut off the British retreat. Outnumbered by more than four to one and facing the French Emperor himself, Moore embarked upon what has been come to be called the Retreat to A Coruña.

As the army turned tail, the light cavalry vanguard became a stalwart rearguard and the 10th Hussars were the next to distinguish themselves. While they skirmished with a regiment of French dragoons near Mayorga on Christmas Day, they learnt that another squadron was forming up on a ridge and preparing to attack. Deciding to seize the momentum, the 10th Hussars charged uphill. Despite hooves skidding through the slush and equine nostrils steaming in frustration, they overwhelmed the surprised French to take another 100 prisoners.

Paget stationed pickets along the swollen River Esla to screen the British retreat while engineers sent the bridge crashing into the raging water. A few hours later, General Charles Lefebvre-Desnouettes was finally able to ford the Esla and push on with 500 or so chasseurs and some colonial Mamelukes. The 18th Hussars - 130 strong - made a hopeless charge, but were repulsed, they tried again with some reinforcements from the 3rd Dragoons of the King's German Legion before they were driven back two miles to the outskirts of Benavente.

The 18th and 3rd having bought them time, Paget brought up some of his stalwart 10th and launched them into an ambush. With the numbers now roughly equal, Lefebvre-Desnouettes ordered a retreat and it was his turn to be driven back over the two miles to the Esla. Around 50 British cavalrymen were killed and 55 French. Lefebvre-Desnouettes and 72 of his chasseurs were taken prisoner.

Though Moore had several opportunities to stand and fight, discipline was decaying rapidly, and it was no longer a given that his orders would be followed, had he risked issuing them. Amplified by the hostile reception the British had received in Spain, 72 hours of constant rain, and being forced to march 36 hours without rest, men billeted at Benavente's Medieval convent gleefully tore the place apart and beat up a friar, while soldiers and their wives raided the wine cellars and rum rations for a fatalistic bout of boozing.

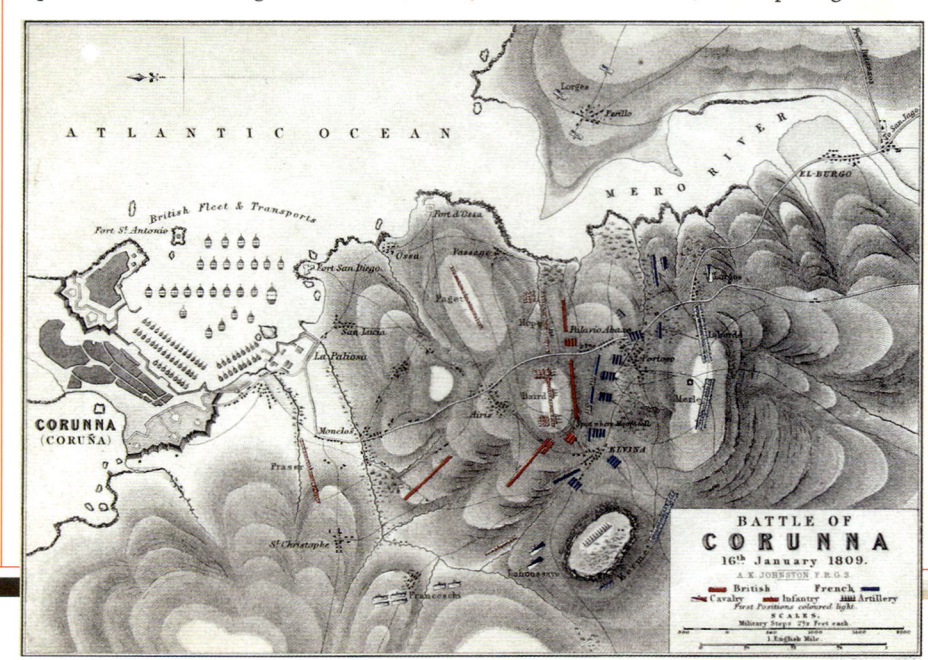

"In the afternoon we passed through a large village which had been completely gutted by fire," wrote Captain Gordon. "The wretched inhabitants were sitting amidst the trifling articles of property they had been able to seize from the flames, contemplating the ruins of their homes in silent despair. The bodies of several Spaniards who had died of hunger and disease or perished from the inclemency of the weather were lying scattered around and added to the horrors of the scene. The village had been burned by some of our infantry."

The Battle of A Coruña

On the surface, Moore had made all the right decisions. He had taken advantage of opportunities as he saw them, and then when the threat of defeat loomed, he had made all haste to extract his army from danger. The problem was that Moore had been repeatedly making the right decisions at the wrong time. His campaign failed not through any want of common sense, but for every want of initiative.

Winter was by now unloading all her torments upon the armies who forced their way through the mountains of Galicia and León. Moore had sent ahead for the Royal Navy to meet them at A Coruña, and the British Army pushed on into blizzards and through fords that had become raging rivers of mud. The French fared little better - the Grand Armée diehards compared it to the campaign in Poland, and some of those who fell behind opted to take their own lives rather than risk a slow death at the hands of Spanish guerrillas.

As the British began to falter, the stragglers became increasingly harassed by the advance guard of the Grande Armée and the road was littered with dead, dying, and discarded. Amid the disgrace were moments of heroism as Sergeant William Newman, 43rd (Monmouthshire Light Infantry) Regiment, gathered up 100 of the most able-bodied wounded and held a narrow point on the road against French cavalry, buying their comrades a four-mile head start on the pursuers. Newman survived, was awarded £50 - effectively a year's wages - and promoted to Ensign (the junior-most commission rank) in the 1st West India Regiment.

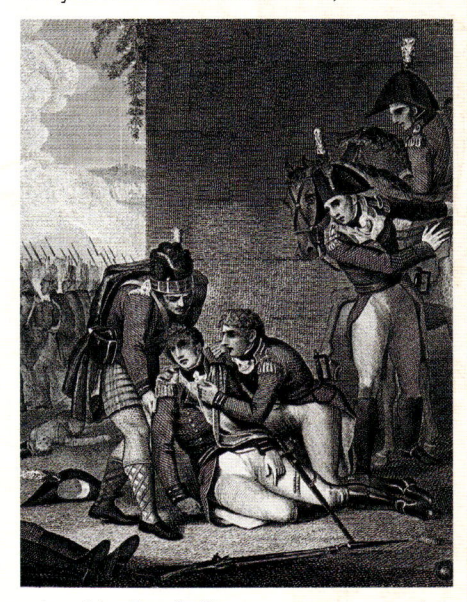

ABOVE *John Trumbull's contemporary engraving shows the death of Sir John Moore, struck by a cannonball in the chest, during the fierce fighting for the village of Elviña.* WELLCOME COLLECTION CC BY

ABOVE RIGHT *The grave of Sir John Moore in A Coruña. Contrary to myth and unlike the battlefield monument, the stonework wasn't commissioned by Marshal Soult.* D ROVCHAK CC BY-SA 4.0

On January 12, 1809, the British limped into A Coruña to see the cold grey ocean stretched out before them. It was empty. The ships they were expecting to rescue them had not yet arrived and the evacuation could not begin until January 14, by which time the French were closing in. Napoléon I, satisfied with the endgame he had set in motion, left the destruction of the British to Soult and returned to Paris, but Soult's army wasn't ready for a pitched battle. The race to the sea had seen the French strung out across the frozen landscape and he needed time to regroup. Once sails had been sighted, followed by the thunderous cacophony of Moore detonating the powder stores, it was clear that Soult had to attack.

The Battle of A Coruña - often written as Corunna in English - began on January 16. The centrepiece of the British line was the village of Elviña, which overlooked the road to the port and here the fighting was the bloodiest as the British sought to cover the evacuation, an operation that deserves to be recalled alongside Dunkirk as a glimmer of hope amid utter hopelessness.

The main line of the defence was the Monte Moro ridge, which although overlooked by the hills to the south - the Palavea and Panesqueado Heights - was a natural fortification. The French quickly took the heights, chasing away the British pickets and seeing off an attempt by the 5th (Northumberland) Regiment of Foot to retake them. The battle now turned to the village of Elviña, which anchored the western flank of the Monte Moro.

It was a contest of irresistible force meeting an immovable object. In the early afternoon, Soult unleashed a thunderous barrage of elite French artillery on the defenders and then charged, driving the 4th (or the King's Own) Regiment of Foot, 42nd Royal Highland Regiment and 50th (or the West Kent) Regiment of Foot from the village. A counter-attack returned the three regiments to the crumbling walls of Elviña, with Moore bringing up the Guards Brigade and leading the defence himself to drive the French back at the point of their bayonets.

Inevitably, given the savagery of the fighting around Elviña, Moore was fatally wounded - struck in the chest with a cannonball. He was buried within the walls of A Coruña, one of the 900 British dead in the battle, with a further 500 killed during the retreat, giving his life to ensure the survivors could evacuate safely. The defenders kept the French at bay until nightfall, which was all the time they needed.

Magnanimous in defeat, Marshal Soult erected a memorial over the spot where Moore fell as a mark of his respect.

The Road to Waterloo — THE OPORTO CAMPAIGN

Pilgrims ON THE DOURO

The Oporto Campaign, April - May, 1809

By the time Lieutenant General Sir Arthur Wellesley returned to the Peninsula on April 22, 1809, having been vindicated by the Cintra Inquiry, the colours on the map told a very different story from the situation on the ground.

The evacuation of the battered and bruised force of the late Sir John Moore had left the defence of the British Army's beachhead in the hands of the nervy General Sir John Cradock and his garrison at Lisbon. Cradock, like many of the military establishment believed that while Portugal's mountainous northern frontier with Spain was ideal terrain for a defender, it was too porous to be effectively held by such a small number of troops. As far as he was concerned, Portugal was lost the second that Moore fell, and he urged a full withdrawal from the Peninsula.

The mood at home was certainly receptive. Weaned on larger-than-life stories of heroic Spain's valiant independence war and the British victory at Vimeiro, the sight of weary

> "Panicked civilians attempted to flee across the pontoon bridges over the Douro River to safety, but they collapsed under the terrible press of bodies."

redcoats stumbling and slipping onto the quay at Southampton was a rude awakening and it knocked the jingo from much of the cabinet.

"Our beards were long and ragged," wrote Rifleman Benjamin Harris, 95th Rifles, "almost all were without shoes and stockings; many had their clothes and accoutrements in fragments, with their heads swathed in old rags, and our weapons were covered with rust."

The war, however, was far from over. The long, hard retreat to A Coruña - while not feeling particularly glorious - had nonetheless drawn substantial numbers of French troops from the business of uprooting the tangled thorns of Spanish resistance. Huge swathes of the country remained in open revolt. Galicia and Asturias were bandit country, Catalonia remained as defiant as ever.

Three Marshals at war

Three French armies were poised to sweep through Portugal, in accordance with the strategy that Emperor Napoléon I had set in motion. Following the Battle of A Coruña (January 16, 1809) Marshal Jean-de-Dieu Soult marched on Portugal's second city and overran the defenders at the First Battle of Oporto (March 29, 1809) - punching through the handful of regular soldiers and the miserably armed citizen militia, the Ordenanças.

Those defenders who attempted to surrender were murdered. Panicked civilians attempted to flee across the pontoon bridges over the Douro River to safety, but they collapsed under the terrible press of bodies. Witnessing what had become of those who laid down their arms, 200 militiamen locked themselves in the bishop's palace and fought to the death.

The taking of Oporto cost Soult's Armée de Portugal around 500 dead, and 8,000 Portuguese soldiers and civilians slaughtered in return. However, whilst he had some 40,000 soldiers on paper, the winter campaign against Moore had cost Soult dearly. Discounting the sick and injured, he could muster only 20,000 effective men.

He had advanced as far as he could for the foreseeable future. Soult was effectively trapped in Oporto, unable to reopen his lines of communication or supply through the countryside where each attempt was rebuffed by regrouped Portuguese forces under the aristocratic Lieutenant General Francisco da Silveira Pinto da Fonseca Teixeira. Soult's men were exhausted and demoralised, numbed by the carnage and conscious of just how far they were from home.

As Soult moved south following Moore's fall, 25,000 men led by Marshal Michel Ney - who Napoléon I called "bravest of the brave" - were dispatched to subdue Galicia and once victorious, cross the frontier into Portugal. This was easier said than done. The remnant of Romana's Spanish Army of

LEFT *Lieutenant General Sir Arthur Wellesley in the uniform of a Major General in India, circa 1804. His service in Asia saw him nicknamed 'the Sepoy General' by his rivals at Horse Guards.*

BOTTOM LEFT *British infantry and cavalry overwhelm the French pickets at the Battle of Grijó, securing the advance to the River Douro and beyond it, Oporto. Painted by Henri Leveque and engraved by the prolific Charles Heath, 1812*

the Left had skirted the Battle of A Coruña and reappeared to mount a series of limited offensives while the countryside thronged with guerrillas who struck from the hills and melted away.

A French victory over the Spanish General Gregorio Garcia de la Cuesta at the Battle of Medellín (March 28, 1809) took Marshal Claude Victor-Perrin and his 18,000-strong force to within striking distance of Portugal's eastern border, but Cuesta had brought the French to the brink of defeat. Victor's army could go no further.

Three Marshals of France had been fought to a standstill. Most bizarrely of all, a 9,000-strong corps under General Pierre Belon Lapisse, which had been detached from Victor's command to join Soult, had been virtually incapacitated by the constant harassment from the energetic 33-year-old diplomat-turned-freebooter Colonel Sir Robert Wilson.

Commanding the 1,600-strong

The Road to Waterloo

THE OPORTO CAMPAIGN

Loyal Lusitanian Legion - a green-clad light infantry regiment of Portuguese exiles recruited and trained in Britain - Wilson chose to ignore the order to evacuate from A Coruña as it would have left northern Portugal undefended. Instead, he strung out half his force as a skirmish line in front of Soult's advance and led the remainder to the formidable fortress of Almeida where they were able to make mischief disproportionate to their number.

In another ringing endorsement of British light infantry doctrine, Lapisse was convinced he was being faced by closer to 12,000 men and was too busy jumping at shadows to link up with Soult.

Against the weakening of nerve in London, Wellesley had reasoned that France would require close to 100,000 men to pacify Portugal alone. Given Napoléon I's commitments elsewhere, those 100,000 men simply wouldn't be available.

Great Britain, meanwhile, wouldn't need vast numbers of men to keep the population in line or to keep supply lines open - they had the Royal Navy and near-complete mastery of the Atlantic Ocean and the Mediterranean. Instead, Wellesley proposed that working with Spain and Portugal (30,000 infantry, 5,000 cavalry and as much artillery as could be spared) would be enough to turn the tide of war

With his close ally Lord Castlereagh, Secretary of State for War and the Colonies, agitating on his behalf, Wellesley's proposal became policy and he was sent to replace the despondent Cradock in Portugal.

Conspiracies and calculations

Wellesley's faith in his war-winning strategy was only strengthened by the view from the ground where it was immediately obvious that his foes had both failed to balance their resources between conquest and occupation and failed to coordinate effectively. The latter was a growing weakness in the Napoleonic French Army, where the rise and fall of marshals was conditional on the personal patronage of the Emperor himself. This encouraged the likes of Soult, Ney and Victor to strike out alone so they could claim the laurels of each great feat for themselves

Including the reinforcements, he had brought with him, Wellesley had around 30,000 men at his disposal, and with Beresford's 16,000-strong Portuguese Army (see boxout), he reckoned he had enough men to pin one opponent in place and confront a second in the field.

The plan was for the main force of 18,500 men and 24 cannons to advance on Oporto with Wellesley, while Beresford took a column of 6,000 to join Lieutenant General Silveira's Portuguese force of 6,000 regulars and 4,000 Ordenanças in the north. They would then outflank the enemy, cut off their lines of communication to the east and permanently block any link-up between Victor and Soult. To further keep Victor at bay, an army of 12,000 was to proceed to Abrantes where they would, wrote Wellesley, either "impede or delay Victor's progress, in case he should come in while I am absent."

The balance of power shifted ever so slightly on two counts. Though Soult had initially no knowledge of the operation that was building to his south, he was preoccupied with mopping up Silveira's rabble along the River Tâmega.

Two attempts by the charismatic and capable General Louis Henri Loison to force a crossing of the Tâmega on April 7 had been rebuffed. In the exchanges that followed, it was Silveira's turn to lick his wounds and he withdrew his army to their strong defensive positions around Amarante, blew all but one bridge and mined the survivor to safeguard against a French crossing. In the early morning fog

Marshal Soult watches the storming of Oporto in this painting by Joseph Beaume, 1839.

38 THE ROAD TO WATERLOO

THE NEW MODEL PORTUGUESE ARMY

With barely 22,000 regular soldiers still in the field (16,000 around Lisbon and 6,000 in the north), the Portuguese government swallowed its pride and asked for British assistance in January 1809. Despite the fierce debate that was unfolding over whether to continue with the Peninsula Campaign at all, Major General William Carr Beresford was proposed based on his reputation as an effective administrator and unyielding disciplinarian.

As a friend of Wellesley's, it's possible that Castlereagh was already putting the return of his protege in motion by nominating the Major General. As his condition for accepting, Beresford insisted that he have control over all Portuguese military appointments and promotions, and face no restrictions when it came to disciplining those who disobeyed his commands.

On March 7, 1809, Beresford was appointed commander-in-chief of the Portuguese Army (with the rank of Marshal) by the government-in-exile, just in time to face difficult decisions as Soult advanced on Oporto. Realising that the city couldn't be held with the army in its present state, Beresford refused to reinforce the defenders.

With morale shattered by invasion, occupation and the flight of the royal family, Beresford's first order of business was discipline and organisation. He appointed several British officers to key positions and rebuilt the army along the lines of the British battalion system (with the commander and second-in-command being British and Portuguese, or vice versa).

Beresford discovered that in some cases, junior officers had been in their posts for as long as 30 years and some were far too infirm for the demands of the field. The radical solution was forced retirement and then promotions by merit, and he either groomed enthusiastic young Portuguese officers or promoted British officers on secondment to 'temporary' brevet commissions.

Beresford insisted on courts-martial for even the pettiest of infractions (streamlining the Portuguese process to speed things up) with a view to firmly stamping his authority on the army and insisted on accurate record-keeping when it came to equipment which was frequently sold on the black market by corrupt officers. The Beresford regime was a shock to the system for officers and men alike - in one early example, a soldier who refused to march was sentenced to ten years hard labour.

BELOW An illustration showing the uniform and colour facings of the new-look Portuguese infantryman under the reforms of Marshal William Carr Beresford.

of May 2, French engineers deactivated the mine and stormed Amarante where the Portuguese defences were unmanned.

Though Silveira escaped the Battle of Amarante (April 7-May 2, 1809) with the greater part of his men, most of their cannon had been seized, and his army was in no position to support Wellesley's grand plan.

Meanwhile, Marshal Soult had been advancing his ambitions to be proclaimed King of Portugal. He arranged petitions to have him accept the crown and started a newspaper to agitate on his behalf. A significant presence within Soult's own force was less than impressed, including the dutiful career soldiers who gathered around General Loison. They went so far as to plan a coup to place Soult under arrest for treason and take command of the Armée de Portugal if he went so far as to declare himself King.

Unlikely support of the man who would be king came from the ardent Jacobins - those whose beliefs in the ideals of the French Revolution made them hostile to the very idea of the French Emperor, less one of Napoléon Bonaparte's character. Mostly younger officers, their ringleader Captain Philippe-Charles Argenton launched a ludicrously unrealistic plot in which the Jacobins would promise to back Soult's claims to kingship if he turned his army against the despotic regime of Napoléon I. Argenton - who had also been in contact with the British, although he received limited enthusiasm on Wellesley's part - approached a French general with his proposal and the mortified general took it straight to Soult. The whole plot counted on the marshal's vanity outweighing his loyalty, but Argenton had made a gross miscalculation. Argenton was pardoned in exchange for naming his co-conspirators and let slip the British offensive looming from the south.

Soult - or "King Nicholas" as he had become mockingly known - immediately ordered Loison to secure a line of retreat through Bragança, northeast of Oporto and placed his screen south of the River Douro on alert, where they scrapped with the British at the village of Grijó. The intention had been for the French retreat to be cut off entirely, but the flanking

THE ROAD TO WATERLOO 39

The Road to Waterloo — THE OPORTO CAMPAIGN

party were delayed on the road. The weight of the battle was carried by Wellesley's advance guard, formed of the 1st Battalion of Detachments, comprising men who had been sick or wounded in Lisbon when their regiments were evacuated from A Coruña.

The Second Battle of Oporto

Unable to escape his understandable fear of British naval superiority, Marshal Soult locked onto the idea that the offensive would come from the sea. He gathered his army to the west of Oporto ready to resist a landing, blew the bridges, brought all the boats on the river over to the north shore, and left the north bank of the Douro thinly defended. Though sentries kept watch from the quays, the eastern suburbs of the city and the rugged terrain to the east were largely ignored.

On the evening of May 11, as survivors of the Battle of Grijó (May 10-11, 1809) galloped into Oporto, Soult decided on a full withdrawal, but he hadn't counted on how quickly Wellesley's army was moving. Early the next morning, Wellesley rode into Vila Nova de Gaia - the town that faced Oporto across the River Douro from the southern bank - virtually unnoticed by the French and surveyed the city from the shelter of the Monastery of Serra do Pilar where he received some encouraging local intelligence.

Firstly, a sunken river ferry had been found a few miles upriver at Avintes, which although damaged by the French, was already being repaired by the villagers for his use. Secondly, a barber had slipped across the water in the night and revealed that four wine barges - Oporto's most famous export being port wine - were intact on the northern shore, just to the east of the city at the Bishop's Seminary. A large stone building, the seminary, was the ideal strongpoint for the taking of the city, and from Wellesley's vantage point it showed no signs of having been garrisoned.

The ferry crossing was entrusted to Major General John Murray, who took two infantry battalions and two cavalry squadrons of his 7th Brigade five miles east to Avintes where they could flank the French in a wide arc and cut off their retreat. Wellesley had encountered Murray's brand of baffling inactivity as

ABOVE *A soldier of the 3rd (East Kent) Regiment of Foot (The Buffs) circa 1812, by the great Victorian/Edwardian military artist Richard Canton Woodville, 1910.*

RIGHT *A trooper of the 14th (or Duchess of York's Own) Light Dragoons, the only cavalry regiment to earn the battle honour 'Douro'.*

Quartermaster General in India and would see nothing in the Peninsula that would force him to reassess the man.

The army's energetic intelligence officer, Major John Waters - who was fluent in both Spanish and Portuguese - was sent across the Douro to secure the wine barges and reconnoitre the seminary in the company of the bold barber, the Prior of Amarante, and some local boatmen who had to be sweet-talked into risking their lives. Waters returned with the boats and confirmation that the seminary was unoccupied. "Well," said Wellesley, "let the men cross."

In the crisp morning light, a light company of the 1/3rd (East Kent) Regiment of Foot (The Buffs) - 25 men per boat - crossed the Douro and occupied the seminary. Meanwhile, Wellesley wheeled his artillery into the monastery gardens, where their elevated position allowed them to scatter all but the northern approach to the seminary with shrapnel. While the Buffs began to secure the seminary gate with an iron bar and improvised firing steps against the walls, more men were ferried across.

As the third boat was mid-way across the river, wrote the historian and Peninsula veteran Sir Patrick Napier, "tumultuous noises rolled through Oporto, the drums beat to arms, shouts arose, the citizens, vehemently gesticulating, made signals from their houses, and confused masses of troops rushing out from the higher streets threw down forward swarms of skirmishers, and came furiously down the seminary."

Roughly an hour after the crossing had begun, Marshal Soult woke to the news that the British had some 1,000 men in the seminary and General Maximilien Foy was leading a suicidal attempt to try and drive them back. Attacking an entrenched position under the view of the British guns across the river, it was a slaughter. The few cannons that the French were able to bring up were quickly silenced and the cut down by volley after volley. With more infantry - the 48th (or Northamptonshire) Regiment of Foot, 66th (or the Berkshire) Regiment of Foot, and a Portuguese battalion - ferried across, after two hours Foy was forced to retreat.

With the bulk of his forces west of the city and too far away to assist, at midday Soult ordered the sentries on the quayside into the fray. The harbour was now unguarded, and the people of Oporto began to take their boats to Vila Nova de Gaia to bring the British across. In less than an hour, the streets were riddled with redcoats and the crack of muskets, and Soult ordered a complete retreat.

Major General Murray was advancing towards the Valonga road as ordered and he should have been able to squeeze the French retreat into a full-blown rout, but he hung back. Only the 14th (or Duchess of York's Own) Light Dragoons bloodied their sabres when Lieutenant Colonel Charles Stewart - Wellesley's daredevil Adjutant General - rode

40 THE ROAD TO WATERLOO

ABOVE *Jean-de-Dieu Soult painted in the early 1800s with the baton of a Marshal of the Empire, a pre-Revolutionary role resurrected by Napoléon I in 1804 and granted to his closest followers among the army.*

up and in frustration, insisted on leading them into the French rearguard himself.

They charged through the retreating column at a bend in the road, knocking one French general from his horse (Henri François Delaborde) and wounding another (the unfortunate Foy) with a wicked sword blow to the shoulder, but paid a price in casualties. One French prisoner told Captain Peter Hawker: "We must be drunk or mad as the brigade we had attacked was nearly 2,000 strong."

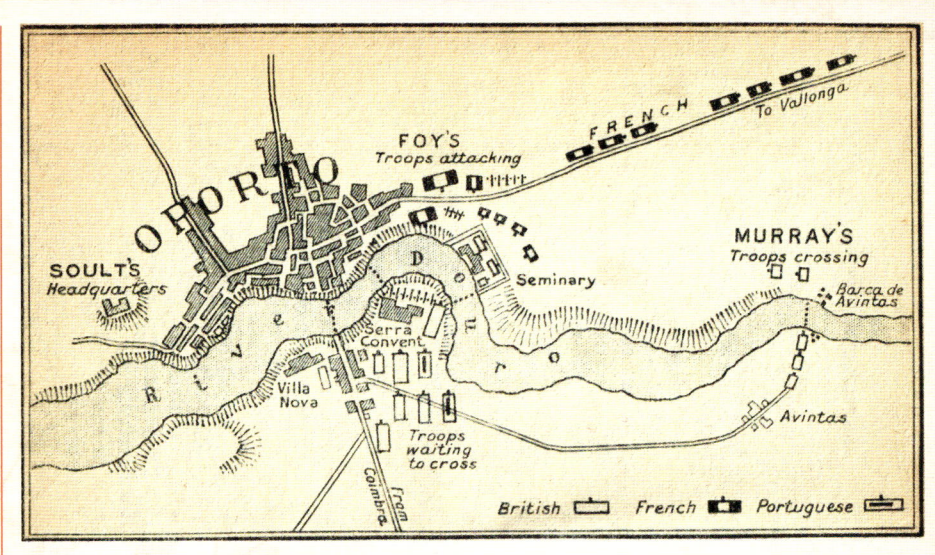

ABOVE *A simplified map showing the French positions in both the First and Second Battle of Oporto, and the British position in the latter.*

LEFT *An 1837 painting of an Oporto street scene dominated by Torre dos Clérigos, the bell tower of the 18th century Clérigos Church, by British artist James Holland.*

BELOW *British infantry stream across the River Douro in the wine barges for the monastery to the east of the city.*

British losses were counted at only 123, around 50 of which belonged to only one regiment: The Buffs, who were permitted to add Duoro to their battle honours. Marshal Soult had suffered an estimated 300 killed and wounded. He had been forced to leave 1,500 wounded in the city's hospitals as prisoners and 70 guns as prizes of war.

THE ROAD TO WATERLOO 41

The Road to Waterloo — THE TALAVERA CAMPAIGN

Fury of the MARSHALS

The Talavera Campaign, June-August, 1809

The army of Marshal Jean-de-Dieu Soult ran like a fox being pursued by hounds across northeastern Portugal, with Major General William Beresford's Portuguese snarling at his right flank, and Lieutenant General Sir Arthur Wellesley at his back. The horrors of occupation and the sight of their occupiers on the run roused the bloodlust of the guerrillas, who took advantage - murdering and mutilating stragglers and patrols.

Beresford seized the planned French escape route, forcing Soult to abandon his wagons and artillery and attempt to force his way through a steep mountain pass and onto a rugged track through the highlands.

Soult made it to the River Misarella, where the bridge was held by Ordenanças. The Passage of the Misarella (May 17, 1809) was easily won in the face of the untrained levies, but it delayed the French Armée de Portugal just long enough for Wellesley to engage the rearguard at the Combat of Salamonde (May 17). There the disordered French broke and bolted across the (different) bridge. Packed tight in desperation they were easy prey for the British cannon.

By the time Wellesley halted his pursuit at the Misarella and turned back for central Portugal, Soult had lost an additional 4,000 men in the flight, while the hounds at his heels took an estimated 500 casualties

Braced for impact

Leaving the border with Galicia and León watched by local militias and the Portuguese Army remnant under Lieutenant General Francisco da Silveira Pinto da Fonseca Teixeira, Wellesley's next target was I Corps under Marshal Claude Victor-Perrin which was within striking distance of southern Portugal.

Before he departed for Oporto, Wellesley had entrusted the containment of Victor to a 12,000-strong Corps of Observation under Major General John Randoll Mackenzie, and already their forward elements had clashed at the Battle of Alcántara (May 14) where a small number of the British-raised Loyal Lusitanian Legion and local defenders had been driven from the Spanish border town.

The 2,000 Portuguese held the vital Alcántara Bridge for three hours before they were finally overrun, their attempt to mine the bridge before they withdrew failed when the hardy Roman engineering withstood the blast. Victor, who was leading the assault himself, had assumed the Loyal Lusitanians were the spearhead of a major British offensive and when he advanced a few miles beyond Alcántara and realised that there was no great army over the hill, he pulled back. It was just as well, his old Spanish sparring partner, General Gregorio García de la Cuesta, had reformed enough of his forces to mount an opportunistic attack on some of Victor's outlying garrisons.

Despite having finally been re-joined by the detached command of General Pierre Belon Lapisse (who knew more than most how much of a nuisance the Loyal Lusitanian Legion could be), he begged Madrid for reinforcements. Madrid was in a state of total ignorance about affairs even a few miles from the city gates - few messengers made it through the insurgent-riddled countryside - and what news did make it through to the so-called 'King José I' was bleak.

Marshal Soult had been thrown out of Portugal by the British, Marshal Louis Gabriel Suchet had been forced to evacuate Aragon after his defeat by a smaller Spanish army at the Battle of Alcañiz (May 23), and Marshal Michel Ney was chasing guerrillas

LEFT *'The Battle of Talavera' by Henri Leveque, created sometime between 1812 and 1815 as part of his series of Napoleonic battles and showing Wellesley overseeing the battle from the high ground.*

ABOVE *Claude Victor-Perrin, painted between 1807 and 1812 by Antoine-Jean Gros. Promoted to Marshal of France only two years earlier, Victor was under immense pressure to prove himself to Emperor Napoléon I.*

LEFT *General Francisco Javier Venegas de Saavedra y Ramínez de Arenzana painted in 1815 by José Aparicio. His actions around the Battle of Talavera are difficult to account for.*

The Road to Waterloo   THE TALAVERA CAMPAIGN

ABOVE *The uniforms of the regular Spanish Army circa 1800, illustrated by Jules Ferrario, 1827.*

BELOW *A matted watercolour by William Heath of the Battle of Talavera, painted between 1818 and 1839 in a more abstract style than is typically the case for military art of the period.*

around Galicia fruitlessly. With no help immediately forthcoming, Victor was forced to retreat behind the River Tagus and take up defensive positions between the towns of Talavera de la Reina and Almaraz. Discovering that supplies were limited, on June 26 Victor pulled back to Talavera de la Reina to consolidate and set the bridge at Almaraz ablaze.

Wellesley meanwhile was reorganising his forces and negotiating with Cuesta for a combined offensive. Despite the momentum having moved against the French, cooperation with the Spanish was still a frustrating business and Cuesta was pushing for a grand encirclement of Victor's I Corps with his 27,000 foot and 6,000 cavalry. Wellesley, who had been marching his men up and down the country ceaselessly, was wary of expecting too much and was in favour of something simpler.

He rearranged his 20,000 men and 30 cannon into four divisions under Major General John Coape Sherbrooke (1st Division), Major General Rowland Hill (2nd Division), Major General Mackenzie (3rd Division), and Brigadier General Alexander Campbell (4th Division). He also entrusted Colonel Sir Robert Wilson and the Loyal Lusitanians to guard his flanks where their mix of British light infantry training and local nous was a particularly effective combination.

Finally, knowledge of Wellesley's whereabouts reached Victor and then Madrid. King José I, who had been previously fixed on supporting operations against General Francisco Javier Venegas de Saavedra y Ramínez de Arenzana and the Spanish Army of La Mancha which had recently emerged from hiding, saddled up his horse and led 11,000 reinforcements to assist the increasingly hysterical Marshal of France.

The best laid plans

Both Wellesley and Cuesta were prickly, self-assured individuals, and any accord was going to be hard-won. What made things more complex is that neither shared the confidence of the Junta Central. They were wary of the generals of the old regime who had so-far treated the civilian government as rivals and leery of the British, who the juntas suspected of facilitating the machinations of men like Cuesta and Romana.

Furthermore, Cuesta believed that the Wellesley wanted to replace him with

> *"Both Wellesley and Cuesta were prickly, self-assured individuals, and any accord was going to be hard-won."*

Venegas, while both Venegas and Cuesta were incensed by rumours that the British government was pushing for Wellesley to be appointed supreme commander of the entire war effort, British, Portuguese and Spanish. That this sort of peacocking and intrigue was the exact reason Britain might want such a thing appears to have passed them by.

The view from the ranks wasn't much rosier. The average British soldier viewed his Spanish counterpart with simmering distrust, and that was reciprocated. Rifleman Edward Costello, 95th Rifles, described Cuesta as a "deformed-looking lump of pride, ignorance and treachery." Old prejudices between Roman Catholics and Protestants played a role (despite the enormous Irish contingent in the redcoat ranks), as did perceptions of Spanish squalor and superstition and British drunkenness and deviance. The British also felt betrayed by the lack of aid given to Sir John Moore's fatal final campaign, just as the Spanish hadn't forgotten that the British had raped and looted their way through Galicia during their retreat.

Venegas was ordered to maintain pressure on the French IV Corps of General Horace François Bastien Sébastiani de La Porta by moving towards Madrid, that way - Wellesley reasoned - they would outnumber Victor by a considerable margin. In theory, Venegas was working from a strict timetable that would leave Wellesley and Cuesta assured of his relative position to their undertaking. There was little margin for error.

Cuesta's Spanish vanguard encountered Victor's forces first and on July 22 they skirmished with a party of startled French dragoons but made little progress until a squadron of British cavalry advanced to threaten the French flanks and scattered them across the River Alberche. Wellesley pushed to engage the French around the town of Talavera de la Reina the next morning while they still had the element of surprise, but Cuesta didn't show up and gave no explanation for his disappearance, and it was only on the morning of July 24 that he finally agreed to an offensive.

In the bright early morning light, they were stunned to discover that Victor had investigated the forces opposing him and had shifted his entire army a further ten miles east of Talavera de la Reina. The furious Wellesley refused to advance any further, while the stubborn Cuesta declared that he would continue alone and ordered his army to make for Toledo. Meanwhile, Venegas had failed to pursue his feint with enough vigour to worry Sébastiani.

ABOVE *Bitter close-quarter fighting at Talavera from Battles of the Nineteenth Century, Vol. I (1896) by Archibald Forbes.*

Theories for this range from personal hatred of Cuesta, that the Junta Central had ordered that both Wellesley and Cuesta should be knocked down a peg, or that it was simply sheer incompetence.

The lion's share of the IV Corps was already in the process of linking up with Victor and including the forces with King José I - aka Joseph-Napoléon Bonaparte - which had arrived from Madrid, the French army around Talavera de la Reina totalled 46,000. In every respect, Wellesley's plan had been tipped on its head and it was getting significantly worse by the day.

Marshal Ney had finally abandoned Galicia to the guerrillas, Marshal François Christophe de Kellermann had done likewise with bandit-ridden Asturias, and their forces were ready to augment Marshal Soult, who had regrouped his own army corps in León. Soult's newly-augmented command of well over 50,000 men was driving south to get behind the British and Spanish forces.

Cuesta was advancing alone into the path of a significantly larger force, and if by some miracle he escaped that massacre, an even larger army was bearing down on them. No less than four Marshals of France and the King of Spain were converging on the two cantankerous commanders.

The Battle of Talavera

One can only imagine the expression on Cuesta's face when the full horror hit him. Victor's reaction was as jubilant as his foe's was crestfallen, and realising that British and Spanish armies had separated, the French cavalry was immediately thrown into action, a steel storm of sabres raining down on the sweat-streaked white tunics of the Spanish.

Without French infantry support, the Spanish managed to hang on for dear life

The Road to Waterloo

THE TALAVERA CAMPAIGN

against the tidal wave of horses and their riders. Cuesta successfully withdrew to the River Alberche where two British divisions frantically moved up to cover their retreat. Springing into action, Wellesley ordered the rest of his army forward to complete a three-mile-long line, anchored on the Spanish right by the town of Talavera de la Reina and the impassable width of the River Tagus in the south, and on the British left by the Sierra de Segurilla mountains in the north.

With the northern half of the battlefield dominated by the Cerro de Medellín (Medellín Hill) and surrounding woodland, French infantry slipped through the trees in the shadow of Medellín where Mackenzie's pickets missed them. The 3rd Division's left and centre were soon shattered by the French assault - the 88th (or Connaught Rangers), 31st (or the Huntingdonshire) Regiment of Foot and 87th (The Prince of Wales's Own Irish) Regiment of Foot fell back in disarray - while only the 45th (or Nottinghamshire) Regiment of Foot held firm.

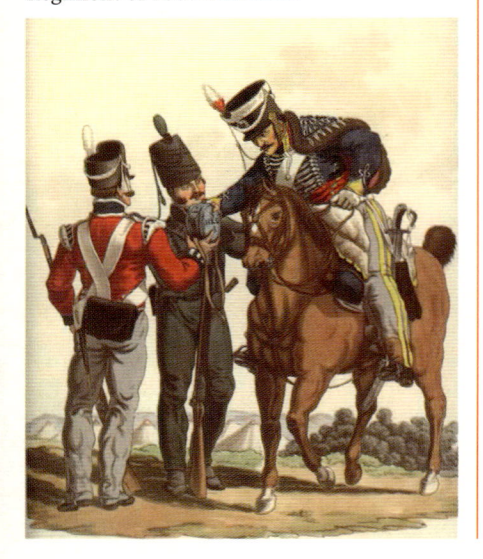

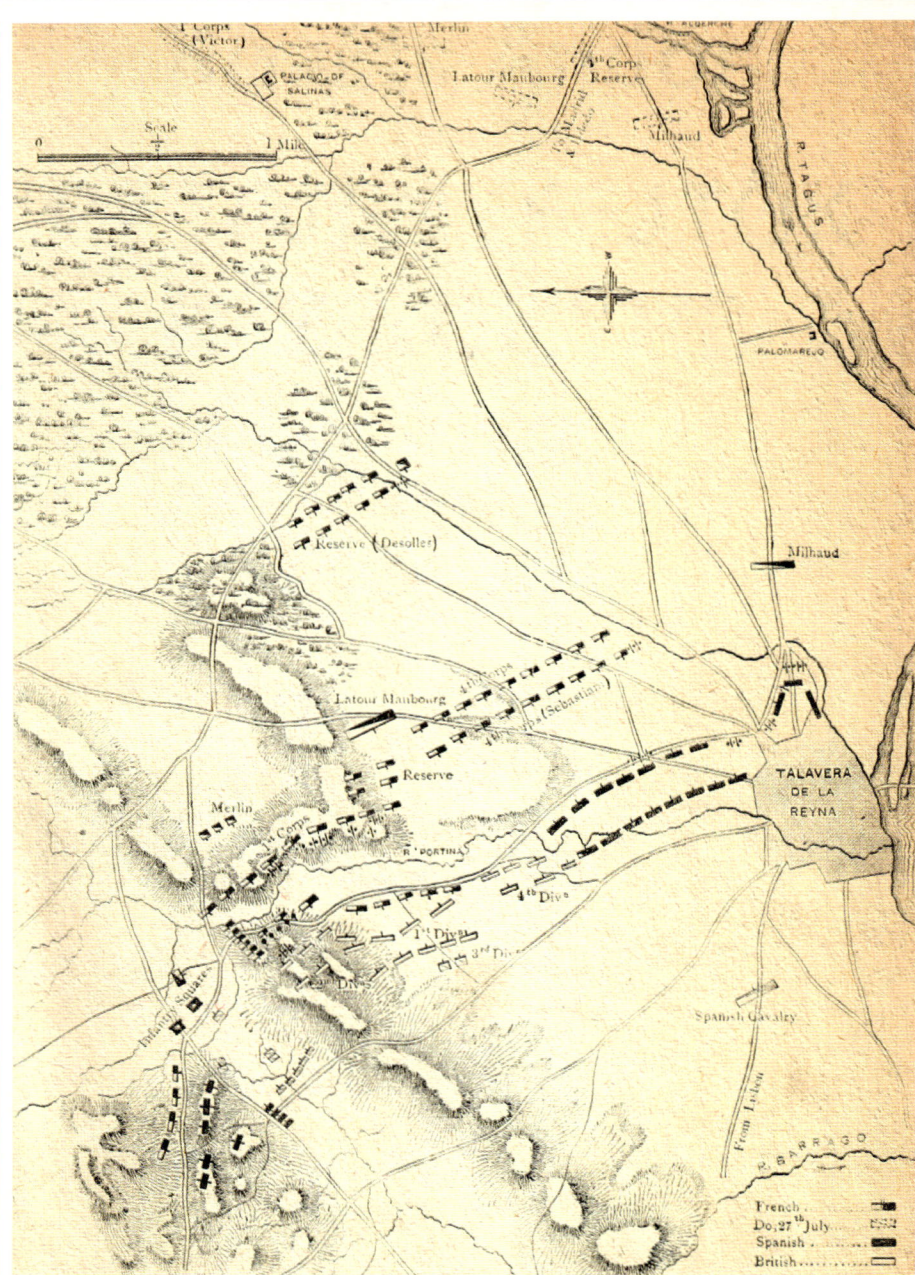

> "A thunderous barrage opened up, shells falling down the length of the British positions from the hateful barrels of over 50 French guns."

Wellesley galloped over to find Mackenzie's command in chaos, and he rallied the broken 31st to the side of the 45th and then managed to regroup the 88th and 87th behind the division's rifle company who doggedly held their position. The bloody battle had begun with 450 casualties - half an entire battalion in a matter of minutes. The 3rd Division was pulled back into reserve, and their position was taken by the 1st Division - somewhere in the bitter scrum Mackenzie himself had fallen, the most senior British casualty of the Battle of Talavera.

A French cavalry squadron proved almost as costly to allied strength without a single round of their own being fired or sword bloodied. As they raced up to the Spanish lines, four battalions of jittery infantry let off a volley in their direction - uselessly, they were still far away - and then turned and bolted, putting the British baggage guard into full flight with them.

With darkness falling and a few shells from both sides falling harmlessly with it, Wellesley and Cuesta steadied their lines, posted pickets and settled down for the night.

ABOVE LEFT *Uniforms of the 14,000-strong King's German Legion, made up of exiled Germans fighting in the British Army. From left to right: a line infantryman, a light infantryman and a hussar.*

ABOVE *The positions of both armies on the afternoon of July 28, the second day of the Battle of Talavera.*

Marshal Victor wasn't finished. The key to the battle was the Cerro de Medellín and he launched a night attack to seize it from the British. However, almost immediately

46 THE ROAD TO WATERLOO

one of the three regiments committed to the attack found itself unable to cross the Portiña, a stream that snaked between the opposing lines. As the watercourse passed through the foot of the hill it ran through a deep chasm that wasn't obvious from the surface, especially not by night. A second column got so lost in the dark that they broke through not into the top of Cerro de Medellín, but a valley to the north.

Only one French regiment successfully climbed the slopes and surprised a brigade of the elite King's German Legion and Major General Hill narrowly avoided being captured as he dashed towards gunfire, getting so close to the French that one made a grab for the bridle of his horse ("I thought it was only the old Buffs making some blunder as usual," he admitted in a letter). Once alerted his 2nd Division were able to send the French battalion tumbling down the hill.

Cannon at dawn

At 5am the boom of a cannon broke the stillness of first light and signalled the start of a second assault on Cerro de Medellín. A thunderous barrage opened up, shells falling down the length of the British positions from the hateful barrels of over 50 French guns. Hill's 2nd Division had taken cover on the reverse slope of Cerro de Medellín when through the rolling clouds of smoke, columns of French infantry threw themselves up the hill. The sheer weight of numbers drove back Hill's skirmishers.

With a manoeuvre that had been used to significant effect at Vimeiro, Hill's infantry suddenly appeared at the crest of Cerro de Medellín. The arrival of their disciplined lines gave the French pause when at a distance of only 40 yards the redcoats emptied a murderous volley down the slope. With only the front rows of the French columns able to fire back, the cascade of close-range musketry tore bloody chunks out of them.

To Hill's right, Major General Sherbrooke watched the French assault and when the charge he was expecting against the 1st Division failed to materialise, he sent one of his battalions forward to open fire into the exposed left flank of the attackers. This was a challenge too many for the men who fought uphill, and they broke, leaving 1,300 dead and dying behind them.

An armistice was called to clear the dead and wounded. It also brought King José I time to consider his options - not that he was getting time to think. While his chief-of-staff advised him to go onto the defensive until Marshal Soult arrived and was able to roll over the enemy from the rear, Victor bellowed himself purple insisting that if they didn't seize the moment then they would all have to answer to the Emperor.

Whatever the reluctant monarch's feelings, two letters arrived to force his hand: one was from Soult, saying that he had been held up trying to replace his guns and wouldn't be there until August 5, and the other was from the French military governor of Toledo, who reported in some agitation that the inscrutable General Venegas was approaching Madrid with the Spanish Army of La Mancha.

It was settled: they had hours to break Wellesley and Cuesta before Sébastiani and the King needed to return to the capital with their men. With the Spanish enjoying a formidable defensive position dug in on the outskirts of the town, the British-held north of the line would take the full force of the attack. In addition to a third frantic frontal assault on the 2nd Division holding Cerro de Medellín and the 1st Division and 4th Division to its south, a flanking manoeuvre would sweep through the northern valley and into the British left.

The lull in the hot summer fighting brought men of both armies to the only water source on the battlefield. Sergeant Andrew Pearson, 61st (or South Gloucestershire) Regiment of Foot, wrote: "The water in the stream, which in the morning was clear and sweet, was now a pool of blood, heaped over with the dead and dying. There being no alternative we were compelled to close our eyes and drink the gory stream."

At about 2pm, the French artillery erupted into life again, forcing the British to seek cover as shot struck the ground all around them. After 30 minutes the rumbling of the guns began to fade as the drums clattered out the advance and rows of French infantry lurched forwards. One regiment lost sight of their comrades in the thick tangle of the olive groves and clouds of smoke and worried they had been left behind, their commander urged them too far forward to catch up. Suddenly very alone, they appeared in front of the 4th Division and were cut down by volley after volley.

The 1st Division to their immediate left was similarly able to push their attackers back with disciplined volleys, but when the French broke, they gave chase, wading through the Portiña and up the bank where they found rows of perfectly intact French infantry waiting for them. Sherbrooke's horrified 1st Division was riddled with shot on three sides and fell back to the steam in panic.

LEFT *A trooper of one of the two highly professional dragoon regiments of the King's German Legion. In 1812 they were redesignated light dragoons.*

THE ROAD TO WATERLOO 47

The Road to Waterloo

THE TALAVERA CAMPAIGN

Wellesley was forced to order up the bruised remnants of Mackenzie's 3rd Division and desperately attempted to rally the 1st Division as they came staggering back over the Portiña.

At the heart of the fight was the 48th (or Northamptonshire) Regiment of Foot and their much-loved commander, Lieutenant Colonel Charles Donellan - known as "Old Charley" and "The Last of the Powderers", because he continued to powder his hair white in accordance with pre-1808 regulations. Alone of the broken 1st Division, Donellan led his men against the flow of the retreating redcoats and according to the Peninsula War chronicler Sir Patrick Napier: "Struck against the right of the pursuing enemy, plying such a destructive musketry and closing with such a firm countenance that his forward movement was checked."

His knee shattered by a musket-ball, Donellan fell and through gritted teeth handed over command to his major "with the same coolness as if he had been on the parade of a barrack-yard." Not only did Talavera become a well-earned battle honour of the 48th, but it was engraved on their cap badges and remained there until the Northamptonshire Regiment was disbanded in 1960.

As the 1st Division regrouped behind Wellesley, the French began to withdraw in turn from the terrible clamour, both sides having cost the other around 1,700 men in the close-quarter carnage.

Defeat from victory

The French flanking manoeuvre in the northern valley was finally in motion, but Wellesley had seen it coming from the high ground. The centrepiece of Victor's strategy was about to hit a composite force of 10,000 British cavalry and Spanish infantry. Having spent the previous hour listening to their comrades fight for their lives. Hooves shuffled impatiently and men toyed with the pommels of their sabres, their eyes fixed ahead.

As the French circled the imposing wedge of Cerro de Medellín they began to see the ominous signs of movement ahead. They formed into squares to meet the British cavalry, but at 150 yards the first row of the 23rd Light Dragoons stumbled into the deep, winding depression of a dried-up stream which was hidden by the long grass. At full gallop, they were unable to pull up and the men behind them piled in on top, a mass of broken bones and punctured lungs.

The 1st Regiment of Dragoons of the King's German Legion charged with greater success, crossing the stream where it was wider and shallower, but they were now dangerously exposed. They wheeled away from the French squares and tried to return to their own lines when General Christophe Antoine Merlin darted out from behind the infantry and rode them down with his elite chasseurs. The 23rd and the 1st Dragoons of the KGL had been all but slaughtered.

It was clear that for the main the French assault had failed. The King needed to make haste for Madrid and although he contemplated throwing his 5,000-strong reserve at the British line to see if that would be the hammer blow that finally broke them, he was conscious that for the most part Cuesta's army was still intact. With a cannon duel continuing until nightfall to cover their withdrawal, when dawn broke on July 27, Wellesley and Cuesta discovered that only Victor's original corps remained, watching them warily from across the Alberche.

The British had taken some 5,500 casualties and the Spanish just over 1,000, but the pressure of around 4,000 wounded on Wellesley's supply train was as catastrophic as the loss of those fighting men themselves, which accounted for nearly a quarter of his entire force. He had no choice but to withdraw from Spain and was forced to race for the Tagus crossing ahead of Marshal Soult, barely scraping across the bridge at Almaraz on August 20.

It would be six months and a whole new year before Wellesley, now ennobled as Viscount Wellington of Talavera, was ready to wage war once more.

'Promoted. On the morrow of Talavera, 28th July 1809' a more sober reflection of the cost of victory by Lady Elizabeth Butler, 1911.

Key Shop

For a great selection of books, DVDs, magazines and models visit:

www.keypublishing.com/shop

Join **BIRD BATTLEFIELD TOURS** on a guided tour of medieval **BRUGES** and the battlefield of **WATERLOO**.

Three nights. Eurostar to Lille. Families and small groups welcome. 'Entertaining and informative'.

For details email Nicky Bird: nick@nickybirddesign.com
www.birdbattlefieldtours.co.uk

BIRD BATTLEFIELD TOURS

LIGNY 1815 MUSEUM

Ligny, the name of this small village appears on all monuments associated with the greatest napoleonian hours from the heights of Ajaccio to the Arc de Triomphe in Paris. On the 16th June 1815, Ligny was the scene of the last victory of Napoleon.

The Ligny 1815 Museum is installed in a historic farm which was used as an infirmary on the evening of the battle.

The museum gives you an outstanding experience by going back in time to this famous battle day, a little over two hundred years ago.

Ligny 1815 Museum

OPENING TIMES

Open from April 1st to November 15th, every day except Tuesday.

Weekdays from 13 pm to 17 pm
Weekends from 11 am to 5 pm

SPECIAL EVENT IN JUNE 2020

12, 13 and 14 June 2020
Historical reenactment
205th anniversary

NEED MORE INFORMATION

Ligny 1815 Museum
Piraux Bridge Street,
23 - 5140 Ligny (BELGIUM)

+ 32(0)71/ 81 83 13
B. Histace: + 32 (0) 477 / 47 38 71

tourisme.ligny@gmail.com
Website: www.ligny1815.be
Facebook: Ligny 1815 Museum

16TH OF JUNE 1815, LIGNY AND THE QUATRE BRAS

An area, in the museum, is also dedicated to the other battle of the 16th of June 1815, Les Quatres Bras, 6 miles west of Ligny, a battle between the French Forces led by Marechal Ney and The Allied Forces managed by the Duke of Wellington. An exceptional collection of items related to the British Army awaits you!

Take the Route Napoleon and travel from one battlefield to the other (15 miles). Seven sites to immerse you in the last hours of the Imperial Army. The battlefield of Waterloo is 25 minutes away from Ligny museum.

THE LINES OF TORRES VEDRAS

The Eagle's CAGE

The Lines of Torres Vedras, September 1809 – September 1810

Whether the Battle of Talavera (July 27-28, 1809) was a British victory or a British defeat is a matter of perspective. As Sir Arthur Wellesley, the newly-anointed Viscount Wellington of Talavera, watched the survivors limp across the Portuguese border he might have briefly considered it the latter.

As they raced to safety with the army of Marshal Jean-de-Dieu Soult at their heels, Wellington had been forced to leave 4,000 wounded to fend for themselves - 500 died on the route and many others were invalided for life by the horrors of the march under the scorching Spanish sun. Another 1,500 of the most severely injured were abandoned for the French to tend to and in this Soult behaved honourably.

Wellington wrote to his brother and gave words to the despair that he kept from his official dispatches: "The soldiers lose their discipline and spirit. The officers are discontented and are almost as bad as the men; and, with the army which a fortnight ago beat double their numbers, I should now hesitate to meet a French corps of half their strength."

The British Army had, however, escaped total annihilation. They would fight another day and although they were in no position to appreciate it, Talavera had to be endured to ensure the victories still to come.

With Wellington off the board in Spain, the French-installed King José I turned back to crushing the widespread resistance. The 30,000 beaten Brits dressing their wounds in Portugal were nowhere near as great a concern to his great reforming project than entire provinces in revolt, a vast rural hinterland crawling with bands of murderous guerrillas and remnants of the Spanish armies, and a rival government dominating the southwest of the country from Seville.

ABOVE AND BELOW *The gun emplacements and stone-lined moat at the Fort of Olheiros as they appear today. The site was significantly restored in 2011.* ROUNDTHEWORLD CC BY-SA 4.0

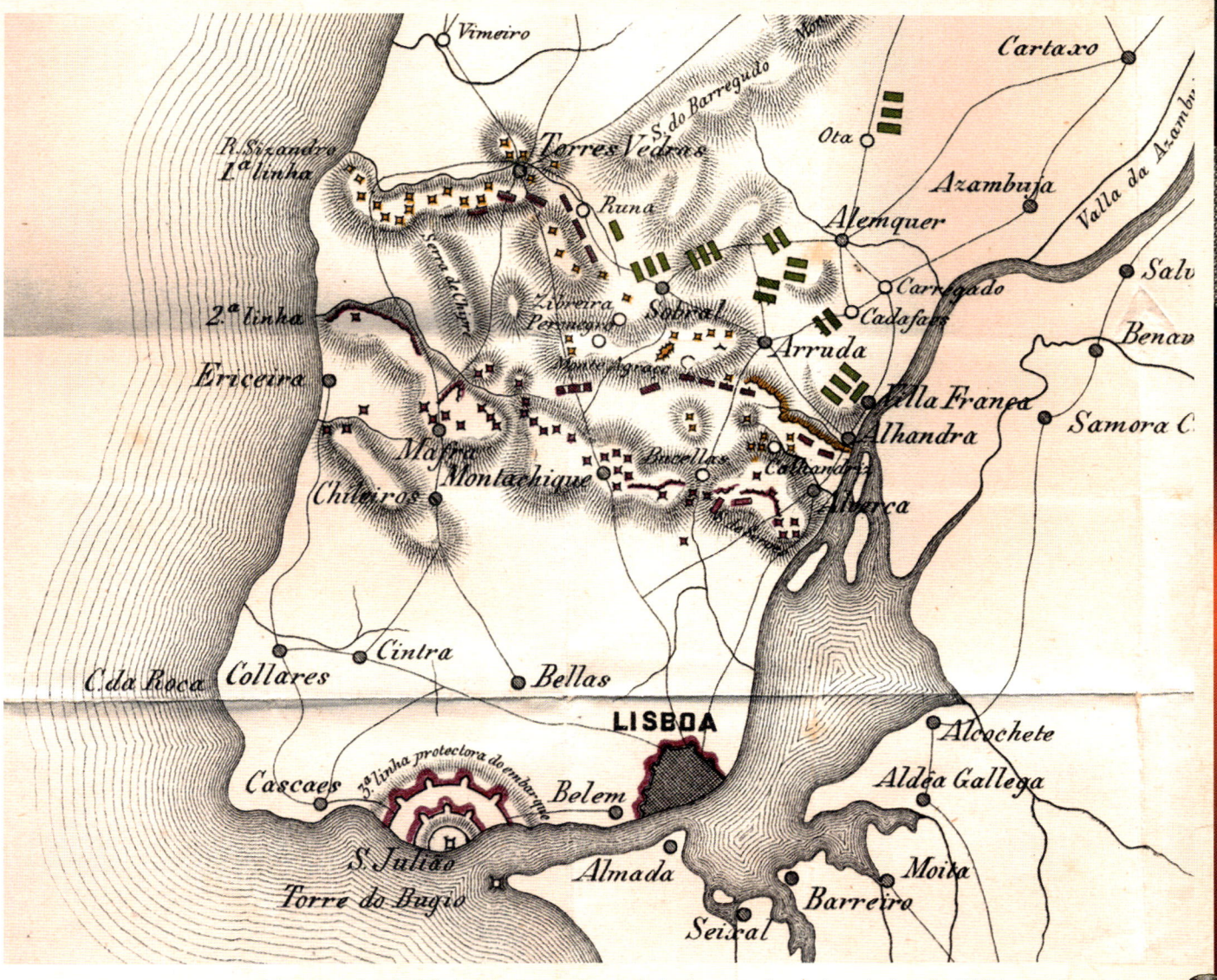

ABOVE *An 1874 Portuguese map of the Lines of Torres Vedras surrounding Lisbon. The First Line is in orange and the Second Line in purple.*

Soult was determined to continue his pursuit and choke off the British will to fight, but with the immediate threat of Wellington neutered, his army was returned to its constituent corps and thrown into engagements elsewhere. General Francisco Javier Venegas de Saavedra y Ramínez de Arenzana - who in doing little had done much to turn Talavera into a bloodbath - decided against marching on Madrid. He did, however, have a fit of late-stage valour and drove his Army of la Mancha to meet their violent end at the Battle of Almonacid (August 11, 1809).

Wellington's jaunt over the frontier alongside the peacocking Gregorio García de la Cuesta y Fernández de Celis, and the desperate flight back the way he came had taught him two important lessons. Firstly, logistics were everything when fighting over great distances in the rugged Iberian interior, and secondly, in matters of material (and indeed, materiel) aid, the Spanish were more foe than friend.

Ill winds and dire straits

News of Talavera and another string of Spanish reversals winded London's enthusiasm for the campaign in the Peninsula, but the news that followed nearly made it a killing blow.

The Austrian Empire's resurgent war with France - inspired by the evident weaknesses laid bare by the Peninsula War - began promisingly with the Battle of Aspern-Essling (May 21-22, 1809). It was the first defeat that Emperor Napoléon I had suffered in person for a decade, but he made sure it wouldn't be repeated and brought the Austrians to heel at the decisive Battle of Wagram (July 5-6, 1809). Britain attempted - not for the first time or the last - a miserable amphibious landing in the Low Countries in support of Austria, but the Walcheren Campaign (July 30 - December 9, 1809) eventually ended with 20,000 sick and weary soldiers being evacuated, riddled with 'Walcheren Fever'.

An estimated 4,000 died during the expedition, mostly of disease and only 100 or so were killed in combat. Even as late as February 1810, 12,000 of the returned troops were still ill and those transferred to Portugal succeeded only in doubling Wellington's casualty list through their presence alone. Worse still, the cessation of hostilities with Austria now made huge numbers of French troops - and possibly the

The Road to Waterloo

THE LINES OF TORRES VEDRAS

Emperor himself - available to reinforce the occupation of Spain and resume the invasion of Portugal.

George Canning - the Secretary of State for Foreign Affairs - asked Wellington gingerly on August 12, 1809 if "a British Army of 30,000 men acting in cooperation with the Spanish armies could be reasonably expected to either effect the deliverance of the whole of the Peninsula, or to make head against the augmented force which Bonaparte might now be enabled to direct against that country?"

This strategy had reached its limits at Talavera and those limits were low. Wellington's response to Canning was diplomatic, but his missive to his old friend and ally Robert Stewart, Viscount Castlereagh, Secretary of State for War and the Colonies, later that month was much less tactful: "Circumstances with which you are acquainted have obliged me to separate myself from the Spanish Army; and I can only tell you, that I feel no inclination to join in co-operation with them again."

If the French were focused on quashing Spanish guerrillas and forcing their way into the Junta Central's prosperous heartland of Andalucía, the British had breathing space. But unless they acted this would only be a stay of execution. Eventually, the French would come marching on Portugal.

Wellington wrote to Castlereagh on August 28, 1809: "Napoléon is reinforcing his armies in Spain, you may depend on it. He and his marshals are desirous of revenging on us the different blows we have given them, and when they come to the Peninsula, their first and great object will be to get the English out."

The Great Wall of Iberia

As early as 1808, Major Jose Maria das Neves Costa of the Portuguese Army had surveyed the hills north of Lisbon for a potential line of fortifications. In early 1809, his proposal was submitted to the exiled government in Brazil and his notes and maps eventually made their way to Wellington. They were of like mind. On his initial arrival in Portugal in July 1808, Wellington rode up to the highlands around Lisbon and mulled over the strategic advantages of the rocky peaks and deep ravines.

He took Neves Costa's survey to his old friend Major General William Beresford, who commanded the Portuguese Army, and then to Lieutenant Colonel Richard Fletcher of the Corps of Royal Engineers, who would ultimately translate their

ABOVE *A private of the Corps of Royal Sappers and Miners, as the Corps of Royal Engineers became known from 1812, in his working dress. Painted by the Victorian artist Charles Lyall, 1890.*

thoughts into reality. On October 20, 1809 the order was issued to begin construction on the Lines of Torres Vedras with a note that all commands issued by Fletcher were to be obeyed without question, no matter the cost.

"The great object in Portugal is the possession of Lisbon and the Tagus," he instructed Fletcher, "and all our measures must be directed to this object."

Built on a wedge of rough, mountainous land with the wide Tagus estuary on one side and the Atlantic Ocean on the other, there was only one realistic approach on Lisbon and the Lines of Torres Vedras consisted of two main rings of fortifications that followed the jagged crests of the hills northeast of the city, plus supplementary defensive positions elsewhere.

Not an unbroken chain, by the end of 1810 the Lines were made up of 126 individual works that were close enough to support each other and block the approaches to the city with their overlapping fields of fire. By 1812, at which point the threat of French invasion was a distant memory, this had grown to 152 works. Military roads were laid down to allow for rapid reinforcement between the forts and a semaphore telegraph - a complex naval construction of masts and lines - was set up that could send a message down the entirety of the line in ten minutes.

Construction on what later became known as the Second Line - but was initially the only line planned - began on November 3, 1809 and was carried out in great secrecy under the supervision of only eighteen military engineers. At least four were from the Portuguese Army, at least two from the King's German Legion, a handful of Royal Military Artificers (later merged with the Corps of Royal Engineers) and eleven Royal Engineers. They were scattered across the countryside with responsibility for as many as 700 workers - men of the Ordenanças, labourers, and later, paid conscripts, all on a day rate higher than the average redcoat.

While Fletcher worked with Wellington, management of the works was entrusted to Captain Stephan Remnant Chapman, and from July 1810, Captain John Thomas Jones, both Engineers. The Royal Engineers regimental history of 1856 notes that Corporal William Wilson and Private James Douglas "rendered themselves conspicuous by their skill and activity.

"[Corporal Wilson] had charge of a work, and a party of the Portuguese Ordenanças militia was placed under his orders to execute it. Two of the men were put to a task to be completed within a certain time; but regarding the work as impossible, they refused to comply and complained to their officer [...] With more manliness than soldier-like propriety, the corporal offered to bet the officer a dollar that he would accomplish the task himself with the time. The bet was accepted. Corporal Wilson stripped, easily won his dollar, and prevented the recurrence of similar complaints during the progress of the Lines."

Once the Second Line had been completed, two of the most two formidable forward fortifications - originally built as strong points for the army fighting in advance of the Second Line - became the foundations of the new First Line which was strung out 10 miles in front.

Despite the great undertaking, there was little confidence that the Lines of Torres

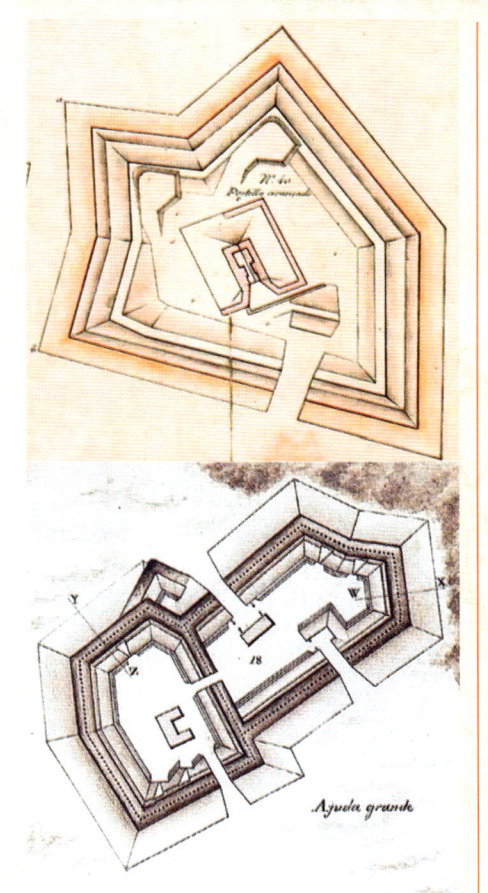

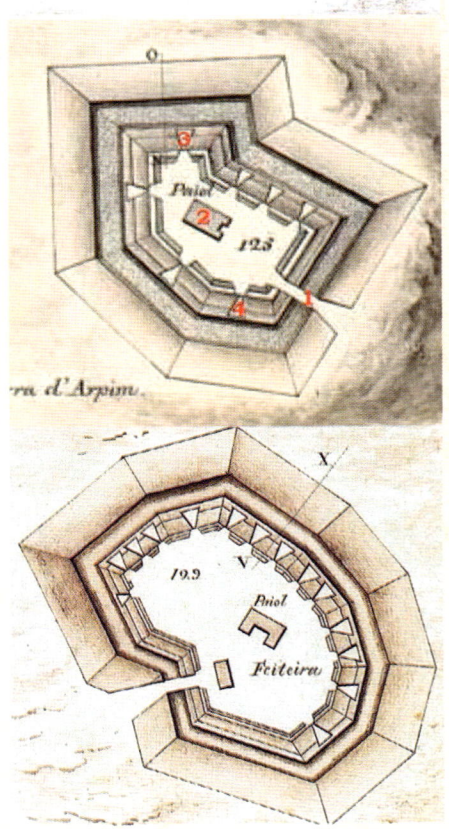

Vedras would be enough. As early as October 6, 1809, Wellington asked Lord Castlereagh for "a large fleet of transports" in case they needed to make an urgent evacuation.

After A Coruña, they were taking no chances and the Third Line was wrapped tight around the coastal Fort of São Julião da Barra, to the west of Lisbon where the army would, if necessary, be able to embark beyond the French cannon. In December 1810 construction also began on the Fourth Line covering the southern bank of the Tagus to prevent an attempted crossing, while the frontier was also reinforced with a number of redoubts.

Moving mountains

The redoubts - usually round towers - made up many of the fortifications in every line and were designed to be held by the militia and Ordenanças, freeing up all available regular soldiers (31,000 British and 26,000 Portuguese) to respond in strength. Around 200 to 300 militiamen and between three and six cannon could shelter in each redoubt, which was additionally protected by a 10-foot deep and 15-foot wide moat, while the largest forts had a capacity of 1,500.

Built at an astonishing rate of three forts per week, the completed 22-mile Second Line had 69 forts and redoubts, with capacity for 215 guns and 15,000 troops. The First Line, which spanned 29 miles, consisted of 70 fortifications, with 319 guns and 18,700 troops. The Third Line protecting the evacuation consisted of 12 forts and redoubts for 94 guns and 5,300 troops, while the Fourth Line on the Tagus had 17 forts and redoubts for 86 guns and 7,500 men.

Lieutenant Edmund Mulcaster, Corps of Royal Engineers, wrote to his friend in excitement: "I wish you could see my entrenchments, unlucky dogs that ever want to attack them if they are defended by Englishmen. They will bite the dust wholesale."

The landscape, already a firm deterrent to invasion, was made as inhospitable as possible to invaders. Farms were cleared - their inhabitants told to take their food and animals as they left - and all buildings and walls were pulled down and crops razed to deny the French cover as well as food sources. The River Ziznadre at the western end of the defensive chain was dammed in multiple places to form a vast wetland, and plans were made to flood a further bed of salt pans that was only paused due to the strong objections of its aristocratic landlady.

Sunken roads and ditches were filled in, olive groves were cleared en masse, and at Alhandra an entire hillside had been sculpted with explosives to ensure it provided no cover. Where valleys and watercourses ran directly through the Lines of Torres Vedras, they were filled with abatis - bundles of olive trees laid on their sides like natural barbed wire - which were slow to traverse and left the attacker vulnerable to fire.

Bridges were either destroyed or mined so that they could continue to be used until the very second of an attack and in the larger countryside plans were made for the large-scale evacuation of civilians and for the Ordenanças to dig in for a guerrilla war. But would it be enough?

Many in the British Army felt not. Lieutenant Rice Jones, Royal Engineers, wrote home on October 22, 1809: "These measures look too much like a determination [...] to defend Portugal to the last extremity; that extremity will certainly arise as soon as the French are able to advance in any force, and we shall then very likely have just such a scramble to get off as the army at Corunna last year."

ABOVE: *The Fort of São Julião da Barra, circa 1860. Constructed in the 17th century, it was significantly modernised during the construction of the Lines of Torres Vedras to serve as an evacuation point for the British Army.*

ABOVE *Plans of some of the forts in the Lines of Torres Vedras made in 1810, from top to bottom they are Aguieira, Ajuda, Arpim and Feiteira.*

THE ROAD TO WATERLOO 53

A Fearful SLAUGHTER

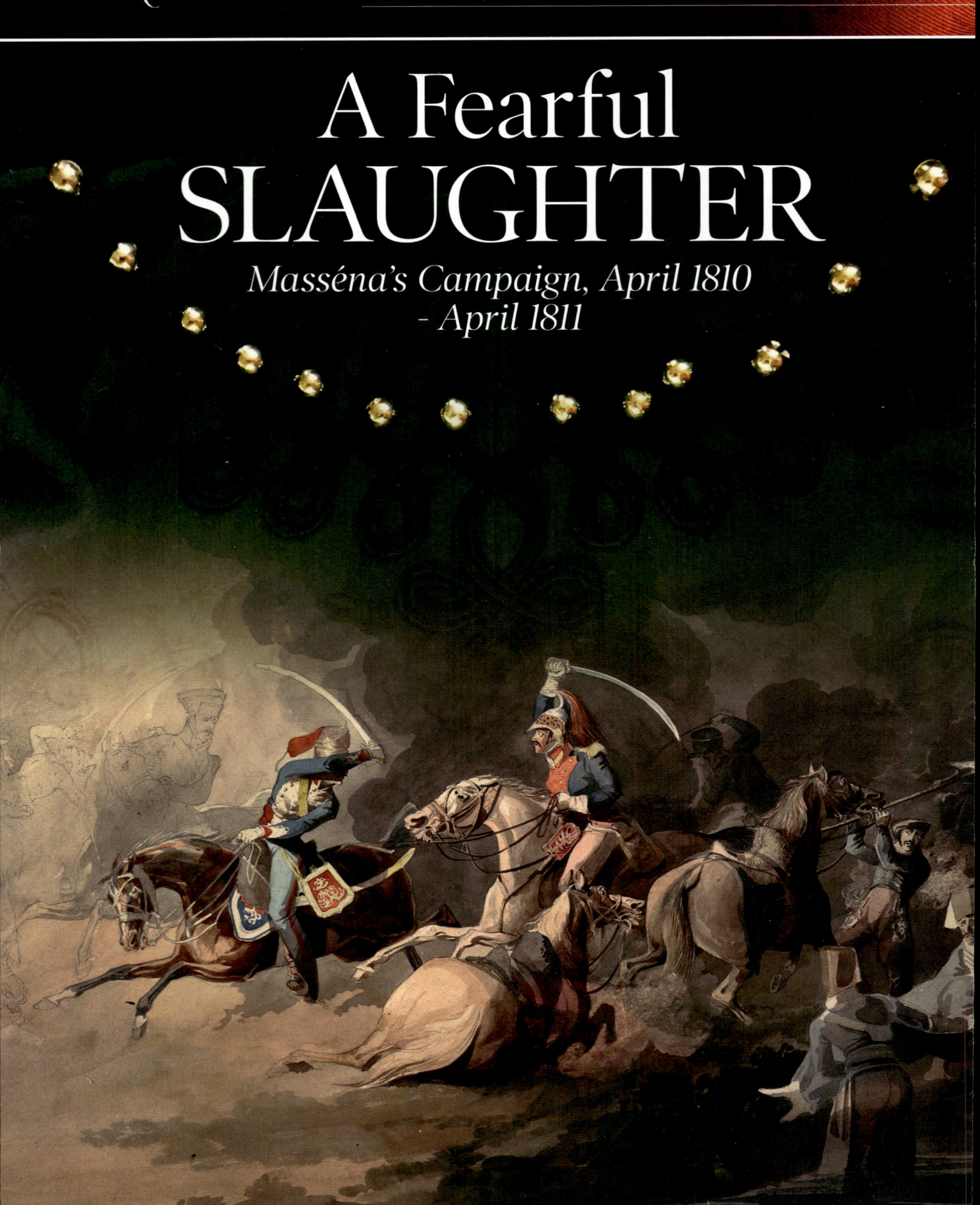

Masséna's Campaign, April 1810 - April 1811

While Wellington busied himself with transforming Lisbon's mountainous hinterland into an impregnable 19th-century Maginot Line (with better results), the influx of French reinforcements from the Austrian front emboldened King José I and the marshals to push on into southern Spain. Their focus was the wide, wealthy province of Andalusia, and its regional capital, Seville - the seat of the Junta Central.

With the Spanish armies in tatters from the devastating body blows of 1809 - chiefly the Battle of Ocaña on November 19, which left the defeated Juan Carlos de Aréizaga with only 32,000 men to hold a 160-mile front - Jaen and Granada fell before the month was out, and Seville capitulated on February 1, 1810, without firing a single shot.

The Junta Central fled to the island citadel of Cádiz, where they were unable to escape much-needed reform. They caved to pressure to restore the elected assembly, the Cortes, and handed over power to a five-man Regency Council before legislating themselves out of existence. Their hosts, the scheming Junta of Cádiz - a cabal of some of the region's most powerful merchants - had little incentive to recognise this new authority and had designs on expanding their influence.

Just as corrupt, inefficient, nepotistic, and self-serving as the old administration, the only upshot of the Regency Council was, in the words of one British officer, that Wellington now had "only five blockheads to transact business with instead of 34."

All's fair in love and war

Napoléon I was convinced that Spanish resistance in the face of constant humiliation was steeled by the British presence in Portugal. Luckily for Wellington, the Emperor's initial designs to lead the offensive himself was derailed by his domestic machinations.

His inability to produce an heir with Empress Joséphine saw the couple divorced on January 10, 1810, with Napoléon I already working his way down a list of eligible princesses. The man who had devoted much of his career to crushing one of the most storied and decadent dynasties in Europe, in the form of the Bourbons, was now fixated on marrying his way into another - the Habsburgs. He immediately opened negotiations with the defeated Austrian Empire, who no doubt had mixed feelings about binding themselves in sickness and in health to the architect of their defeat.

Command of the new Armée du Portugal went to Marshal André Masséna, whose actions against Austria had seen his star ascend. Masséna was less than thrilled ⟫

BELOW 'The Divorce of the Empress Joséphine in 1809' in oils by Henri Frédéric Schopin, 1843. A domestic affair with global repercussions.

LEFT A trooper of the 15th Hussars trades blows with a French dragoon during the Battle of Buçaco.

"His inability to produce an heir with Empress Joséphine saw the couple divorced on January 10, 1810, with Napoléon I already working his way down a list of eligible princesses."

The Road to Waterloo

MASSÉNA'S CAMPAIGN

by the prospect, and his subordinates were less than thrilled to receive him: General Jean-Andoche Junot suspected he was being punished for his failures in 1808, and the haughty Marshal Michel Ney simply didn't play well with others.

Masséna's invasion force was made up of the II, VI and VII Corps - numbering 70,000 men - with the newly-raised IX Corps en route. Though not conducting the operation in person, Napoléon I was very much conducting it in spirit. He had given Masséna strict instructions on how the campaign was to be carried out, to avoid the catastrophes that followed previous attempts to drive out the British. Advancing southwest from central Spain, the citadels of Astorga, Cuidad Rodrigo and Almeida were to be secured as they advanced.

The first two were in the hands of the Spanish, and Almeida - which was right on the border - was held by a Portuguese garrison under Lieutenant Colonel William Cox and supported by a screen of the Light Division under Brigadier General Robert Craufurd, known as 'Black Bob' for his expletive-laden mood swings. The Light Division, which included two regiments of brown-jacketed Portuguese Caçadores (meaning 'hunters', like the German Jaegers) as well as the battle-hardened 1/95th Rifles, 43rd (Monmouthshire Light Infantry) Regiment and 52nd (Oxfordshire Light Infantry) Regiment, had been Wellington's eyes and ears on the frontier since late 1809.

From the outset, Masséna found his resources being stretched by events elsewhere. Hoping to keep guerrillas from interfering with his Portuguese offensive, a pre-emptive strike was launched at Asturias, which despite quickly securing the regional capital of Oviedo became bogged down in an attritional series of raids and bloody reprisals which only served to drive more peasants to take up arms.

Elsewhere in Northern Spain, British and Spanish

ABOVE *A bust of Brigadier General Robert Craufurd, commander of the buccaneering Light Division, who was described by Rifleman Benjamin Harris as having "a severe look and a scowling eye."*

ABOVE RIGHT *André Masséna, depicted sometime around 1807, was one of Napoléon I's eighteen original Marshals of France and nicknamed by him, "l'Enfant chéri de la Victoire" - "The Dear Child of Victory."*

RIGHT *Sharpshooters of the 4th Caçadores give the British covering fire in this 1812 watercolour by Denis Dighton. They were finally equipped with Baker rifles in August 1810.*

RIGHT *A map of the costly Combat on the Côa in which the Light Division attempted a delaying action on the outskirts of Almeida.*

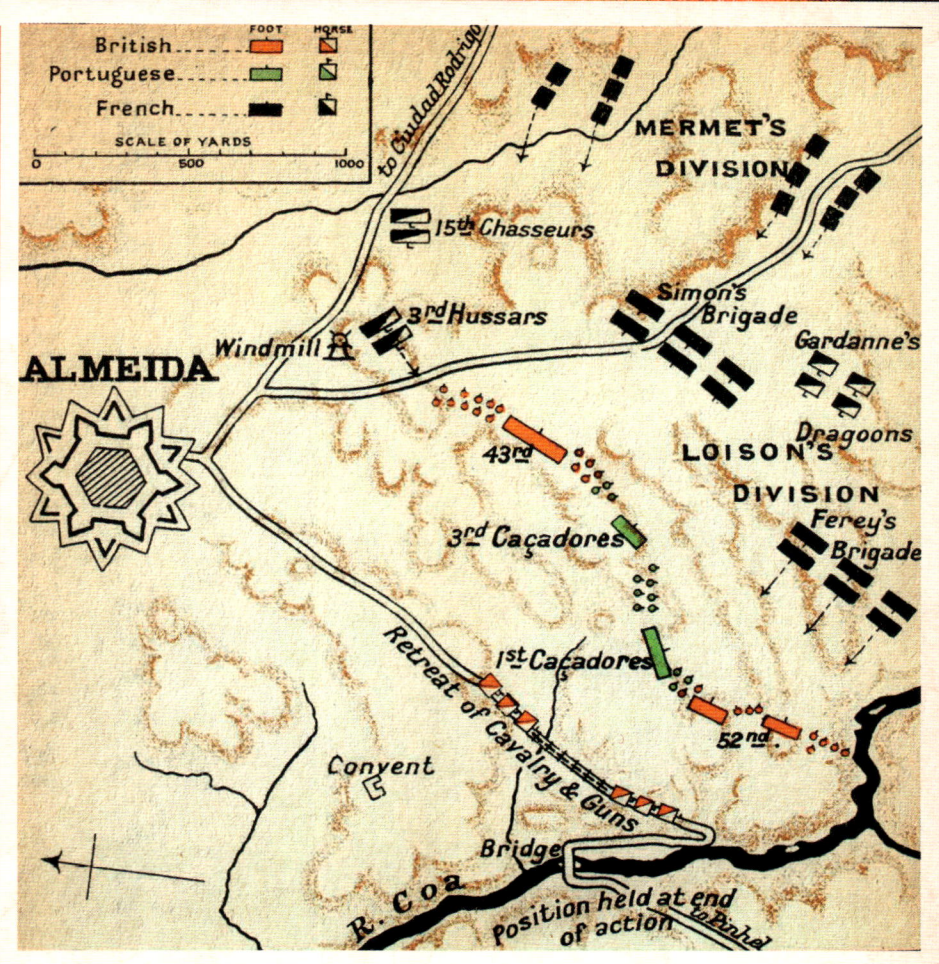

ships marauded up and down the coastline, landing detachments of 2,000 or so Marines at a time to strike at targets inland and depart as suddenly as they had arrived. Keeping the lines open in spite of harassment by sea and by land was incredibly labour intensive, and reinforcements bound for Masséna were peeled off in transit to garrison obscure Spanish coastal forts or vital supply dumps.

After a month-long siege - so long because the French had to wait for their siege guns to arrive, more than any defiance by the defenders - Astorga fell on April 21 and the French turned on the walled town of Ciudad Rodrigo, which held out until July 10 under its elderly but determined governor, Don Andrés Perez de Herrasti.

With only 5,000 militia at his disposal, Herrasti repeatedly asked Wellington for reinforcements. Not unreasonably, the Spanish had assumed that the British would relieve them - after all, if Ciudad Rodrigo fell, they would be next. His heart hardened by Talavera, Wellington refused. A march over the mountains and into Spain would bring every French marshal within a hundred miles dashing to cut him off and throw his strategy into tatters. The battle of Cuidad Rodrigo had to be lost so that the war could be won.

Combat of the Côa

The bloody breaching of the Spanish citadels in the Siege of Astorga (March 21 - April 22, 1810) and the Siege of Ciudad Rodrigo (April 26 - July 10, 1810) had cost Masséna a month and over 1,500 casualties.

The day after the fall of Ciudad Rodrigo, Craufurd's Light Division scrapped unsuccessfully with a French foraging party at the Combat of Barquilla (July 11, 1810). Too slow in bringing up the light infantry and too hasty in throwing his cavalry at the French square which quickly formed up as they broke cover, the Light Division took 30-odd casualties and inflicted none.

Craufurd's orders were to pull back behind the Côa if the French marched on Almeida, but the opportunity for the sort of dashing and disruptive action that the Light Division had been composed for was simply too tempting. With Almeida at his flank, Craufurd waited on the eastern bank of the River Côa. He was expecting the first French attack to be light, but as a torrential downpour in the early hours made the waterway at their back treacherous and

Craufurd's orders were to pull back behind the Côa if the French marched on Almeida, but the opportunity for the sort of dashing and disruptive action that the Light Division had been composed for was simply too tempting.

left the high, narrow bridge as their only retreat, Masséna smelt blood and sent Ney forward with his entire army corps. The cavalry led the way, followed by a second line of 13 battalions, a third line of 11 battalions, and a reserve of three.

Facing them were barely 5,000 men - five infantry battalions and two squadrons of cavalry - and with the courage of the ignorant, Craufurd held them off for over an hour, the British left taking the brunt of the assault until it finally buckled. With French hussars in pursuit, the 95th Rifles broke and bolted. As they passed under the anxious guns of Almeida, the defenders mistook their dark green tunics for the dark blue of the enemy and opened up on the retreating riflemen. The 95th were all but wiped out and only a drystone wall prevented the 43rd suffering the same fate.

Despite his determination to hold on, Craufurd was becoming increasingly conscious that the French columns in front of him stretched on for further than was healthy, and that the bridge behind them was a vulnerable line of escape. He sent the cavalry and horse artillery off first and then ordered the infantry to follow.

In its drivers' haste, a wagon crashed on the bend, adding to the panic of the retreat. A company of the 52nd dropped behind, risking being cut off from their comrades. Acting fast, Major Charles McLeod, 43rd, and Colonel John Charles Beckworth, 95th, urged the retreating men back and they turned with all the fury they could muster. The sudden counter-attack stunned the French, who halted in confusion for long enough for the stragglers to slip across the bridge.

Nor were they done showing the French what a British light infantryman was

THE ROAD TO WATERLOO 57

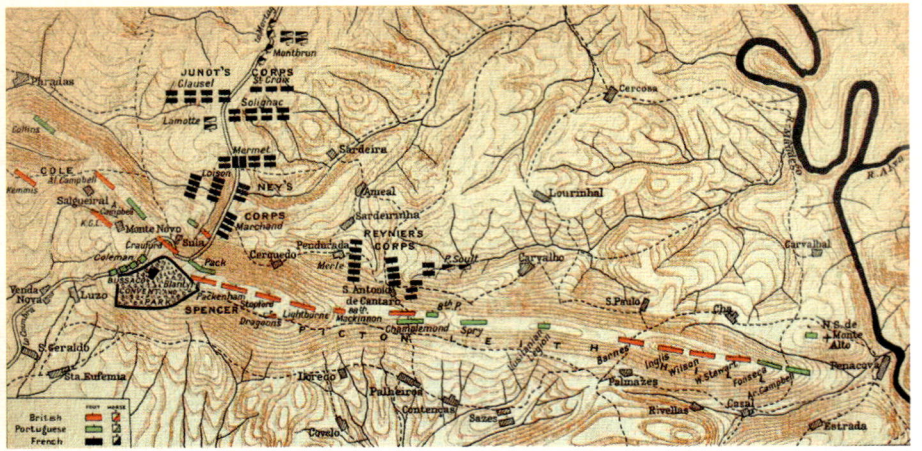

The Road to Waterloo — MASSÉNA'S CAMPAIGN

ABOVE *The initial positions of both forces during the Battle of Buçaco, with the more numerous French clearly unsure how far the British lines extended along the ridge.*

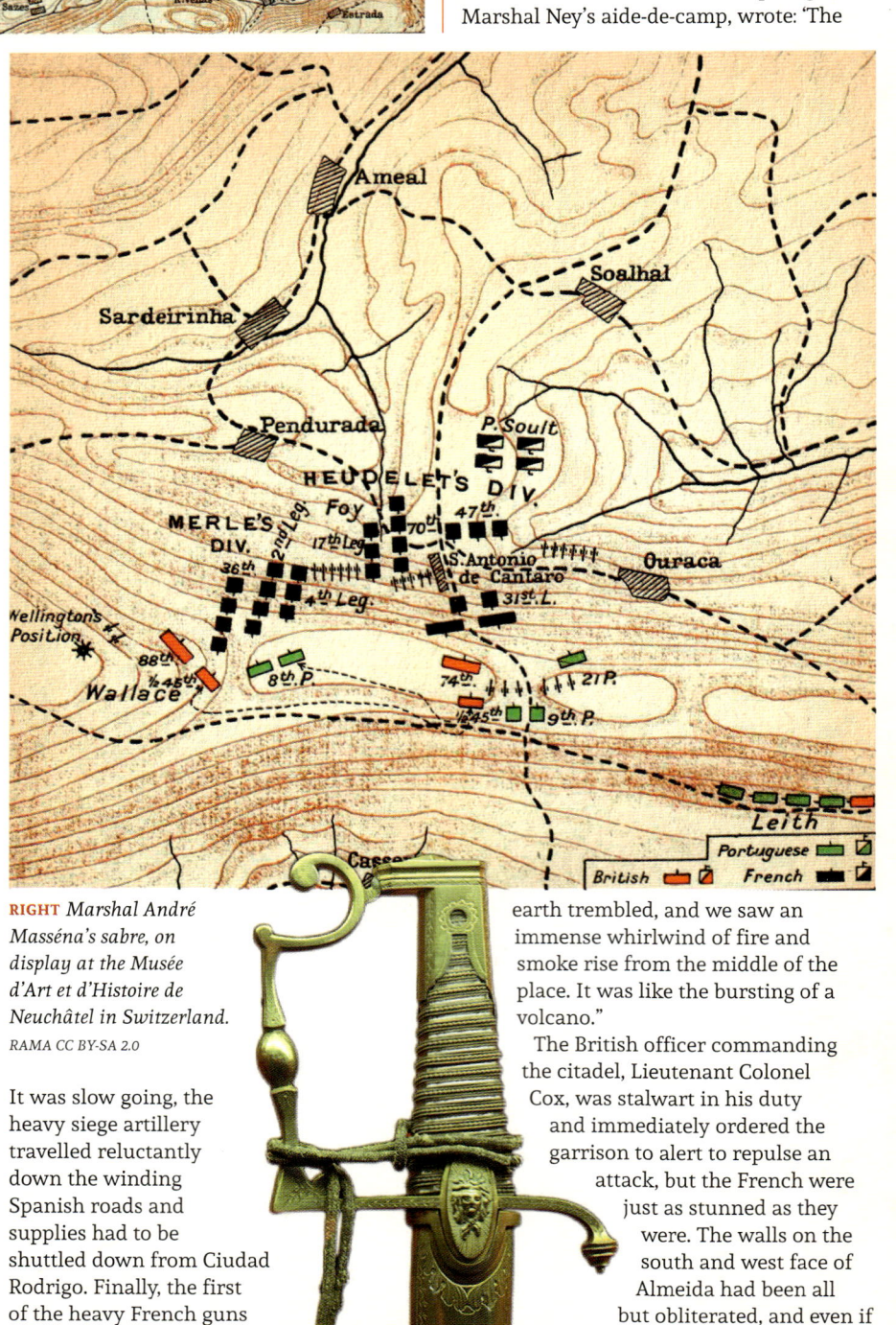

RIGHT *The II Corps under General Jean Louis Ebénézer Reynier pour into the relatively lightly held positions of Major General Thomas Picton's 3rd Division, nicknamed the 'Fighting 3rd'.*

capable of. Thinking the British were broken, Marshal Ney ordered his infantry across the bridge in triumph, not expecting that the Light Division had rallied on the western bank. Colonel Jonathan Leach, 95th Rifles, wrote: "A few hundred French grenadiers, advancing to the tune 'Vive l'Empereur!', 'Evan avant, mes efans!' and so forth were not likely to succeed in scaring away three British and two Portuguese regiments, supported by artillery."

The first crossing was repulsed at the half-way point, and the second attempt saw 300 French soldiers march up to the bridge and only 70 limp back in the opposite direction. Unwilling to pay the bridge's bloody toll, Ney withdrew his men and turned to besiege Almeida instead.

Wellington raged to his brother in a letter dated July 27: "I had positively forbidden the foolish affairs in which Craufurd involved his outposts [...] and repeated my injunction that he should not engage in an affair on the right of the river."

The siege of Almeida

Despite desertions (mostly to tend to the harvest) bringing the number of defenders down to 3,000, spirits were high. Almeida was a robust fortification, centred on the Medieval castle at the heart of the town, and its stern profile dominated the hard granite of the plateau. Supplies were plentiful and the defenders were confident that Masséna could be kept at bay for months.

The Siege of Almeida began on July 25 with the digging of trenches and batteries.

RIGHT *Marshal André Masséna's sabre, on display at the Musée d'Art et d'Histoire de Neuchâtel in Switzerland.*
RAMA CC BY-SA 2.0

It was slow going, the heavy siege artillery travelled reluctantly down the winding Spanish roads and supplies had to be shuttled down from Ciudad Rodrigo. Finally, the first of the heavy French guns opened up on August 26 and within hours the citadel had been cracked open.

A million-to-one mortar shell struck the subsidiary magazine in the castle, setting light to 4,000 prepared charges which were in the process of being delivered to the Portuguese batteries. Within seconds the first explosion triggered a far greater one as 150,000 lbs of gunpowder detonated, destroying the castle and the cathedral outright, killing around 800 of the defenders instantly, and 500 civilians unlucky enough to still be in the town.

Colonel Emmanuel-Frédéric Sprünglin, Marshal Ney's aide-de-camp, wrote: 'The earth trembled, and we saw an immense whirlwind of fire and smoke rise from the middle of the place. It was like the bursting of a volcano."

The British officer commanding the citadel, Lieutenant Colonel Cox, was stalwart in his duty and immediately ordered the garrison to alert to repulse an attack, but the French were just as stunned as they were. The walls on the south and west face of Almeida had been all but obliterated, and even if

58 THE ROAD TO WATERLOO

Wellington had planned to reinforce them, what exactly would they be fighting for?

For two days Cox pushed for the most generous terms for the defenders, demanding that the militia be allowed to return to their homes and the regular soldiers be permitted to re-join Wellington. Not exactly negotiating from a position of strength, the increasingly impatient Masséna opened up one final barrage to hurry him along and Cox reluctantly capitulated.

Already Masséna was feeling the strain of the two sieges and he lingered around the smouldering ruins of Almeida for a while, waiting for his supply lines to catch up and for the II Corps of General Jean Louis Ebénézer Reynier to reinforce them.

Wellington had selected the village of Ponte de Marcella along the main road south from Almeida towards Coimbra as the first location for his fighting retreat to the Lines of Torres Vedras. Suspecting an ambush, Masséna opted to take a miserable road north through the mountains that would avoid Ponte de Marcella completely. Wellington marvelled: "There are certainly many bad roads in Portugal, but the enemy has taken decidedly the worst in the whole kingdom."

On September 18, the weary French columns began trooping slowly into the walled town of Viseu, sitting proudly and picturesquely on a rolling plateau amid the hills and mountains. Whatever comfort they felt at the sight of civilisation after days on the road was void when they encountered the first signs of Wellington's 'scorched earth' policy. Viseu was deserted and the inhabitants had taken every scrap of food with them as they departed.

For reasons known only to the marshal himself, Masséna chose to rest the army at Viseu for six days and rumours were that this was because his mistress - a one-time dancer at the Paris opera - Henriette Leberton was tired from her journey.

While the French watered at Viseu, another strange decision brought another stroke of good fortune for Wellington. British scouts reported that an advance guard of Ney's VI Corps - rather than moving south along the road to Coimbra - had in fact moved west towards the cruel granite ridge of Serra do Buçaco.

The Battle of Buçaco

"We are in an excellent position," wrote Wellington on September 24. "Indeed, one which cannot be easily attacked in front; and if they wait another day or two, they will be unable to turn it on the only vulnerable point. I shall do everything in my power to stop them here."

Serra do Buçaco was a bleak and inhospitable range utilised only by a handful of rugged goatherds and a remote convent of the Barefoot Carmelites who had their tranquil contemplation of nature rudely interrupted by the arrival of thousands of crude and obnoxious fighting men.

On September 25, the first French troops approached the slopes of Serra do Buçaco to find it thronged with British and Portuguese troops. From the high ground, the arriving French columns made for an impressive sight: "Far as the eye could stretch," recalled Lieutenant Moyle Sherer, 34th (or the Cumberland) Regiment of Foot, "the glintering of steel and clouds of dust made by the cavalry and artillery proclaimed the march of a countless army."

It took two days for Masséna to arrive at the battlefield and again it was rumoured that his mistress was responsible. There was a sharp exchange of words between Masséna and Ney, who had been pushing for an immediate offensive from the second he arrived, but the time had already been wasted and the British had taken their positions in force.

From right to left, the British deployed the Loyal Lusitanian Legion and two guns to hold the flank, followed by Major General Rowland Hill's 2nd Division, then Major General James Leigh's 5th Division, and then Major General Thomas Picton's 'Fighting 3rd' Division. The furthest left where the ridge gave way to a steep slope was held by Major General Sir Brent Spencer's 1st Division, supported by three independent Portuguese brigades and protected by a screen of Craufurd's Light Division, and to their left, Major General Lowry Cole's 4th Division.

It was an estimated 50,000 men - many of them untested in battle and Portuguese regiments integrated throughout - facing 65,000 French soldiers. As had become his custom, Wellington positioned the bulk of his men on the reverse slopes to conceal their numbers.

Masséna issued his orders: the Battle of Buçaco would begin on the morning of September 27 with an attack on the British right by Reynier's II Corps. They were instructed to gain the high ground and sweep north through the convent and get behind the Anglo-Portuguese. Ney's VI Corps would then assault the centre along two roads that crept up towards the ridge, the hammer striking at Reynier's anvil. The smaller VIII Corps would hang back to offer support where needed.

Craufurd's trap

As the dawn light filtered through the low-lying fog, II Corps advanced behind the skirmishers towards the British right. As the columns climbed, the mass of French voltigeurs forced their British light infantry counterparts further uphill. At the top ⟫

The Portuguese 8th Regiment charges down the hill to drive II Corps back. From 1810, because of Beresford's reforms, they wore dark blue tunics and British-style shakos.

> "On September 25, the first French troops approached the slopes of Serra do Buçaco to find it thronged with British and Portuguese troops."

THE ROAD TO WATERLOO 59

The Road to Waterloo

MASSÉNA'S CAMPAIGN

ABOVE *The French Brigadier General Édouard Simon is wounded and taken prisoner during the counter-attack by the 43rd (Monmouthshire Light Infantry) Regiment 52nd (Oxfordshire Light Infantry) Regiment.*

RIGHT *A triumphal illustration celebrating Wellington's victory at the Battle of Buçaco.*

of the ridge, the 3rd Division could hear the shouting and the shooting but saw nothing below. Straining their eyes for the sight of approaching infantry, the Portuguese artillery opened up as the massed blue columns emerged from the gloom.

"The bullets were flying as thick as a hail storm," wrote Sergeant Andrew Pearson, 61st (or South Gloucestershire) Regiment of Foot. "Two guns charged with grape had been brought to bear on the columns of the French, and notwithstanding their ranks were mowed down they still held their ground. We saw there was only one alternative left and bringing our bayonets to the charge we rushed on with a shout. The 45th, 48th and 8th Portuguese most gallantly did their work, hurling the enemy over the brow of the hill with a fearful slaughter."

A further attack was thrown back just as savagely. With their line of sight obscured by the crest of Serra do Buçaco, the French believed that the 3rd Division was the end formation in the Anglo-Portuguese line (as opposed to being slightly right of the centre). Untouched by the offensive, Leigh manoeuvred his 5th Division north to back up the 3rd catching the French column in the flank and decimated them with close-range volleys.

The fog of war didn't discriminate and at two miles or so through the thinning mist at the French lines, Ney saw what appeared to be II Corps taking the crest of the wicked ridge. Following his orders to the letter, he spurred his VI Corps of two great columns into action.

Advancing behind a hornet's nest of skirmishers as far as the village of Sula, General Jean Gabriel Marchand's division on the left was to follow the winding path up to the convent and General Louis Henri Loison's division on the right was to take a far more daunting track that grew steeper the closer it got to the crest. The skirmishers were almost immediately engaged by the 4th Caçadores, who beat a fighting retreat. On the slope beyond the village, Craufurd had made his HQ in the windmill, where his battery of Royal Horse Artillery primed their charges and listened to the sound of combat roll towards them.

As the French chased after the 4th Caçadores towards Sula, they were suddenly hit by a volley of fire from both the 95th Rifles and the 3rd Caçadores. They retreated again, leading the enemy deeper into the gauntlet. Passing through the village, the Royal Horse Artillery opened up from the vicinity of the windmill and the King's German Legion artillery opened up from the other side. Loison ordered his men onwards to take the windmill and silence the terrible cannon. The trap baited, the French column got within 65 feet of their prize when the 43rd (Monmouthshire Light Infantry) Regiment and 52nd (Oxfordshire Light Infantry) Regiment emerged above them from a sunken path and fanned out in an arc.

Sergeant Pearson recalled: "The ardour with which the enemy rushed up the hill, under a heavy fire of musketry and artillery, astonished our men. They hoped to gain a footing on the swelling ridge of rock, and there make a determined stand; but they were surprised by the 43rd and 52nd Regiments, who, at the word of command, came from their hiding place which was the very position they sought to have gained. The appearance of these two regiments caused the French to lose heart and a murderous fire being opened upon then, they fell back, when our brave comrades charged the retreating foe down the hill and strewed it with their dead and wounded."

In the 20 minutes since the 43rd and 52nd broke cover, Loison's division had suffered some 1,200 casualties, while the Light Division suffered only 150. Craufurd's payback for Côa was complete. Following the easier route from Sula, Marchand's division soon found themselves taunted by sharpshooters and embroiled in a bitter firefight in the undergrowth around the convent. Although advancing with marginally more success they were unable to ignore Loison's division in full flight to their right.

Sore losers

At 8am, Marshal Masséna sounded the retreat. In only a couple of hours, the Battle of Buçaco had cost them dearly - they counted close to 5,000 casualties and in response had inflicted only 1,252. Unwilling to double his losses in another fruitless assault on Wellington's superior positions, Masséna turned north and pushing through the harassing bands of militia found their way onto the Oporto-Lisbon road.

Wellington meanwhile pulled his triumphant army back to Coimbra, the

60 THE ROAD TO WATERLOO

next stage in the fighting retreat to the Lines of Torres Vedras, but finding the streets choked with panicked refugees elected to keep moving.

On October 1, Masséna took Coimbra and his humiliated army tore the city apart in a drunken rage. The scientific instruments in its ancient university were smashed and the gold panelling in its cathedral levered off and looted. Those Portuguese who had refused to pull back to the Lines suffered for their courage and the Bishop of Coimbra recorded that 2,969 men, women and children had been murdered and 1,144 homes set ablaze. Leaving a garrison to hold the city and offloading 4,000 of his inconvenient wounded, Masséna continued onwards in Wellington's wake.

On October 11, after seeing nothing of the enemy but distant scouts and cavalry skirmishers, he caught sight of the Lines of Torres Vedras for the first time. His eyes wide, he cast around for some weakness but saw only "steeply scarped mountains and deep ravines [...] crowned with all that could be accomplished by way of field fortifications garnished with artillery."

He attempted to probe the lines at the Battle of Sobral (October 13-14, 1810), but this only confirmed his suspicions, the redoubts were costly to take and impossible to keep and following a British counter-attack, Junot's VIII Corps retreated with nothing to show from his folly but another 267 needless casualties. His despair made total by the news that one of Portugal's roving bands of peasant militia had seized Coimbra, Masséna penned an apologetic letter to his Emperor and began his withdrawal.

By November the autumn rains, the constant skirmishes with Ordenanças and British scouts, the lack of forage, and sheer exhaustion of the march had reduced the army to 40,000 who could be considered fit for duty. The rain kept falling and Wellington still refused to come out and fight. Morale plummeted and couldn't be rescued by the dribble of reinforcements that made it from Spain. Finally, on March 5, 1811 Masséna began a full retreat - they dumped their wagons and made for the border, leaving a trail of atrocity in their wake.

The population ravaged by starvation from Wellington's scorched earth doctrine and labouring under the cruelty of the French took their revenge. During the retreat, the wounded, sick, fatigued or hungry fell when they could walk no more and were left by the roadside. Those who were unlucky enough to be alive when the peasants found them were stripped naked, stoned, kicked to death, and their bodies mutilated.

"Here and there," wrote Sergeant Pearson, "a broken-down cart would be met, and in and around it a body of French soldiers wearing out a miserable existence and crying to be put to death. For what they had done to others, they were repaid tenfold."

The final encounter of the campaign, the Battle of Sabugal (April 3, 1811), saw the French take up position strung out uselessly along the Côa River in the damp and fog, desperate for some sort of reckoning. With 8,000 men set aside to distract the shattered Armée du Portugal, Wellington set upon Reynier's II Corps and drove the French over the border into Spain.

Marshal Masséna's star, once so glorious in ascent, was now hurtling towards the ground and his replacement, Marshal Auguste Frédéric Louis Viesse de Marmont was on his way from the Adriatic where Napoléon had him governing the French Empire's Balkan provinces.

BELOW *'Subuqal on the Riva Côa' by Thomas Staunton St Clair, 1812. A deceptively serene panorama of dragoons at rest along the River Côa, now safely back in British and Portuguese hands.*

The Road to Waterloo — BERESFORD'S CAMPAIGN

The Wages of DOUBT

Beresford's Campaign, March - June 1811

Defeated and humiliated by the long months of retreat, the only French presence remaining in Portugal was the garrison at Almeida, reinforced by Marshal André Masséna as he limped back to Spain.

While Masséna was being kicked up and down the length of Portugal, Marshal Jean-de-Dieu Soult had been engaged in a major offensive against the Regency Council in Andalusia. Ordered to relieve pressure on his fellow marshal, Soult gathered some 20,000 men and pulled them away for an attack on the fortified fortress city of Badajoz.

Hoping to draw some of Wellington's forces out from their Portuguese redoubts, Soult first attacked the town of Olivenza en route to Badajoz. The Siege of Olivenza (January 19 - 22, 1811) ended with 4,000 men of the Spanish Army of Extremadura taken prisoner. Now forced to send men back to Seville to escort the prisoners, he was left with only 5,500 infantry to besiege Badajoz.

As the objective was not to capture Badajoz, but to induce Wellington to divide his forces and give Masséna an opening, Soult went ahead, and the First Siege of Badajoz opened on January 27. Soult didn't even have enough men to encircle the city.

Instead of the British, on February 5 Soult was confronted by 15,000 men marching with General Gabriel de Mendizábal Iraeta's Spanish Army of the Left. Mendizábal had replaced Pedro Caro, 3rd Marquis of la Romana, who died of a syphilis-induced heart attack. Rather than immediately attack the smaller French force, Mendizábal set up camp on the opposite bank of the wide Guadiana River, believing that his mere presence would send them packing. At the Battle of the Gebora (February 19, 1811), Soult launched a surprise attack on the Spanish camp - advancing over a pontoon bridge and causing almost instant panic. The French lost 400 men and the Spanish a staggering 8,000.

The death of Badajoz's stalwart defender, Don Rafael Menacho y Tutlló, weakened resolve and Menacho's successor capitulated, despite his ample provisions and sizeable garrison. The First Siege of Badajoz (January 25-March 11, 1811) ended with an unexpected victory for the French, one that only served to reinforce Wellington's prejudices, writing that the defeat could have been avoided "had the Spaniards been anything but Spaniards."

62 THE ROAD TO WATERLOO

The Battle of Campo Maior

Soult's instincts were correct though. Wellington had dispatched men to relieve Badajoz, and when the shocking news broke that the Spanish garrison had laid down its arms, the orders were amended. The 18,000 men under the Major General William Carr Beresford had a new mission: throw the French out.

Marshal Soult had returned to Seville where the Spanish were manoeuvring against the provincial capital and left the defence of the frontier citadel to Major General Armand Philippon and his 4,000 men.

Beresford's advance guard arrived at Campo Maior where he surprised the small contingent of French troops holding the town in the Battle of Campo Maior (March 25, 1811). The French were already in the process of abandoning the old Medieval castle and were moving the cannon up to Badajoz when a cavalry charge by Brigadier General Robert Long and 700 of the 13th Light Dragoons, 1st and 7th Portuguese Dragoons threw them into a rout.

The 7th Portuguese Dragoons under Captain Loftus Otway, on loan from the 18th Light Dragoons, gave chase over seven miles, capturing the convoy of siege guns, and some of them even ran within firing range of Badajoz itself, where the infantry was turned out to see them off. Beresford was blamed for not releasing the heavy cavalry to run down the retreating French, while Beresford maintained that Long was about to throw them into a suicidal action against infantry squares.

As the army approached Badajoz (retaking Olivenza on the way), it was the turn of the British to struggle with the lack of supplies that awaited them in this barren hinterland. Only by April 13 did they finally scrounge up enough raw materials to build a pontoon bridge across the Guadiana River only for it to be swept away by flooding and for three days Beresford's vanguard was trapped on the hostile opposing bank. Large numbers of Spanish had also joined the army - the surviving battalions from the Spanish armies which had disintegrated in the French offensives of 1810 - and promised siege guns were coming up from the Portuguese fortress of Elvas, nine miles southwest of Campo Maior.

ABOVE *William Carr Beresford, in the uniform of Lieutenant General in 1812. Although responsible for the successful reform of the Portuguese Army, he found himself unsuited to independent command.*

LEFT *The Anglo-Portuguese forces embellish their siege works during the fruitless final stages of the Second Siege of Badajoz by Charles Tuner, 1812.*

The second siege of Badajoz

On April 25, Beresford finally opened the Second Siege of Badajoz (April 25 - June 11, 1811) but it was slow going in the heavy rains.

The obvious high ground was far too rocky to dig into and as they worked, the pioneers were exposed to a hornet's nest of snipers that picked off a third of the army's engineers in one day alone. When they finally arrived, the siege guns from Elvas proved to be impressive only as historical artefacts - with four of them dating from the 17th century - and even the more recent pieces lacking modern sights, elevation and being of uncertain calibre.

Only a token force was arrayed against the south wall which had been breached by Soult and hastily repaired. Instead, the detached Fort of San Cristóbal on the high ground had been selected by Wellington as the primary target. It was logical in that it had commanding views over the entirety of Badajoz and whoever possessed it would be free to lob shells into the town with impunity, but it was a more sophisticated fortification in a superior position that wouldn't surrender easily to Beresford's motley crew and their antique artillery.

Beresford's indecision was a constant cause of frustration. For all his strengths as an administrator, he was proving less than impressive as a field officer, and the desperately slow progress of the siege bought Marshal Soult ample time to gather some 25,000 reinforcements and begin marching to the relief of his garrison.

On April 16, 1811, Wellington's brother-in-law and adjutant-general Lieutenant Colonel the Honourable Edward Pakenham wrote: "Beresford is a clever man but no general; his anxiety is too great, and he cannot allow an operation to go through by its first impulse without interference, which generally on such occasions mars everything."

The Battle of La Albuera

Finally coerced into action, Beresford raced 12 miles south to join the Spanish army blocking Soult's progress at the village of La Albuera and the Second Siege of Badajoz was briefly lifted so that the Battle of La Albuera (May 16, 1811) could begin.

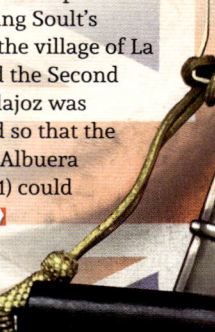

The Road to Waterloo

BERESFORD'S CAMPAIGN

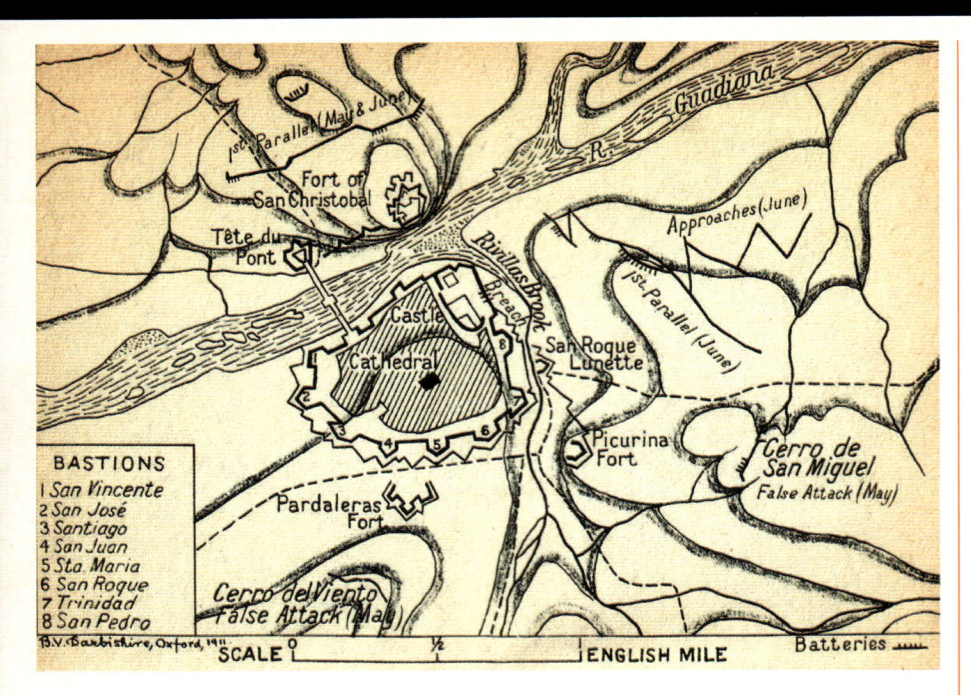

ABOVE A map showing the phases of the Second Siege of Badajoz in May and June 1811, which included several costly diversions.

BELOW An unfinished panorama of Badajoz with collection of Spanish irregulars killing time in the foreground. The view is from the east, with the target Fort of San Cristóbal immediately to the right of the town, marked with an 'F'.

and the marshal saw an opportunity to outflank Beresford's right.

With a strong thrust towards La Albuera at the centre to distract Beresford and his Spanish counterpart, Lieutenant General Joaquín Blake y Joyes, two French infantry divisions and a brigade of cavalry slipped across the Arroyo Chicapierna stream into the hills occupied by the allies. Both Beresford and Blake reacting sluggishly

and he moved up Major General William Stewart's 2nd Division and Major General Lowry Cole's 4th Division to support the Spanish. It was already too late, four Spanish infantry battalions and a single battery of artillery were being buffeted by 8,000 French infantry and cannon advancing in mixed order, the guns alongside the foot soldiers. Confident in their superior firepower, rather than greet the Spaniards with a bayonet charge, they slowed and exchanged shots.

Few things are less decisive than a standing musket duel and despite the terrible bloodshed, the Spanish held their nerve, buying time for Blake to send up more of his infantry to bolster their ragged lines. Beresford planned a counter-attack with both the 2nd and 4th to push the French off the hill, but the eager Stewart - who had replaced the more reliable but ailing Major General Rowland Hill - immediately tossed his 1st Brigade forward in lines against the oncoming foe.

The 3rd (East Kent) Regiment of Foot (The Buffs) led, followed by the 48th (or Northamptonshire) Regiment of Foot, 66th (or the Berkshire) Regiment of Foot and 31st (or the Huntingdonshire) Regiment of Foot, firing and advancing into the fray with bayonets levelled. While the Spanish flanks were protected by artillery, the 1st Brigade

Beresford's force took up positions along a low-lying chain of hills just behind La Albuera, with the Anglo-Portuguese on the left and the Spanish on the right, while the village itself made a natural strongpoint in the centre of the line. Despite being outnumbered three-to-two, Soult's right flank was masked by a thick, wiry tangle of olive groves and ilex trees,

to this change in fortunes, the former left it entirely for the latter to deal with and Blake wheeled about only 1,000 infantry to halt the flanking manoeuvre that risked rolling over their entire positions.

Saved only by the time the French divisions spent changing formation, Beresford finally realised that their right flank was the real target of Soult's plan

RIGHT An unfinished panorama of the Battle of La Albuera from behind the British and Spanish lines. The French flanking manoeuvre can be seen on the hill marked with an 'E'.

marched forward totally exposed and the Vistula Lancers, a Polish cavalry regiment, peeled off from the French columns and tore them apart, with only the final

THE BATTLE OF BAROSSA

Since February 1810, Cádiz had been under a blockade, but it was really the intemperate Marshal Victor who found himself between the devil and the deep blue sea. His army had dwindled to around 19,000, a bulk of which were sappers and artillerymen, whilst the defenders had been reinforced by sea to the tune of 20,000 Spanish and 4,500 British soldiers.

If Victor lifted the siege to retreat, there were enough of the enemy to immediately fall upon his army and tear it limb from limb. A combined offensive was almost inevitable. Using their naval superiority, Lieutenant General Thomas Graham and General Manuel Lapeña Rodríguez y Ruiz de Sotillo landed a force of 5,000 British (some troops had joined from Gibraltar) and 8,000 Spanish at Algeciras.

With sallies from the defenders of Cádiz, putting Victor firmly on edge and giving his men some sleepless nights, Graham and Lapeña marched through the rain to attack the siege lines from the rear. The Battle of Barossa - also known as the Battle of Chiclana - took place on March 5, 1811 and Marshal Victor was prepared, marching east with 10,000 men to confront them on the main road to Cádiz, he strung one division across the road and sent two others north to flank the enemy.

Lapeña's force moved down the main highway, while Graham's men followed a parallel track through the pine. The French blocking the road were quickly driven off by the Spanish, but outnumbered two-to-one, the British were forced to fight off the flanking columns alone - dishing out 2,400 casualties to 1,240 British and 400 Spanish.

Throughout the exchange, Lapeña refused to support the Anglo-Portuguese force and instead held the main road to the isthmus and the relationship between the two generals was now so acrimonious that the British garrison at Cádiz withdrew to León. Graham won the Battle of Barossa, but Lapeña lost the Blockade of Cádiz and the siege would continue for another 18 months.

Vastly outnumbered, the British infantry charge uphill to confront the flanking French.

THE ROAD TO WATERLOO 65

The Road to Waterloo

BERESFORD'S CAMPAIGN

RIGHT *A map of the Battle of La Albuera, showing the initial deployment as well as the French diversion and the French flanking attack.*

battalion, the 31st, having enough time to form squares. Two-thirds of their total strength was killed, wounded or captured, and five regimental flags and eight cannon were seized by the Polish.

Major William Brooke, 2/48th (or Northamptonshire) Regiment of Foot, was among the prisoners and later recalled: "Part of the victorious French cavalry were Polish Lancers: from the conduct of this regiment on the field of action I believe many of them to have been intoxicated, as they rode over the wounded, barbarously darting their lances into them. Several unfortunate prisoners were killed in this manner while being led from the field to the rear of the enemy's lines."

The scrum on the hill had reached a stalemate as more men were thrown into the line, the Spanish losing all cohesion as they became a single mass of barking muskets. The 4th Division were now advancing into the line, among them Sergeant John Spencer Cooper of the 7th or Royal Fusiliers, who wrote:

"Having arrived at the foot of the hill, we began to climb its slope with panting breath, while the roll and thunder of furious battle increased. Under the tremendous fire of the enemy our thin line staggers, men are knocked about like skittles; but not a step back is taken. Here our colonel and all of the field officers of the brigade fell killed or wounded, but no confusion ensured. The orders were 'close up'; 'close in'; 'fire away'; forward'. This is done. We are close to the enemy's columns; they break and rush down the other side of the hill in mob-like confusion."

All courage and no judgement

Not through any great strategic thinking on the part of the allies, the Battle of La Albuera was won through sheer brute force and iron will of the line infantry. The British, Portuguese and Spanish lost a combined 5,380 dead and wounded - with 4,159 of them being British. Of that number, at least 1,258 were lost during Stewart's sacrifice of his 1st Brigade.

Soult had lost as much as a third of his army and the French morale, both in the field and back at beleaguered Badajoz was shattered. He finally withdrew

RIGHT *Major General Beresford disarms a Polish Vistula Lancer during the fierce fight for the allies' right flank.*

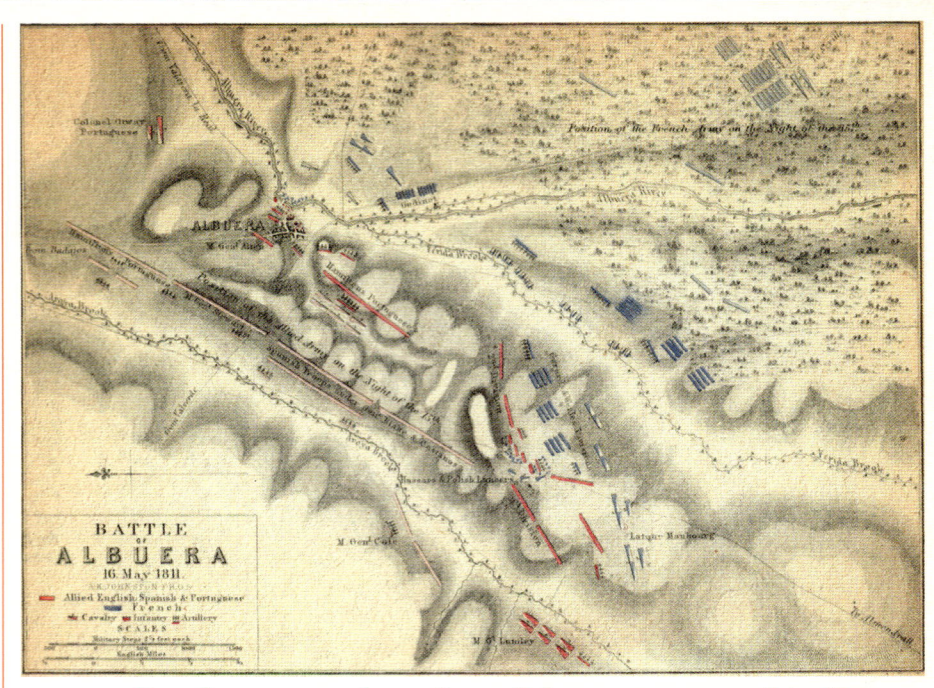

> *"Under the tremendous fire of the enemy our thin line staggers, men are knocked about like skittles; but not a step back is taken. Here our colonel and all of the field officers of the brigade fell killed or wounded..."*

once it became clear that Beresford was reinforcing the Spanish line

As for Beresford, he was showing signs of being in the grip of a nervous breakdown and his report on the battle was substantially edited by Wellington - always loyal to his subordinates - before it was sent onto London. Major General Stewart escaped censure, although the contemporary historian Sir Patrick Napier noted diplomatically that his "boiling courage overlaid his judgment," and Wellington ensured that the gifted brigade general was spared further burdens of a divisional command.

Wellington arrived at Badajoz on May 19 and on May 27, Major General Rowland Hill took command of the southern front from Beresford. The Second Siege of Badajoz would lumber on for another fortnight, costing the British many dead and wounded in desperate assaults upon the impregnable Fort of San Cristóbal.

On June 10, Wellington cut his losses and withdrew the besieging army for better use elsewhere. Badajoz could wait.

GREAT SUBSCRIPTION OFFERS FROM KEY

SUBSCRIBE TO YOUR FAVOURITE MAGAZINE AND SAVE!

A History of Conflict

As the UK's best-selling military history title, **Britain at War** Magazine is dedicated to exploring every aspect of the involvement of Britain and her Commonwealth in conflicts from the turn of the 20th century through to the present day. With at least 116 pages in every issue, **Britain at War** prides itself on well-researched and eye-catchingly designed historical content, aiming to provide new and fresh perspectives on Britain's wars.

www.britainatwar.com

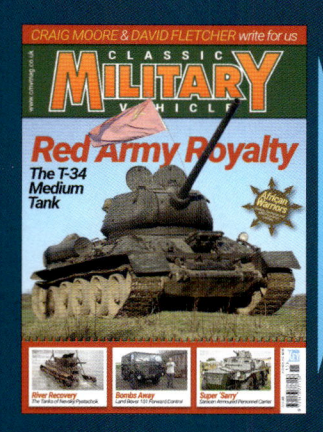

The UK's best-selling historic military vehicle magazine

Classic Military Vehicle magazine covers a comprehensive range of military vehicles from the beginning of mechanisation at the start of the 20th century and continues up to the recent Gulf and Afghanistan conflicts. It concentrates on wheeled and tracked military hardware that featured in conflicts around the world.

www.cmvmag.co.uk

Britain's Top-Selling Aviation Monthly

FlyPast is internationally regarded as the magazine for aviation history and heritage. Having pioneered coverage of this fascinating world of 'living history' since 1980, **FlyPast** still leads the field today. Regular profiles include British and American aircraft type histories, as well as those of squadrons and units from World War One to the Cold War.

www.flypast.com

ALSO AVAILABLE DIGITALLY:

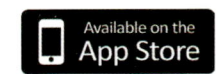

Available on iTunes   Available on the App Store   Available on Google play   Available on kindle fire   Available on PC, Mac & Windows 10

Available on PC, Mac and Windows 10 from pocketmags.com

756/19

FOR THE LATEST SUBSCRIPTION DEALS

VISIT:
www.keypublishing.com/shop

PHONE:
(UK) 01780 480404   (Overseas) +44 1780 480404

The Road to Waterloo — THE ALMEIDA CAMPAIGN

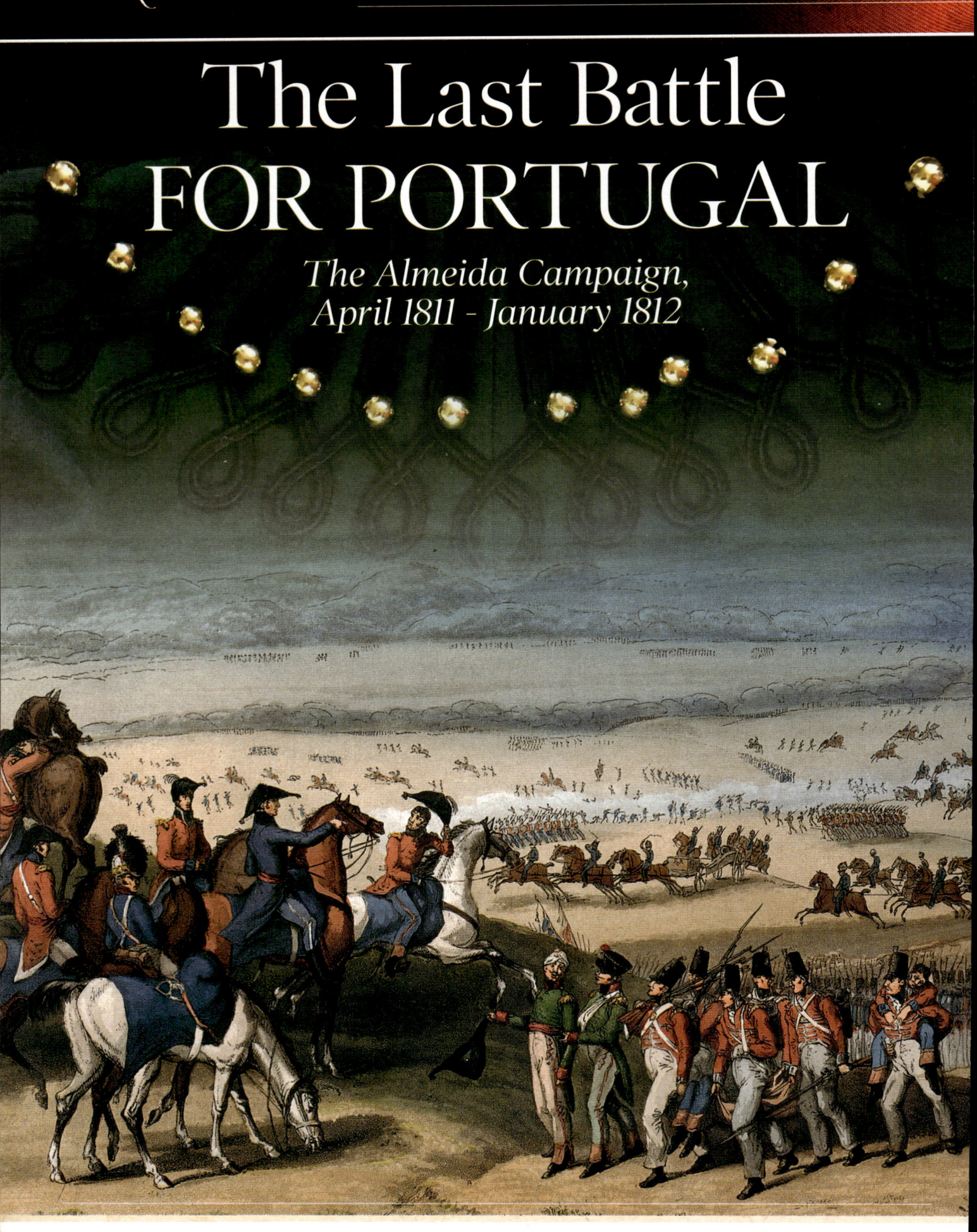

The Last Battle FOR PORTUGAL

The Almeida Campaign, April 1811 - January 1812

Marshal André Masséna's shattered Armeé du Portugal was no longer capable of any serious offensives and he was weeks away from handing over his command to the freshly dispatched Marshal Auguste Frédéric Louis Viesse de Marmont. Though in full retreat, Masséna's garrison in the Portuguese border citadel of Almeida and its Spanish counterpart Ciudad Rodrigo still acted as a formidable deterrent to any Anglo-Portuguese ventures into central Spain.

Almeida had been under British blockade since April 14, 1811. It was not technically a siege, as no artillery were available to threaten the casements so the British concentrated on severing the lines of communication and supply to starve out the garrison of 1,400 French under General Antoine François Brenier de Montmorand. The same undertaking had begun at Ciudad Rodrigo, but the Light Division under Major General Sir William Erskine weren't proving as effective as they had been under Brigadier General Robert Craufurd - who was on his way back to the Peninsula after wintering in Britain - and a large supply column slipped through. Disappointed, Wellington pulled the Light Division back and focused his efforts entirely on Almeida.

Reputations were won and lost in accordance with the whims of Emperor Napoléon I and Masséna felt under immense pressure to reverse his fortunes and secure his standing. As resourceful as he was determined, Masséna departed Salamanca on April 26 with an army of 48,000 to relieve Almeida and Ciudad Rodrigo. Lacking the supply train to remain in the field for long - let alone provision the defenders of Almeida - their only purpose was to prove that without the shelter of the Lines of Torres Vedras or the hard ridge of Buçaco, Wellington could be broken.

The Battle of Fuentes De Oñoro

It's true that the plains of the Spanish-Portuguese frontier offered Wellington neither a chain-link fence of purpose-built fortifications or a hard, high escarpment, but it wasn't without its topographical advantages.

The village of Fuentes de Oñoro was built on a gentle slope that rose from the river of Dos Casos up onto a low plateau that ended at the River Côa. The British would have the high ground, while the village itself was sturdy enough to offer cover for the right flank and the ruined Fort de la Conception anchored the left, which was additionally protected by a deep gorge which rendered the Dos Casos impassable as it wound north.

Around Fuentes de Oñoro at the southern end of the seven-mile Anglo-Portuguese line was Major General Sir Brent Spencer's 1st Division, to their left at the village

BELOW *The view from behind the lines of the 1st, 3rd and 7th Divisions during the Battle of Fuentes de Oñoro, which ended the third and final French invasion of Portugal. Painted in 1811 as part of a series on Wellington's victories by the artist Charles Turner.*

The Road to Waterloo

THE ALMEIDA CAMPAIGN

THE 'MADNESS' OF SIR WILLIAM ERSKINE

Only in the less-than-meritocratic upper echelons of the early 19th-century British Army could the deterioration of Major General Sir William Erskine, 2nd Baronet and MP for Fifeshire have gone untreated.

His poor eyesight - a murderous affliction in a cavalry officer - and his alcoholism were the least of his problems and the military lawyer Francis Seymour Larpent alleged in his journal that Erskine had spent two years in a lunatic asylum. After Erskine was dispatched to the Peninsula in autumn 1810, Wellington questioned the choice, writing to Horse Guards that he "was generally understood to be a madman."

The military secretary replied laconically: "No doubt he is a little mad at intervals, but in his lucid intervals he is an uncommonly clever fellow, and I trust he will have no fit during the campaign, although I must say he looked a little wild as he embarked."

His 'lucid intervals' seemed to be few and far between. After getting lost in the fog at the Battle of Sabugal (April 3, 1811), failing to maintain the blockade around Ciudad Rodrigo, and pocketing the orders to secure the bridge at Barba del Puerco, Wellington shunted him from role to role, looking for one that wouldn't endanger the entire war. Finally, he was asked to leave the army.

Erskine was reported to have fallen - or jumped - out of a window in Lisbon during a "fit of delirium" on February 13, 1813. His last words were said to have been, "Why on earth did I do that?"

Regiment of Foot even followed them over the river and up the eastern bank but retreated before they could get themselves into too much trouble.

The cost of assaulting Wellington's light infantry over ground that favoured the defender was correspondingly heavy. A reported 642 French troops had fallen in the battle, compared to 259 of the enemy. Before they lost the light, Masséna's scouts made a full reconnaissance of the British lines and reported that the enemy couldn't be turned on their left flank, but south of Fuentes de Oñoro, the village of Pozo Bello was held by a single battalion and a screen of cavalry pickets.

Three divisions totalling 17,000 men were detailed to undertake the flanking manoeuvre through Pozo Bello on the British right, while the rest of the army had to keep so much pressure on the line - 14,000 men hammering the village and a series of probing attacks by II Corps - that Wellington would be unable to reinforce until it was much too late.

of Villar Formosa was Major General William Houston's 7th Division and Major General Thomas Picton's 3rd Division, aka the 'Fighting 3rd'. Further left above the village of Alameda (not to be confused with Almeida) was Campbell's 6th Division, while Erskine's 5th Division and Craufurd's Light Division held the line around the ruined fort. Craufurd had returned and resumed command, no doubt to the relief of Wellington.

Almeida itself was to the northwest. To relieve the siege, Masséna would have to force his way through the line at Fuentes de Oñoro and his army advanced in two huge columns: VI Corps and IX Corps marched directly on the village with 30,000 men, and on the French right II Corps marched towards the Alameda and beyond it, Fort de la Conception. The diminutive VIII Corps, only a division strong, marched towards the centre.

The Battle of Fuentes de Oñoro began on May 3, with Masséna ordering a division of General Jean Gabriel Marchand's VI Corps to attack the village and II Corps to make a show of strength towards the British left. Wellington rightly read this as feint, but he moved Craufurd forward to interrupt General Jean Louis Ebénézer Reynier and his men.

By early afternoon six battalions of French infantry converged on Fuentes de Oñoro where they were met by a reception committee of skirmishers under Lieutenant Colonel William Williams. He advanced with four companies of riflemen from his own 5/60th (Royal American) Regiment of Foot, a company of 3/95th Rifles, and a sea of British, Portuguese and King's German Legion light companies - 1,800 troops in all. The red, green and brown coats were soon pushed back by sheer weight of numbers, and the French drove on through the village as far as the sturdy stone chapel.

Wellington, who was watching from above, called up reinforcements from Spencer's 1st Division and three battalions raced down the slope to rally the skirmishers and retake Fuentes de Oñoro. The eager 71st (Glasgow Highland)

ABOVE *A map showing the initial positions and the main attack on the village of Fuentes de Oñoro itself.*

The second day at Fuentes de Oñoro

The French movements were nowhere near as covert as Masséna had supposed. Clearly weighted towards the south, Wellington suspected that the new plan was a flanking march through Pozo Bello, and he sent his four British cavalry regiments out with Don Julio Sanchez's mounted Spanish guerrillas to act as the first line of defence.

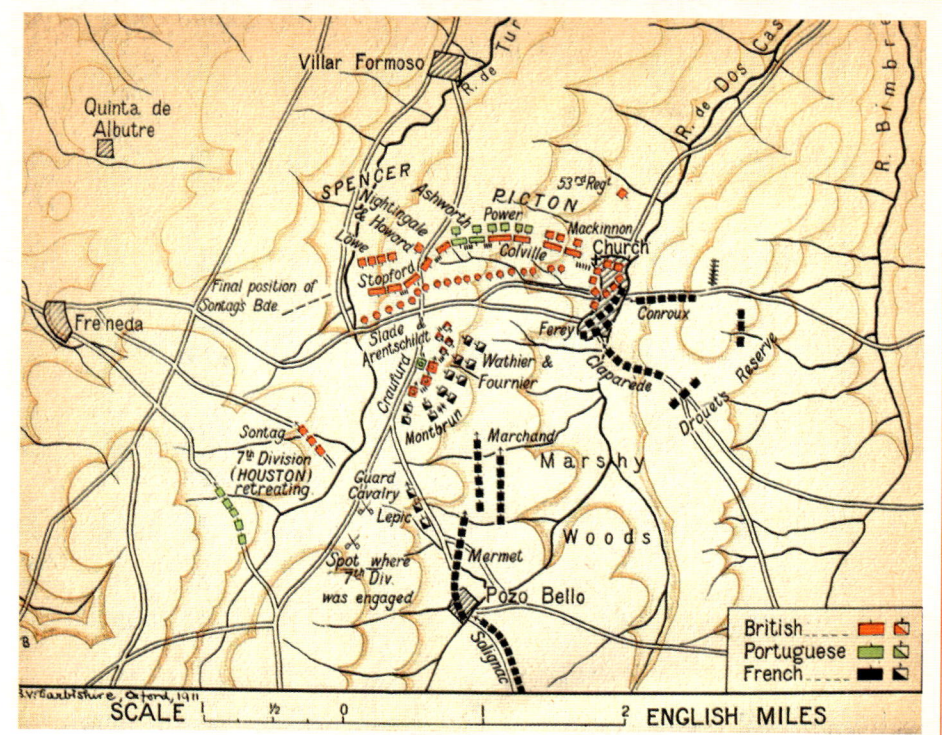

LEFT The movements of the second day of the Battle of Fuentes de Oñoro, with the British line reduced to defend against the French flanking movement.

BELOW Pursued by French cavalry, Captain Norman Ramsay of the Royal Horse Artillery desperately tries to get his guns to safety during the 7th Division's withdrawal. Painted by William Barnes Wollen, 1924.

"The non-combatants, who had gathered behind the first line, were hurrying away panic-stricken, and with lamentation were driven by French cavalry across the plain. The whole of the vast plain was covered with confused multitudes, amongst which the squares appeared but as specks, for there was a great concourse composed of commissariat animals and followers of the camp, servants, baggage, led horses, and peasants, and finally broken pickets and parties coming from the woods."

The skirmishers in Pozo Bello were next to meet the French advance and quickly tried to retreat but were set upon by the French cavalry who swept in on their flanks through the rolling fog and cut down 150 of their number. Salvation came with a German accent as the 1st Hussars of the KGL boldly barrelled in to their rescue, distracting the French for just long enough that the two battalions of shaken skirmishers were able to consolidate a more orderly retreat.

Now realising that the 7th Division was in danger of being cut off as the advancing French columns wheeled north, Wellington ordered the Light Division and the 1st Division into a new line running west from Fuentes de Oñoro. He then ordered the 7th to fall back to the new position.

> "The non-combatants, who had gathered behind the first line, were hurrying away panic-stricken, and with lamentation were driven by French cavalry across the plain."

Houston's 7th Division was stationed behind Pozo Bello and two battalions of light infantry - the 2nd Caçadores and the 85th (Bucks Volunteers) (Light Infantry) Regiment - took up positions in the village itself.

At daybreak, the guerrillas encountered a large number of dismounted French dragoons advancing surreptitiously through the fog. They immediately saddled up and charged. Two nearby squadrons of 14th (or Duchess of York's Own) Light Dragoons made a fighting retreat towards Pozo Bello and further along the line, the 16th or the Queen's Light Dragoons and 1st Hussars of the King's German Legion formed up and charged the French, before realising how vastly outnumbered they were and pulling back in desperation.

Sergeant Andrew Pearson, 61st (or South Gloucestershire) Regiment of Foot, wrote:

THE ROAD TO WATERLOO 71

The Road to Waterloo
THE ALMEIDA CAMPAIGN

The Light Division was the last of the three to arrive and they moved up as the 7th pulled back. True to form, Craufurd was heading where the fighting was at its thickest. Packed tightly into squares with the cannon between them, the Light Division peppered the approaching French cavalry with shot whilst the French guns which were brought up were quickly run down by British dragoons. Finally, Wellington called Craufurd back into the line which then batted aside the oncoming foe with its wall of musketry.

Seeing the French cavalry sweeping behind Fuentes de Oñoro and ignorant of Wellington's new line, Masséna ordered the assault on the village. The streets choked with dead and dying as thousands of French infantry attacked and forced the defenders back, Wellington poured Picton's 'Fighting 3rd' in and sent the weary 6th Caçadores to join them. Fixing bayonets, the 88th (or Connaught Rangers) and 74th Highland Regiment charged down the hill to drive the French back from the church, exhausted beyond all measure, the Caçadores gave covering fire as their comrades drove their bayonets home.

By early afternoon, the battle was over. Records show that 1,452 British and Portuguese had fallen, but in doing so they had cost the enemy 2,192 men.

The escape from Almeida

Watching the enemy warily across the watercourse, the French began to withdraw in stages to Cuidad Rodrigo. As he departed, Masséna dispatched a message for General Brenier, which was smuggled through the blockade and over the walls of Almeida with the promise of a 6,000-franc bounty. Brenier's instructions were to sabotage the defences and make an escape from the citadel, and on the night of May 10, 1811, they spiked their guns, destroyed the stores, blew a series of mines that blasted great holes in the northern and eastern walls, and bolted through the gate.

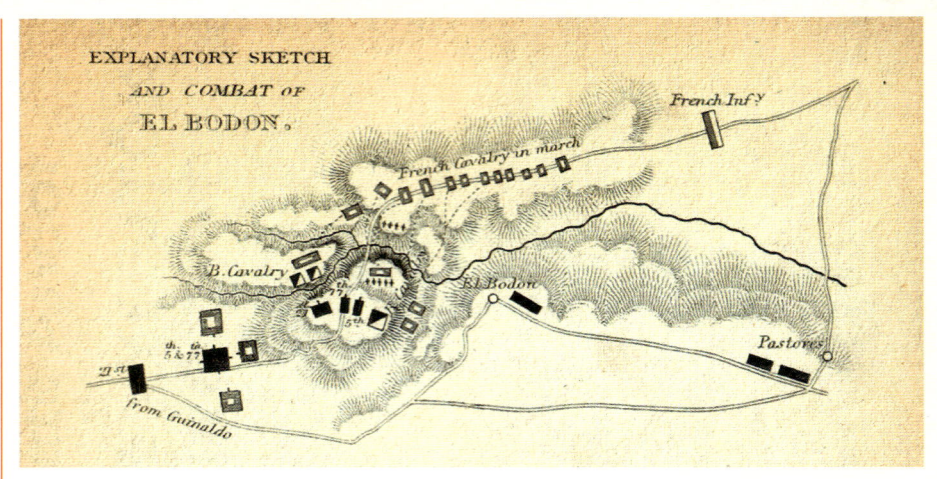

The besiegers' pickets had been posted too far back to observe their escape, and Brenier led his men in two columns to the weak join between the Portuguese 1st Regiment and the 2nd (Queen's Royal) Regiment of Foot. Overpowering the scattered sentries, they pushed on for the bridge at Barba del Puerco. Earlier that same day, Wellington had ordered the line extended to cover the bridge, but Major General Erskine didn't pass the orders on until close to midnight - around the same time the garrison were making good on their escape plan - and the 4th or the King's Own Regiment of Foot weren't where they were supposed to be.

ABOVE *A map showing the 3rd Division elements facing the French cavalry on the hillside and then marching to Fuenteguinaldo in squares.*

Brenier got 960 of the 1,400 French defenders to safety through a mixture of courage, good fortune, and British incompetence. Lieutenant Colonel Charles Bevan of the 4th was blamed for failing to secure the bridge and he asked for a Court of Inquiry to clear his and his regiment's name. Wellington refused.

Private John Timwell of the 43rd (Monmouthshire Light Infantry) Regiment, wrote: "Poor Bevan was censured by Lord Wellington, which circumstance preyed so much on his mind, knowing he had done his duty, that he blew his brains out." His cause of death was reported as fever and it wasn't until 1843 that his family learned the truth.

The third and final French invasion of Portugal was over. Confident that it would be a long time before Masséna - in fact, the newly installed Marshal Marmont - would

The French cavalry fall upon the infantry squares formed in Wellington's new line.

be able to take to the field, Wellington rode south with reinforcements to help resolve Major General William Carr Beresford's increasingly laborious Second Siege of Badajoz (April 22 – June 10, 1811).

The Battle of El Bodón

Although Ciudad Rodrigo was the most obvious target for Wellington after the fall of Almeida, he had no intention of bringing down its walls - he lacked the firepower - but he knew that even a blockade would eventually force a response from the French and so on August 11, 1811 he sealed off the city.

His real intention was to draw out the French from Salamanca and then fight defensively at Fuenteguinaldo, a village in the rolling hills 14 miles to the southwest. With the French defenders being so plentifully provisioned, Marmont didn't consider the situation at Ciudad Rodrigo particularly pressing until a train of British siege guns was landed at Lisbon and started its crawl towards the frontier.

Marmont combined the Armée du Portugal with the Armée du Nord and marched close to 58,000 men east and Ciudad Rodrigo was relieved without a fight on September 23. Rather than set up camp in the shadow of the walls as the British had expected, Marmont immediately sent his entire cavalry forward to probe their whereabouts, surprising Wellington who had carelessly strung his army out across the east and south.

Each of Wellington's isolated divisions was in danger of being cut off long before they made it to Fuenteguinaldo - which contained only Wellington's HQ and the 4th Division.

Two French cavalry brigades under General Frédéric-Louis-Henri Walther reconnoitring west of Ciudad Rodrigo stumbled upon pickets of 14th (or Duchess of York's Own) Light Dragoons and 16th (or the Queen's) Light Dragoons guarding the road to Almeida, close to the village of El Carpio. The dragoons retreated behind the stream and lured the French towards the edge of a wood, which immediately struck Walther as the ideal site for an ambush. The Combat of El Carpio (September 25, 1811) ended with British victory when the 14th suddenly charged from the treeline while three light companies of British infantry opened fire. The French were driven back with 48 killed and captured, but Walther had forced Wellington's infantry to reveal themselves.

Ten miles to the south at the Battle of El Bodón (September 25, 1811), elements of the 3rd Division - barely three battalions of infantry - found themselves facing four brigades of French cavalry under General Louis-Pierre Montbrun. Six miles from the next three battalions in the cordon, the British were holding the main road to Fuenteguinaldo, and only sheer bloody-mindedness saved them from not only total annihilation but from the capture or death of Wellington, the rout of Fuenteguinaldo, and myriad other potential catastrophes.

The 1/5th (Northumberland) Regiment of Foot, 77th (East Middlesex) Regiment of Foot and the Portuguese 21st Regiment - with cavalry support from 1st Hussars of the King's German Legion - held a plateau at the top of a steep slope against - according to one report - 40 individual attacks despite being outnumbered two-to-one. Without infantry support, the French were repeatedly thrown back by concentrated volleys or tightly packed bayonet charges. The exchange bought enough time for the rest of 3rd Division to withdraw to Fuenteguinaldo before the heroes of El Bodón were forced to make their own retreat, crawling across the countryside in their prickly squares.

Rather than run them down, Montbrun was apparently disquieted by the discipline of their withdrawal. He held his men back and periodically shelled them with horse artillery. Now with 15,000 of the 3rd and 4th Division at Fuenteguinaldo, Wellington's position looked marginally more robust - although it would take a miracle to save them from a force many times that number.

That miracle was his infamy. Wary of attacking Wellington at a location of his own choosing and despite his apparent weakness, Marmont withdrew and in the night the British slipped away to an even stronger position further west. The frontier battles of Almeida, Ciudad Rodrigo, and Fuentes de Oñoro may have had the makings of a frustrating stalemate, but it proved that the initiative was now firmly in the hands of the British.

THE SIEGE OF TARIFA

In subjugated Andalucía, only three towns remained as safe havens for the Spanish army. The mighty bastions of Cádiz and Gibraltar could hold out indefinitely, their defences too potent and their lines of supply endless so long as Britannia ruled the waves. Tarifa, at the southernmost tip of Iberia, was a different affair.

Its Moorish walls were built for arrows rather than shells and it was overlooked by high ground. Despite being reinforced by a British brigade under Colonel John Byrne Skerrett, the approach of an 8,000-strong French force looked like nothing but certain defeat for the defenders.

Skerrett requested evacuation by sea for the Anglo-Spanish defenders. He was opposed by the real architect of Tarifa's defiance, Captain Charles Felix Smith of the Corps of Royal Engineers. He noted that ground level inside the walls was much lower than the ground outside the walls and cooked up a plan.

The pickets were pushed back on December 19 and settling on the high ground to the northeast, the French prepared their trenches on December 22 and by December 29 were ready to open fire. Within hours the walls had been breached and the French rushed forward to discover a 14-foot sheer drop down the other side. The defenders had made firing positions of the surrounding houses, barricading the narrow streets to trap the French against the walls where they were unable to escape.

Two more attacks followed before torrential rain flooded the French siege works, made the approaches an impassable swamp and spared Tarifa further assault. The siege was lifted on January 5 and unable to move them through the mud, the French were forced to destroy their guns as they withdrew.

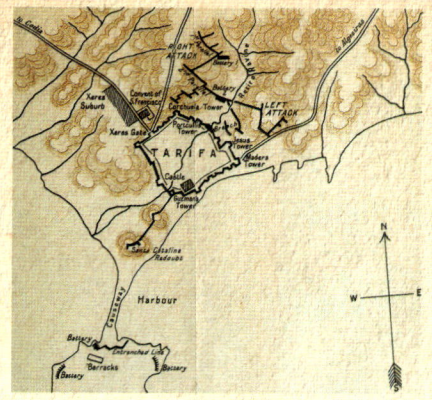

A map of the rugged landscape around Tarifa, which allowed the attackers to lob shells at the town with impunity.

THE ROAD TO WATERLOO 73

The Road to Waterloo — THE SALAMANCA CAMPAIGN

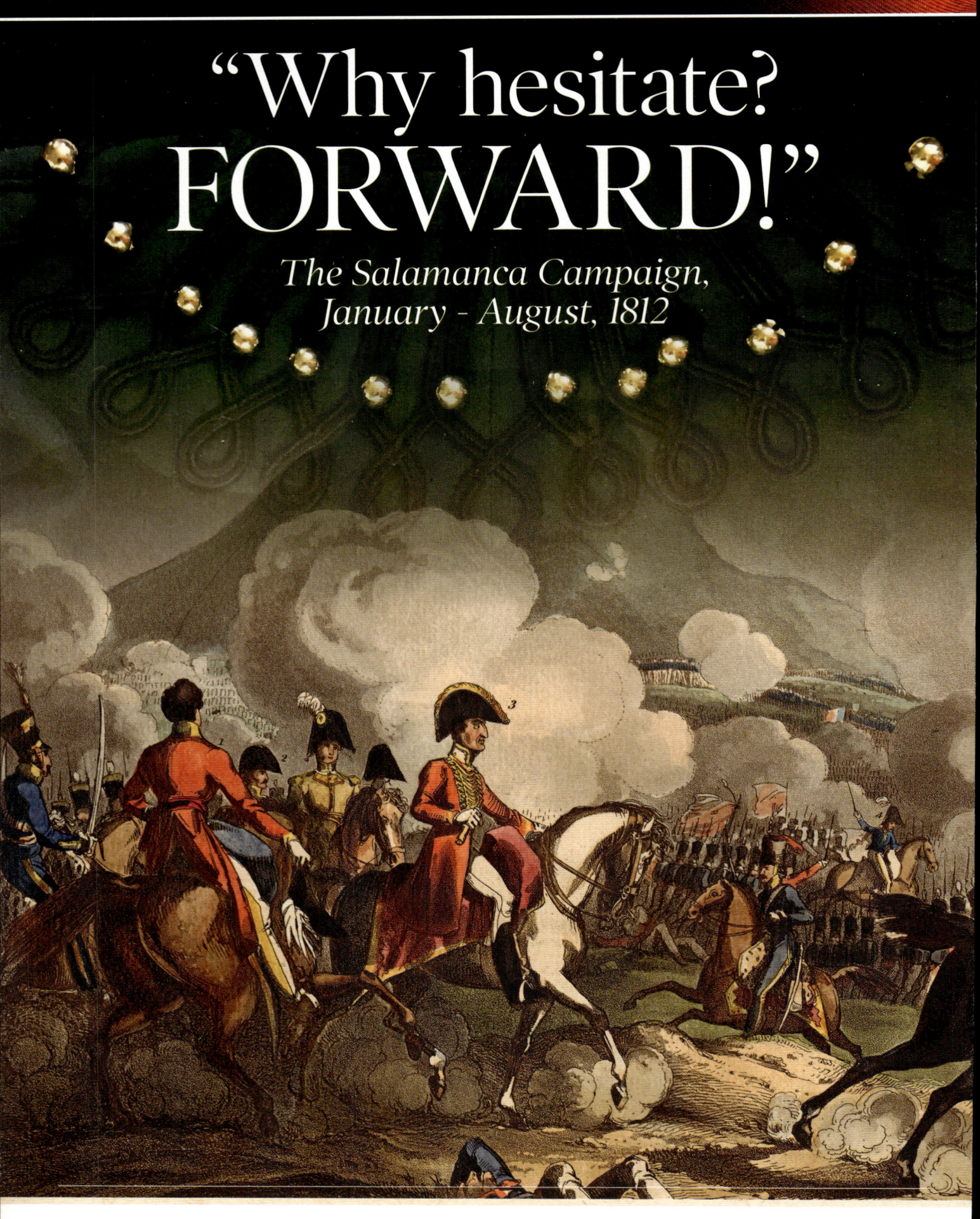

"Why hesitate? FORWARD!"

The Salamanca Campaign, January – August, 1812

After his cautious retreat from Fuenteguinaldo, Wellington wintered the army in the vicinity of Almeida. His hands were full fighting off the attendant disease and hardship that followed the season, but he followed the French movements in Spain with an eye for an opening to finally silence the border fortress of Ciudad Rodrigo.

Although Marshal Auguste Frédéric Louis Viesse de Marmont remained in the vicinity of Salamanca, two recent developments convinced Wellington - now the Earl of Wellington - that his time for action was nearing. The Grande Armée was assembling in Central Europe for an offensive against Russia, an undertaking that would result in some 685,000 men marching east in the largest army ever assembled in Europe.

Closer to home, Emperor Napoléon I's newest marshal, Louis-Gabriel Suchet, had successfully besieged Valencia, but the demands of pacifying a new province on top of the myriad fronts elsewhere in Spain and the build-up of troops in Poland was leaving them dangerously over-extended. With no chance of reinforcements until the war with Russia had played out, troops could now only be drawn by robbing Pierre to pay Paul.

Joined by the heavy siege artillery which trundled in his army's wake and a newly formed commissariat department, Wellington's siege began on January 8, 1812.

The Siege of Ciudad Rodrigo

Despite his garrison of only 2,000, General Jean Léonard Barrié was confident that Ciudad Rodrigo could hold out until Marmont raced to the rescue. This was exactly what Wellington wanted to avoid and he wasted no time. On the first night of the Siege of Ciudad Rodrigo, the Light Division seized the Renaud Redoubt which had been thrown up to prevent attackers using the high ground of the Greater Teson.

Using his infantry as navvies - a costly exercise that saw many fighting men felled by cannon from the ramparts - and working all through the night and day, by January 11 the siege guns were dug in and pressed into action. On the night of January 13, the French were cleared from the outlying Convent of Santa Cruz and the second line of trenches was dug in 200 yards from the west walls leading onto the second hill, the Lesser Teson.

Despite an attempt by Barrié to raid the siege works, the damage was swiftly repaired and on January 15, the guns of the British siege batteries opened fire. They targeted those patches on the wall that had been repaired following the French siege, where the brickwork soon proved to be brittle for want of lime in the mortar.

On the evening of January 19, the 3rd Division under Major General Thomas Picton rushed the larger breach, while the Light Division under the newly promoted Major General Robert Craufurd stormed the smaller breach which had been caused by a collapsing tower.

At the exact same time, 2nd Caçadores and the light company of the 2/83rd Regiment of Foot led by Lieutenant Colonel Bryan O'Toole crossed the River Agueda, slipped into the gatehouse and finding that Barrié lacked the numbers to hold both the north and south of the citadel simultaneously, scaled the walls and began advancing towards the main breach where Picton's 'Fighting 3rd' were fighting for their lives.

Charging into the very eye of the storm, the 3rd Division found that from the breach to street level was a 25-foot drop, one

BELOW *General Sir Arthur Wellesley, Earl of Wellington, directs his rows of redcoats into action at the Battle of Salamanca, by William Heath, 1821.*

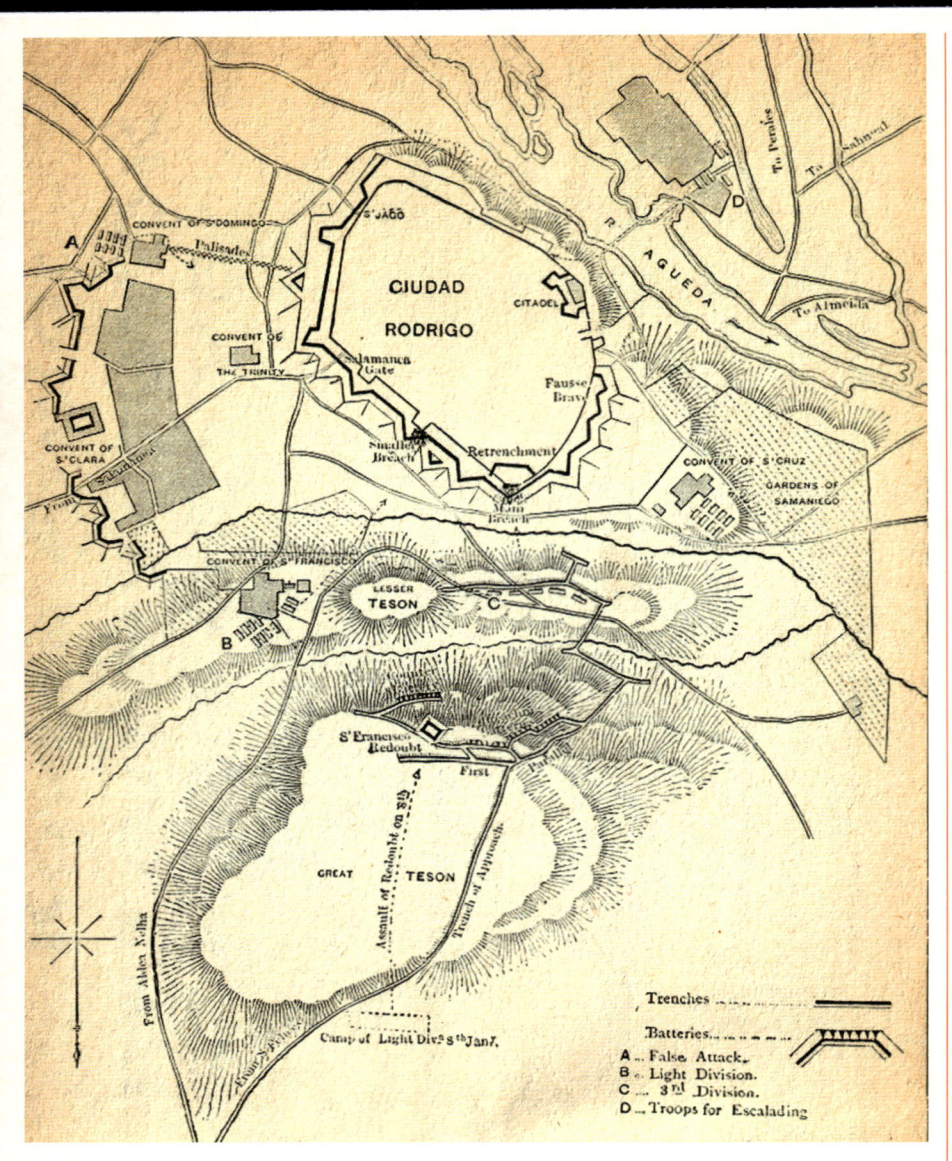

The Road to Waterloo — THE SALAMANCA CAMPAIGN

LEFT A map of the Ciudad Rodrigo siege works and defences with the north - the Great Teson and the Renaud Redoubt - at the bottom of the image and the south at the top.

> *"Whilst Marmont's situational awareness was compromised, by the time information reached his distant master, Emperor Napoléon I, it was even more wildly out of date."*

they had to make under the muskets of the French. As the first into the breach - the 'forlorn hope' of the 94th Regiment of Foot - teetered indecisively at the edge, a canister fired from a French cannon showered them with shrapnel. Bloodied but determined, the 94th tried again but were sent back again by the heavy fire, while the 88th (or Connaught Rangers) managed to push on, crawling through a ditch with only their bayonets to seize one of the enemy cannon.

Seeing that the tide was beginning to turn and that the Light Division and O'Toole's contingent were both converging on the forlorn hope, the defenders detonated a mine under the breach - the explosion tossing hapless redcoats to their deaths, among them the 88th's Major General Henry MacKinnon. The bold 'Black Bob' Craufurd fell in the attack too, fatally wounded by the debris from a canister. The Second Siege of Ciudad Rodrigo (April 26 - July 10, 1812) was over.

The British took 1,121 casualties, while the French defenders suffered 530 killed or wounded, and another 1,360 taken captive. The British celebrated with a two-hour orgy of drunkenness, violence, and vandalism before they were brought under control

The folly of the French

Intelligence of events unfolding over such a great and hostile landmass always arrived late to the invaders, and it wasn't until

ABOVE Auguste Frédéric Louis Viesse de Marmont, Marshal of France and Duke of Ragusa (now Dubrovnik), by Jean-Baptiste Paulin Guérin, 1837.

January 15 that Marmont became aware the siege had even begun. By the time he received news that the Spanish flag had returned to the battered battlements of Ciudad Rodrigo, the relief column was at Salamanca and it was clear to Marmont that Badajoz, which had so far resisted Wellington for want of siege artillery, would be next.

Whilst Marmont's situational awareness was compromised, by the time information reached his distant master, Emperor Napoléon I, it was even more wildly out of date. Just as the marshal wheeled south to intercept Wellington's march to Badajoz, he was ordered over the border into Beira which Napoléon I believed would 'contain' Wellington and force him to return to Portugal. The province was a remote, rugged landscape and in the hands of the Portuguese militia.

Marmont wrote icily: "[Wellington] knows my army is not in a position to cross the Côa, even if no-one opposes me, and that if we did so we should have to turn back at the end of four days, unable to carry on the campaign, and our horses starved to death."

The winter had not been kind to Marmont, his commitments in Spain had expanded significantly as part of the Emperor's Iberian drawdown and his Armée du Portugal - as it was still laughably known - was now responsible for maintaining several garrisons in Léon and maintaining communication with Marshal Jean-de-Dieu Soult's Armée du Sud in Andalucia. Marmont only had four divisions ready for immediate action against Wellington.

While Wellington marched to Badajoz, Marmont marched to Ciudad Rodrigo and found it as he had expected: the British had repaired the walls, which were manned by 3,000 Spanish troops and all the artillery that the Armée du Portugal had entrusted to the garrison. With his siege guns on the wrong sides of the wall, Marmont had no choice but to press on to Almeida, where he was similarly unable to menace the garrison. Onward into Portugal he marched, skirmishing with militia and achieving little more than, as Wellington wrote, "the murder and plunder of the inhabitants of a few villages in lower Beira."

Only when news of Badajoz reached Paris, was Marmont finally ordered back, by which time it was too late.

The Third Siege of Badajoz

On March 14, a 60,000-strong Anglo-Portuguese army laid a pontoon bridge across the wide and forbidding River Guadiana and began to cross.

In terms of preparation, Wellington had met his match in the defender of Badajoz, General Armand Philippon. Since Wellington and Beresford had withdrawn from the Second Siege of Badajoz (April 22 - June 10, 1811), the French commander had reinforced the breaches with stone blocks, the eastern approach had been mined with a lattice of explosives and the Rivallas Brook had been dammed to flood the southeastern approach with an artificial lake. The walls were defended additionally by nine bastions and the Medieval castle at the northeastern corner of the city.

Once the keen eye of Lieutenant Colonel Richard Fletcher, Royal Corps of Engineers, had surveyed the citadel, Wellington decided to target the southeastern corner, between the bastions of Santa Maria and Trinidad. To bring his siege works close to the walls, he first needed to suppress the outlying

ABOVE LEFT *Wellington's siege artillery opens up on the walls of Badajoz, incorrectly shown to be from the north. Most likely this is the perspective of the citadel the artist was most familiar with.*

ABOVE *Another dramatic Victorian depiction of the storming of the breach, from Cassell's Illustrated History of England, Volume 6, 1865.*

BELOW LEFT *The 'Folorn Hope' throw themselves into the breach of Ciudad Rodrigo on the night of January 19, 1812. The wounded officer in the foreground is Captain John Dobbs, 94th Regiment of Foot, who died in the assault.*

The Road to Waterloo
THE SALAMANCA CAMPAIGN

earthwork of Fort Picurina. On the night of March 17, the 2,000 troops dug their first parallel 200 yards from the fort, with the early morning fog affording them enough cover to continue their works by daylight - the defenders fired off the odd shot testingly into the gloom.

The dense fog was followed by four days of torrential rain which flooded the Guadiana and washed away the pontoon, turned the British earthworks into a swamp, and reduced the poor bloody infantry to skidding around in the mud, shoring up their liquid walls with sandbags. On March 19, Philippon launched a sortie to drive off the working parties, collapse the trenches and capture the tools, with a bounty paid out for each tool his men spirited away.

Fletcher was in the thick of the fighting to defend his siege works and was hit in the groin by a musket ball, which was deflected by a fortuitously located silver coin before it took his life (although the coin was driven two inches into his groin so that quality of life may be debatable). Fletcher was laid up in his camp bed for the duration, Wellington consulted him every morning for the remainder of the siege.

Although their progress had been delayed by both the French and the weather, the siege guns were soon ready and at 11am on March 25 they unleashed a merciless barrage onto Fort Picurina, silencing its cannon one by one. That night, 300 men of the 3rd Division and Light Division, guided by Royal Engineers and accompanied by miners with axes and ladders, stormed the fort and overwhelmed the defenders.

Extra muskets had been placed on the walls, so each soldier could fire multiple times without reloading and at close range, the French unloaded a hail of fire upon their attackers. The operation cost the British 54 dead and 265 wounded, a casualty rate of over 60 per cent and yet again the 'Fighting 3rd' and the Light Division were expected to foot the bill.

By March 30, the batteries had been moved forward far enough to target Trinidad, Santa Maria and the curtain wall which linked the two. Days upon days of relentless hammering by Wellington's heavy siege guns eventually caused the masonry to crumble and by April 5, it was now or never. The ditches hadn't been filled, nor had the defences been tested but Soult's army was approaching from the south.

The Light Division and the 4th Division were to attack at the southeast corner, while the 3rd Division and the 5th Division launched a diversionary attack at the eastern and western walls, with a

ABOVE *The 3rd Division advance into the French guns at the Second Siege of Ciudad Rodrigo, the horrific loss of life confirming that sieges weren't Wellington's forte.*

RIGHT *An unfinished panorama of Badajoz viewed from the west with the River Guadiana and the Fort of San Christóbal on the left.*

further feint by the Portuguese against the impregnable Fort of San Christóbal in the north.

The bloodiest night

Ill fortune and haste worked together. Although set to begin at 10pm, Picton's 3rd was spotted creeping into their start positions in the trenches and the garrison opened up, forcing them to attack the eastern walls immediately, without fighting elsewhere to draw fire. Meanwhile, the 5th Division didn't get into place until 11pm, allowing the defenders to concentrate their fire on the 3rd and then on the main attack, which had been lured into a killing ground.

As the Light Division and the 4th Division closed on the bastion of Santa Maria from the east, the mines were detonated and around 1,000 men were incinerated in seconds. One anonymous officer recalled: "The earth trembled - a mine was fired, an explosion, and an infernal hissing from lighted fuses succeeded, and like the rising of a curtain on the stage, the hellish glare that suddenly burst out round the breaches, the French lining the ramparts in crowds, and the English descending the ditch, were exposed as distinctly visible to each other as if the hour were noontide."

With many officers dead or dying, the remainder of the main attack descended into chaos with the two divisions losing all formation as they desperately raced for the walls and piled headlong into the ditch in front of them. Those who managed to reach the breaches found their passage blocked by the murderous blades of the chevaux de frise, improvised barricades of wooden planks with swords driven through.

With 2,200 men killed or wounded in two hours, Wellington grimly withdrew the Light Division and the 4th Division from their fruitless assault.

Far from the main breach, the 3rd Division scaled their ladders up the unbroken walls, where they were easily thrown back with a bayonet to the eye, while rocks, grenades and logs were tossed from the parapets onto the redcoats below. Though the 300 defenders on the eastern walls had the advantage, they lacked the numbers to defend at multiple points.

Lieutenant Colonel Harry Ridge of the 5th (Northumberland) Regiment of Foot grabbed a ladder and took it to the wall some distance to the left, with his grenadier company in pursuit. His sword aloft, Ridge became the first of the attackers onto the walls and behind him poured a torrent of bayonets and blades that drove the French down into the castle.

The defenders outnumbered 13-to-one had no stomach for a level field and fled through the gates and into the city.

While his comrades secured the keep, Lieutenant James MacPherson, 45th (or Nottinghamshire) Regiment of Foot, forced his way onto the roof. With two ribs broken from a musket ball that had glanced off one of his silver buttons, he breathlessly overcame the defiant French sentry and hauled down the Tricolore. Without a flag on his person, MacPherson ran his crimson tunic up the flagpole instead.

RIGHT *The 3rd Division storm the ramparts of Badajoz, with the hatless officer in the front of the image most likely Lieutenant Colonel Harry Ridge of the 5th (Northumberland) Regiment of Foot. From a painting by the Victorian artist Richard Caton Woodville.*

"The earth trembled - a mine was fired, an explosion, and an infernal hissing from lighted fuses succeeded, and like the rising of a curtain on the stage, the hellish glare that suddenly burst out round the breaches, the French lining the ramparts in crowds

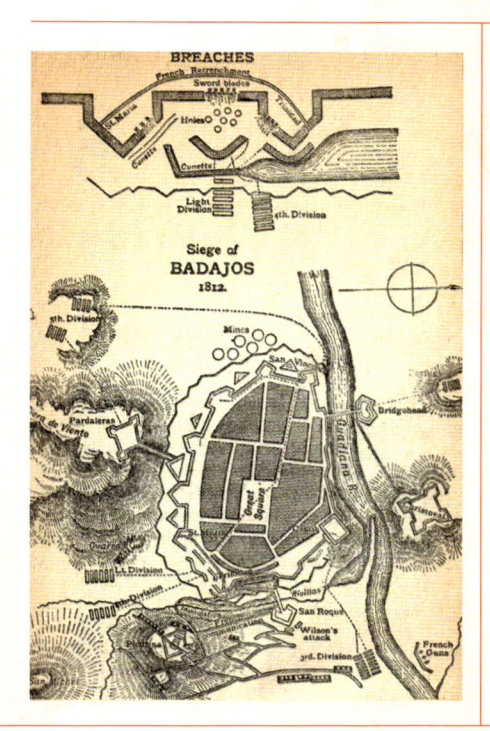

Over 700 of 3rd Division had been killed or wounded in the assault, including the valiant Ridge - whose last words were "Why hesitate? Forward!" - and Picton, who was wounded in the foot but survived. Elsewhere, the 5th Division successfully took San Vincente and filed out along the walls, joining 3rd Division in flanking the defenders, just as the Light Division and 4th Division renewed their assault on the breach.

Philippon made one desperate attempt to scatter the 5th Division before he saddled up his horse and bolted with his cavalry through the Las Palmas gate and across the river to the protection of San Christóbal where he later surrendered. Wellington, who had been watching the assault on the breach with a growing despair, was as stunned as the French when the news reached him and he exclaimed in disbelief: "Then the place is ours?!"

The defenders laid down their arms and the Anglo-Portuguese forces swept into the citadel, flushed with bloodlust and victory. In the offensive, 4,670 British and Portuguese soldiers had fallen and the rage once uncorked had to run its terrible course.

Captain Robert Blakeney, 36th (or the Herefordshire) Regiment of Foot, wrote: "There was no safety for women even in the churches, and any who interfered or offered resistance were sure to get shot. Every house presented a scene of plunder, debauchery and bloodshed committed with wanton cruelty."

LEFT *A map of the Siege of Badajoz showing the various assaults on the fortifications, with a close-up showing the three breaches at the bastions of Trinidad and Santa Maria.*

THE ROAD TO WATERLOO 79

The Road to Waterloo

THE SALAMANCA CAMPAIGN

RIGHT *An extremely crowded contemporary depiction of Lieutenant General Rowland Hill's daring Raid on Almaraz.*

The raid on Almaraz

The capture of Badajoz - and Philippon's cache of correspondence which he hadn't had the time to destroy, so sudden was his defeat - revealed to Wellington just how weak his opponents were. Not only had he now decisively secured the Spanish-Portuguese frontier, but had an opportunity to permanently sever the link between Marshal Marmont in the north, and Soult in the south.

The River Tagus bisected Spain almost neatly from east to west and the major transit point for the French was the pontoon bridge they had erected near the village of Almaraz to replace the 16th century stone bridge destroyed by the retreating Spanish. Without it, artillery and wagons would be required to journey an extra 160 miles to the bridge at Toledo.

The French had taken no chances with this vital link in their supply chain and the north bank was protected by Fort Ragusa and the south by Fort Napoléon which was on a hill previously occupied by a Spanish hermitage. Each fort was supported by a single flèche, a triangular earthwork that offered a rudimentary firing position for both cannon and infantry. Further south along the main road was the tower of Miravete, which had been fortified with a wall and linked to a farmhouse on the opposite side of the road to form an effective stronghold.

Major General Rowland Hill, known affectionately to his men as 'Daddy Hill', took 7,000 men to the Miravete Pass, where he quickly concluded that assaulting the position outright would be costly. Instead, he took most of his force along a mountain track to the east - the Cueva Pass - while those left behind mounted a diversionary assault on Miravete.

Making their way through the hills under the cover of darkness and dragging siege ladders behind them, Howard's column was still only halfway from Fort Napoléon when the sun began to rise. With no time to gather his men and the attack on Miravete having begun at dawn, Hill had no choice but to begin the battle on May 19, 1812.

Despite many of his men still scattered along the trail, Hill's column quickly overran Fort Napoléon. Once the first fortification had been taken, the rest of the garrison began to panic and their commander Colonel Aubert was left to fight on alone. Captain John Patterson of the 50th (or the West Kent) Regiment of Foot, recalled:

"Being resolved to sell his life as dearly as he could, he placed his back against the round tower in the centre of the work where with his sabre he chopped away right and left, cutting down any rash desperado who ventured to approach his weapon. At length Sergeant Checker [...] exasperated by the stubborn obstinacy of the Frenchman, put an end to his existence with his halberd, giving to the valiant governor the fate which, in his despair, he so resolutely courted."

Bolting across the bridge for the sanctity of Fort Ragusa, the weight of the sudden charge across the pontoons caused it to collapse. As men flailed around in the icy river, the garrison on the opposite bank fled. Hill briskly set about destroying the remainder of the pontoons, the shells for the guns were thrown into the river, and Fort Napoléon was dynamited. The French defenders lost 400 men, many drowned,

ABOVE *A crude lithograph from the 1812 'Victories of Wellington' series, showing the British cavalry sweeping in on the French at Salamanca.*

RIGHT *A grenadier company of the 3rd Division charge into the battered French flanks at the Battle of Salamanca.*

to the British count of 178 dead and wounded.

The Battle of Salamanca

The sudden destruction at the Almaraz crossing threw Marshal Soult into a state of utter panic and he repeatedly petitioned for more troops from King José I of Spain - the Emperor's older brother, Joseph-Napoléon Bonaparte - insisting that tens of thousands of redcoats were making a beeline for Andalucia. Marshal Marmont, meanwhile, had returned to Salamanca and was convinced - with greater probability - that Wellington was marching his way with 37,000 infantry and 3,500 cavalry.

José I, overly-cautious through years of being brow-beaten by his brother, prevaricated over the reports. Eventually, he went with Marmont and ordered Soult to reinforce his colleague - Soult being Soult, refused and Salamanca was left to its fate.

Over June and July 1812, the British and French armies danced around the rolling plains of León, entirely reluctant to face one another in the field. In this Wellington had found in Marmont, a commander who was just as keen as he was to fight exclusively on his own terms. Not numb to the irony, Wellington complained on July 3: "It appears certain that Marmont will not risk an action unless he should have an advantage; and I should certainly not risk one unless I should have an advantage."

The British pushed on into the city of Salamanca, which had been vacated of the Armée du Portugal, save the stubborn defenders of three fortified convents, San Vicente, San Cayetano, and La Merced, which guarded the bridge over the River Tormes. Unsurprisingly, given that Ciudad Rodrigo and Badajoz had been such costly bloodbaths under Wellington's command, it took ten days and disproportionate cost for the British to finally dislodge the 800 defenders in the Siege of the Salamanca Forts (June 17-27, 1812).

Wellington's reluctance to engage had given Marmont time to consolidate his forces, bringing their numbers up to 43,000 infantry, 2,200 cavalry, and 78 cannon. His army now in a significantly better state than it had been in June, Marmont drew closer and the two commanders continued their manoeuvres over the landscape, each one attempting to goad the other into attacking to their disadvantage.

The turning point

Aside from a brief moment on July 18 when Wellington had ridden back to supervise the rearguard himself - and suddenly the senior staff of the Anglo-Portuguese command found themselves drawing swords as French dragoons raced in among them - the first weeks of July had been almost slapstick.

Marmont had wheeled south and was trying to flank Wellington on his left, but each move would be met by a counter from the British, until finally on July 19 both armies were marching parallel under the hot Spanish sun on opposite banks of the River Guarena. Wellington changed direction first and coming to a tributary called the Poreda, the British pulled slightly further to the right. As both armies continued on their sullen way, between them to the British left a wedge of land was opening up where the Poreda parted from the Guarena.

The two armies lost sight of each other and the business of manoeuvre and counter continued, until they both wheeled back towards Salamanca - Wellington edging back towards the city and Marmont constantly attempting to outflank him. The night of July 21 blew through the camps, waking the men from their slumber with a thunderstorm that threw the horses into panic and eased the terrible heat - a small mercy ahead of the impending slaughter.

The terrain was wooded and undulating, broken enough to obscure each army's true intentions and when Marmont spotted skirmishers from Lieutenant General Sir John Hope's 7th Division advancing along a ridge to the west, he thought the British were in full retreat. He immediately dispatched his voltigeurs to drive the 2nd Caçadores and 68th (Durham Light Infantry) Regiment back, while the rest of the army raced rapidly westward to outflank them by taking the hills of the Southern Apariles.

Rather than being in full retreat to the west, Wellington had drawn his divisions up into two tight lines, one shorter line running north to south along the River Pelagarcia - where the two sets of skirmishers were scrapping - and the longer line running east to west through the village of Los Alpariles. They were deployed so closely that each division could be effortlessly reinforced, while the French had strung themselves out in their eagerness to outflank the British on their right.

THE ROAD TO WATERLOO 81

The Road to Waterloo — THE SALAMANCA CAMPAIGN

At 2pm, the French attacked Los Apariles itself, which Wellington had anticipated and he had withdrawn the 7th Division from the left to reinforce the centre, replacing them with the Light Division. He was feeling so nonchalant about it, that he was taking lunch when he noticed just how far the westward march under General Jean Guillaume Barthélemy Thomières had drifted from the rest of the French army. "By God," he uttered, lowering his telescope. "That'll do!"

There was a gap of nearly six miles and Wellington immediately launched an all-out attack. Advancing along the low wooded hills, Brigadier General Benjamin d'Urban's three Portuguese cavalry squadrons suddenly burst into the front rows of Thomières' column, their heavy sabres carving up the stunned infantry like offal. In their wake came the 3rd Division - Colonel Edward Pakenham, Wellington's brother-in-law, having replaced the wounded Picton - who drove the French infantry into a rout. The French cavalry attempted a counter-charge but being relatively recent recruits on untested mounts, they could do little against the battle-hardened 'Fighting 3rd' and they turned tail. Thomières himself was killed in the retreat.

The first French assault on Los Apariles had been beaten back at a terrible cost - Marmont having underestimated just how densely Wellington had arranged his line. As the marshal galloped down from the Greater Alaprile to take command of his now exposed left flank, an exploding shell swept him from his saddle and he rolled down the hill, his ribs and arm shattered. His second-in-command, General Jean-Pierre-François, Comte Bonnet was also wounded within minutes, and in less than an hour of fighting the Armée du Portugal was on its third commander, General Bertrand Clauzel.

With the French left collapsed and the survivors pouring east back across the Lower Alpariles, Major General James Leith's 5th Division in the British centre advanced on what was now the left flank. In a crude imitation of Wellington's favourite ploy General Antoine Louis Popon de Maucune pulled his division back onto the reverse slope of the hill, but out of fear of the nearby cavalry division they were formed into nervous squares rather than lines. As the 5th passed the ridge, both divisions fired volleys at each other - a thunderous meeting of musketry at close range, that added Leith to the fallen - and then the British charged, the line of furious bayonets putting Maucune's division to flight.

The squares shattered, Major General John le Marchand's cavalry division finally thundered around the hill and cut the retreating French down. The 3rd (King's Own) Dragoons, 4th or Queen's Own Dragoons, and the formidable 5th (or Princess Charlotte of Wales's) Dragoon Guards tore through Maucune's men and barrelled into the French vanguard, who opened up with a volley, before they too were pitched east in panic.

To the right of Clauzel, four French divisions were standing firm, and he was torn between covering his army's retreat and pressing his advantage. Having just thrown the 4th Division into retreat with a bayonet charge that left Major General Lowry Cole severely wounded, Clauzel scented glory and pushed on.

Wellington pitched in the reserves, and with huge numbers of redcoats sweeping across the Southern Alpariles, Clauzel ordered the retreat. As night fell and the woods burned, the French made a desperate fighting retreat. Arguably the greatest battle of Wellington's career to date had been won and the Armée du Portugal destroyed.

At a cost to his own forces of only 4,800 - still a lot of casualties, with a number of his most capable generals among them - the French had lost 13,000: 6,000 casualties and 7,000 captured.

The gates of Madrid

The elite cavalry of the King's German Legion gave chase, tearing chunks out of Clauzel's survivors at the Battle of García Hernández (July 23, 1812) where even squares failed to protect the battered French. Despite vengeance coming quickly at the Combat at Majahalonda (August 11, 1812) in which the watering KGL were surprised by a French column, losing 200 men in less than an hour, nothing could keep Wellington from advancing towards the Spanish capital.

King José I had been demanding reinforcements from Marshal Soult, who true to form was paying no attention to his irrelevant monarch and instead suggested he'd be better off abandoning Madrid. In reply, the king demanded Soult resign, which he was no likelier to obey than any other order he had seen fit to issue thus far. Defeated, the short-lived and largely meaningless King of Spain evacuated for Ocaña and on August 12, 1812, Wellington entered Madrid in triumph.

BELOW *French prisoners are marched back to Salamanca under guard, following the battle. Engraved by JH Clark and M Dubourgh circa-1813.*

WWW.KEYPUBLISHING.COM/SHOP

GREAT GIFT IDEAS - TREAT YOURSELF OR A FRIEND

Flight Book

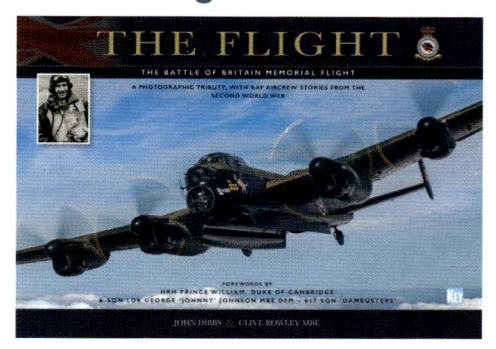

A photographic commemoration of the Battle of Britain Memorial Flight. Hardback, 192 pages.

ONLY £19.99   Code: B510

Spitfire Construction Set

Build Your Own Aviation Legend.

ONLY £22.99   Code: G009

SPECIAL OFFERS

Vulcan Test Pilot
Inside the Cockpit of a Cold War icon. Softback, 224 pages.

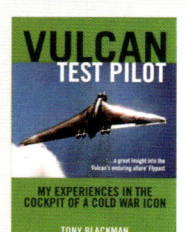

ONLY £9.99   Code: B493

D-Day 75
The Story Behind Operation Overlord

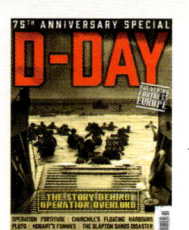

ONLY £5.99   Code: SPECDD75

Schooldays to Spitfire
The story of the legendary Spitfire. Softback, 384 pages.

ONLY £9.99   Code: B564

Britain At War Binder
Keep your Britain At War collection in pristine condition with these high-quality binders.

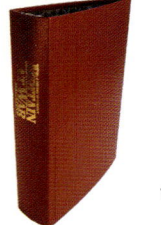

ONLY £9.49   Code: BAWBINDER

From £19.99

Why not subscribe to Britain At War?

See our website for the latest subscription deals
www.britainatwar.com

TWO EASY WAYS TO ORDER

757/19

ORDER ONLINE
www.keypublishing.com/shop

CALL US NOW
(0)1780 480404

Lines open Monday to Friday 9.00am until 5.30pm GMT

Customer code: RTW011219

Credit and debit card payments will show as Key Publishing. Key Publishing will hold your details in order to process and service your supscription only.

The Road to Waterloo THE LIBERATION OF SPAIN

The Liberation OF SPAIN

The Pyrenees Campaign, May - August, 1813

With Wellington's advance, the pressure eased from the French in one vital respect: he had freed his opponents of territory they were struggling to control, enabling them to concentrate their forces against him.

General Bertrand Clauzel had been far more decisive than the wounded Marshal Auguste Frédéric Louis Viesse de Marmont, and the Armée du Portugal - such as it was - relieved the French garrisons of Zamora, Toro and Astorga from their Spanish opponents, and resupplied his force from the depot at Burgos. He was down to 25,000 men, but despite Wellington's best efforts, the Armée du Portugal was still in the field.

Attempting to run Clauzel down, the Anglo-Portuguese army was too heavily laden with guns and supplies to manage more than six miles a day. Arriving at Burgos to find Clauzel long gone - and the garrison embellished with a large number of the Armée du Portugal's wounded - Wellington took 21,000 men and embarked upon his most disastrous and ill-advised siege in a growing list.

Now suffering from a chronic shortage of artillery, the Medieval castle at the heart of the town was able to hold out against successive attempts to mine it and Wellington's army suffered 2,059 casualties for no gains. The Siege of Burgos (September 19 - October 21, 1812)

84 THE ROAD TO WATERLOO

was followed by the equally dismal Battle of Venta del Pozo (October 23, 1812) and Battle of Tordesillas (October 25-29, 1812) in which the rearguard scrabbled to hold onto their fallback line along the River Carrión.

Forced to limp back through the sleet to Ciudad Rodrigo and abandon Madrid, the Salamanca Campaign ended with a whimper, with most of the gains wiped away by the autumn showers. Sick, weary, and with their supply chain now in tatters, only the reluctance of King José I - Joseph-Napoléon Bonaparte - to risk an open battle with Wellington saved them from being utterly decimated.

Huge numbers of men dropped or deserted on the road, and of the remainder, 18,000 were listed as sick. Added to this logistical nightmare, Wellington had also taken on responsibility for the reform and reorganisation of the Spanish army. It was overdue, but it did little to enhance the general's mood and being appointed

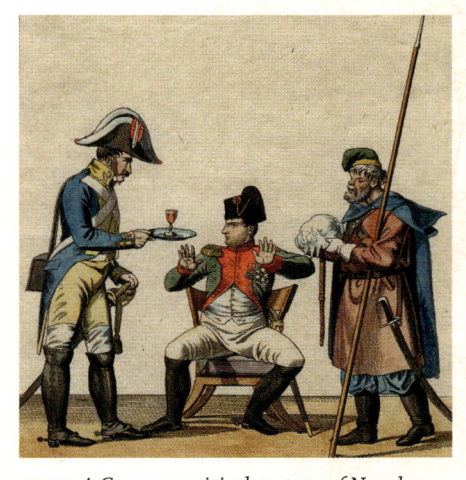

ABOVE A German satirical cartoon of Napoleon I refusing Russian ice and a glass of Spanish bitters. The Emperor replies of his situation in 1813: "No, no! The one is too cold, and the other makes me too hot."

LEFT A scene of fierce mountain combat between the British and the French at the Battle of the Pyrenees, by William Heath, 1836.

Spain's commander-in-chief simply exposed him to the inner workings of a corrupt and self-serving institution he had long despised.

"They are," he wrote, "in general, the most incapable of all the nations that I have known. The most vain, and at the same time the most ignorant, particularly of military affairs and above all of military affairs in their own country."

The view from the ground may have been gloomy, but from London, everything

ABOVE 'Portrait of the Duke of Wellington' by Francisco Goya, which he began in 1812 when Wellington liberated Madrid. Despite the title, this painting shows him in the uniform of an earl, but the two later portraits in the set updated his regalia.

looked as though it was proceeding according to plan. Against all expectation, the Grande Armée of Emperor Napoléon I had been destroyed by Russia in the Patriotic War of 1812, Wellington had recovered or destroyed a string of vital fortresses, and the provinces of Andalucia, Asturias and Extremadura had been liberated.

Over the winter, Wellington had done much to ease the suffering that visited the army the previous year and had largely shrugged off the damage incurred during the retreat from Burgos. He took a personal interest in improving medical care, he saw that fresh uniforms were finally issued, the men were drilled throughout the quiet months, and had even set about micro-managing the equipment each company took into the field to ensure that they met future downpours with tents and cooking pots.

The coastal road

Thanks to the pressure of the Royal Navy along the northern coast, the tiny province of Biscay - wedged between Asturias and the Pyrenees - and its inland neighbour, Navarre, had emerged as a particularly jagged thorns in the side of José I. An estimated 14,000 guerrillas, who were even being supplied with artillery by Britain, had brought communication between Madrid and Paris to a virtual standstill and had tied down the Armée du Nord - now commanded by Clauzel - and a large chunk of the Armée du Portugal.

Using all the tools now at his disposal - the guerrillas, the Spanish, the Royal Navy, and his bloody-knuckled Anglo-Portuguese army - Wellington prepared his final Spanish campaign, a decisive operation that would drive the French from Iberia. While the

The Road to Waterloo

THE LIBERATION OF SPAIN

ABOVE *A portrait of Lieutenant General Sir Thomas Graham painted in 1823 by Sir George Hayter, following Graham's elevation to the peerage.*

RIGHT *Joseph-Napoléon Bonaparte's most trusted military advisor and his chief-of-staff as King of Spain, Marshal Jean-Baptiste Jourdan.*

BELOW RIGHT *A watercolour by Adam Neale showing the distant signs of the battle in the rolling valley floor with the town of Vitoria beyond, 1813.*

guerrillas tied down Marshal Jean-de-Dieu Soult in Catalonia, the formidable Anglo-Portuguese-Spanish force advanced in two columns. Marching on the southern bank of the River Douro, 30,000 men under Lieutenant General Rowland Hill returned to Salamanca on May 26, 1813 to draw the attention of the French.

Setting off later, the larger 64,000-strong column under Lieutenant General Sir Thomas Graham (who had received his OBE over the winter after recuperating in Scotland) marched along the northern bank of the Douro. With General Augustin Daricau anxiously transfixed by the progress of Hill's column from Zamora, he only became aware of Graham bearing down on the rear of his division at the very last minute and narrowly escaped to warn the King of a much-reduced Spain.

Initially gathering 51,000 men around Valladolid, news that the two allied columns had merged into a single 90,000-strong force gave José I cause to rethink his strategy to fight them in the field and on June 3 he retired to the fortress at Burgos, where the only movements from Wellington seemed to be detachments of noisy cavalry.

Like Daricau a month earlier, José I realised almost too late that Wellington was in the process of encircling Burgos. He withdrew again, abandoning the citadel on June 13 and took up a defensive position behind the River Ebro where he bet all his chips on Wellington being unable to march such a large army over such barren terrain in the unrelenting Spanish summer. The French now occupied only a fifth of Spain, if that.

It's true that Wellington's previous campaigns through central Spain had been fraught by difficulties in supply and reinforcement. However, by switching to the north he was able to be resupplied by sea, using depots established at Santander by the energetic Commodore Sir Home Riggs Popham, whose relentless buccaneering along the northern coast had done much to drive the French to distraction.

Captain George Wood, 82nd Regiment of Foot, wrote: "Our march for the first two or three hundred miles was like a party of pleasure in comparison to others we had encountered: we passed through a most delightful level country, abounding in all the verdant beauties of nature [...] Everything and every countenance now wore the aspect of joy - the men singing and telling their jocose stories, as they passed along hill and dale."

Through their sheer presence, Wellington's army had cleared New Castile, Old Castile and Léon of their occupiers. By June, Wellington was descending on wayward Biscay, forcing the French to fight a series of panicked rearguard actions at the Battle of San Millan-Osma (June 18, 1813). José I resolved - if you can use such a strong word to describe such a notorious flip-flopper - to hold the allies at Vitoria. If he failed, they would be able to advance up the Bayonne highway through the Pyrenees Mountains and into France.

> *"Our march for the first two or three hundred miles was like a party of pleasure in comparison to others we had encountered: we passed through a most delightful level country, abounding in all the verdant beauties of nature*

The Battle of Vitoria

With the various army formations that he had gathered en route, José I's army was now over 60,000. The town of Vitoria sat in the middle of a deep valley that -

86 THE ROAD TO WATERLOO

ABOVE *William Heath's 1836 depiction of the Battle of Vitoria, showing the British advancing over the undulating valley floor towards the town.*

LEFT *Lieutenant General Sir Thomas Picton painted by William Heath, 1814. Wellington described him fondly as "as a rough foul-mouthed devil as ever lived."*

he believed - offered only one westerly approach for the enemy, while the River Zadorra held the French right and the Pueblo Heights secured the left.

That José I and his advisor, Marshal Jean-Baptiste Jourdan, expected Wellington to obligingly saunter down the middle of a valley to face him when almost every great British victory of the previous four years involved a bold flanking manoeuvre, is surely evidence that strategy wasn't a family trait.

The Zadora was bisected at regular intervals by bridges and fords, and José I gave no thought to their destruction - instead, he busied himself ensuring that his wagons of loot had ample escorts for their journey through the mountains, taking the total strength down to 57,000. Additionally, the French forces were invested over 12 miles of the undulating valley with significant gaps in their lines.

Wellington's forces were now closer to 75,000 - the 6th Division having been detailed to secure the road to Santander and one of the Spanish corps had been sent to Bilbao - but it was immediately obvious that the French position was porous. Only at the very last minute did José I get jittery about the reports that the approaching army was far smaller than expected and sent his bodyguard and some cavalry back to reinforce Vitoria itself. Jourdan, meanwhile, gave some idle thought to what their fallback position might be if the allies attacked from the north, but was feeling under the weather and didn't bother to send the orders.

At 8 am on June 21, 20,000 men under Lieutenant General Rowland Hill - the 4th Division, a Portuguese division, and a Spanish division - flung themselves at the hillside and filtered east along the heights. Rather than the rows of redcoats they expected to see marching towards them from the west, the first the French were

THE ROAD TO WATERLOO 87

The Road to Waterloo
THE LIBERATION OF SPAIN

SIR HOME POPHAM: BRITAIN'S BISCAY BUCANEER

In many ways, Commodore Sir Home Riggs Popham was a man after Wellington's own heart. Like Wellington, he came from a distinguished family fallen on hard times - in Popham's case, his father incurred massive debts and brought his diplomatic career little glory as British consul to Morocco.

Ironically, his father's falling out with the Emperor of Morocco was a consequence of his inelegant attempt to curb the monarch's support for piracy, and not only did his son go on to join the Royal Navy but would do so in a manner that would have delighted a Barbary pirate captain.

At one extreme in his colourful naval career, his ship was seized for smuggling contraband through the East India Company monopoly in South Asia, he was accused of corruption by the Admiralty for running up a suspiciously high bill for repair in Calcutta but cleared his name in Parliament, and he was later court-martialled for embarking on his own expedition to foment revolution in Latin America. This last high-profile case prompted a doggrel poem of support from Jane Austen, of all people, and saw him awarded a ceremonial sword by the City of London at the same time as he was being rapped on the knuckles by the Admiralty.

Thanks to the patronage of the Duke of York, Popham was able to hold on to his blue jacket, and he proved his worth by creating the Sea Fencibles, a coastal defence militia. He also developed a code using double-backed flags that increased the navy's alphabet from twelve 'words' to 24. It was in this cypher that Vice Admiral Horatio Nelson's famous "England Expects..." message was communicated before the decisive Battle of Trafalgar (October 21, 1805).

Perhaps the perfect alignment of his unique skillset came in the Peninsula War. In 1812, Popham was stationed on the Atlantic coast of Spain, where he worked with guerrillas to harass the French occupiers and landed detachments of Royal Marine Light Infantry to raid French-held ports. Using Santander as his regional hub, Popham was able to establish an intelligence network through Basque country that allowed him to keep Wellington informed about French activity in northern Spain.

Responsible for tying up an entire French army corps for the best part of a year, as well as a part share in the success of Wellington's 1813 campaign, Popham's role remains largely unrecognised and unappreciated. Resented by many at the Admiralty and too dependent on his politically influential patrons - again there are parallels with Wellington - the Peninsula War turned out to be Popham's last active command.

An engraving of Commodore Sir Home Riggs Popham by Anthony Cardon, 1807.

---

aware of Hill was when the first of his divisions immediately opened fire on their left.

Now convinced that Wellington's masterplan was to flank them from the south, José I and Jourdan hastily pulled troops from elsewhere and flung them at the heights. Whilst the fierce firefight erupted in the southwest corner of the valley, the real flanking manoeuvre began in the north. Not so much a pincer as it was an iron maiden, with Wellington slamming the lid shut - the 1st and 5th Division erupted from the mountains to the immediate north of Vitoria itself where a single French infantry division was holding the road, and to the right of the frontline, the Light Division, the 7th and the 'Fighting 3rd' crept through the mountains and the woodland.

The Light Division - as ever - were first into the fray, slipping across the undefended bridges, but they were soon in danger of being overwhelmed for want of reinforcement. The 3rd was supposed to be following the 7th Division, but Major General George Ramsay, 9th Earl of Dalhousie - a man whose nobility was in inverse proportion to his competence - dithered in the undergrowth. Lieutenant General Sir Thomas Picton, who was already irritated at having to follow Dalhousie, cast precedence on the fire and advanced with a shout of, "Come on, ye rascals! Come on, ye fighting villains!"

Squeezed from the right and coming under increasing pressure from the left as more of Hill's divisions advanced along the hillside, the French were desperately being driven back. Frantically, José I ordered them into new defensive lines across the valley, but under the sheer concentration of enemy fire, the lines disintegrated as quickly as they were formed. Fairly confident that he wouldn't have to worry about the King of Spain's opinion on anything ever again, General Honoré Théodore Maxime Gazan de la Peyrière, decided his divisions had done all they could and withdrew.

Scenting blood, Hill's divisions pushed on into the gap left by Gazan's men and levered the French line into fragments. With the route to the northeast blocked by Graham's column, the French poured down the eastern road to Pamplona which quickly became clogged with refugees.

Only the allure of the wagons they left in their wake saved them from a massacre, but although the casualties were fairly even - an estimated 5,000 on either side (plus 3,000 French prisoners taken) - the chaos and the despondency was total. All but one piece of artillery had been lost, five million francs in coinage, barrels of wine, the endless papers, documents, and works of art were scattered by the roadside for redcoats to squabble over.

Securing The Frontier

Wellington was furious with the indiscipline, which he felt had cost them total victory, but in the wake of the Battle of Vitoria, what remained of the French occupation in Spain collapsed almost entirely. General Clauzel pointed his two divisions toward the Pyrenees, Marshal Soult ordered the evacuation from Navarre, and finally, the man who was once king, Joseph-Napoléon Bonaparte, was instructed

LEFT This cartoon by the early 19th-century master satirist George Cruikshank celebrates the Battle of Vitoria. Note Joseph Napoleon Bonaparte sneaking off on a mule in the top right: "O vat de devil vill Brother Nap say?"

BELOW A view of the Siege of San Sebastián from the east across the River Urumea showing the sandy estuary that the forlorn hope were expected to cross at low tide.

to hand over what remained of his army to Soult and disappear into ignominy.

A few garrisons remained in French hands as optimistic beachheads which they hoped would endure until more favourable winds blew across the mountain. On June 25, Wellington blockaded Pamplona and dispatched Graham to tear chunks out of the retreating General Maximilien Sébastien Foy, who had been previously standing watch over the Basque coast with a 5,000-strong division. Graham had aspirations to sever Foy's line of retreat and scattering a number of French detachments who were caught on the wrong side of the Bayonne road before him, the column advanced towards Villafranca.

To the surprise of both commanders, an entire French division was resting at Villafranca. General Antoine Louis Popon de Maucune had been returning to Vitoria from escorting Bonaparte's booty when news of the battle reached him and he immediately wheeled around for want of a purpose. Now Maucune had found one, and he covered Foy's retreat. The two detachments, totalling 16,000 men, bloodied their tormenter at the Battle of Tolosa (June 26, 1813) and then retreated at their own discretion for France.

Convinced Pamplona's defenders could be starved into submission, Wellington decided to besiege the small but strategically vital fortress of San Sebastián, which stood watch over the Bay of Biscay. Although already under Spanish blockade following the retreat of Foy and Maucune, the seaward operation was less than fastidious and throughout the siege, the defenders were able to be resupplied by the French navy.

With 40 pieces of siege artillery brought up the coast, Wellington detailed Graham to conduct the Siege of San Sebastián (July 7 - September 8, 1813) with 9,000 men from Major General John Oswald's 5th Division and a Portuguese brigade under Brigadier General Henry Bradford.

The city clung to a narrow isthmus between the ocean and the River Urumea, with the walls and batteries at their most formidable on the south face. Wellington noted that on the eastern side, the walls had been steadily deteriorated by the river currents and at very low tide the Urumea was almost dry. The fortified Monastery of San Bartolomé covered the approach

> "The city clung to a narrow isthmus between the ocean and the River Urumea, with the walls and batteries at their most formidable on the south face. Wellington noted that on the eastern side, the walls had been steadily deteriorated by the river currents and at very low tide the Urumea was almost dry."

The Road to Waterloo — THE LIBERATION OF SPAIN

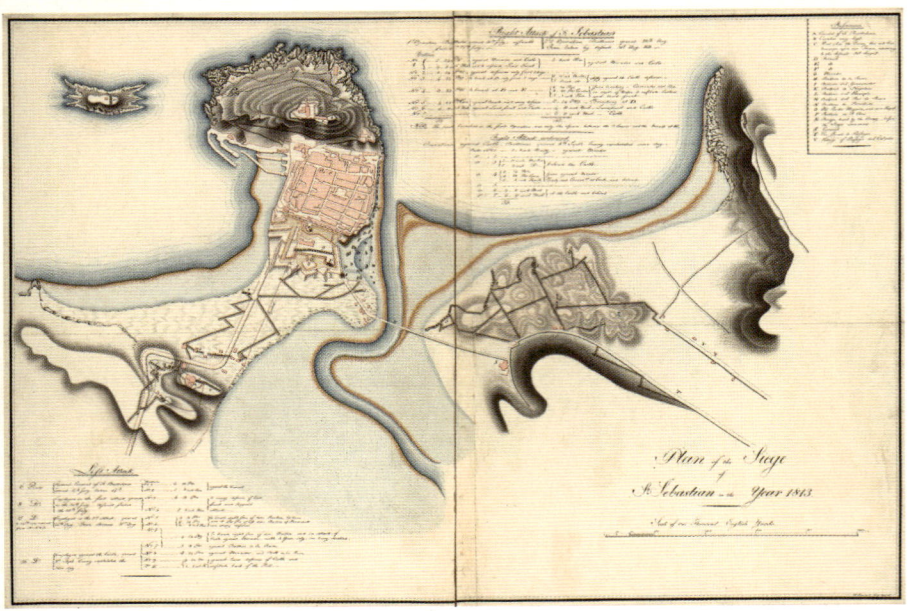

ABOVE *San Sebastián and the locations of the disastrous attacks on the left and the right of the hornwork on the morning of July 25, 1813.*

LEFT *A private of the 1st Regiment of Foot or Royal Scots, who suffered greatly during the attack on San Sebastián. Painted by military artist JD Shakespeare.*

sewer and the eastern end faced the Anglo-Portuguese batteries the other side of the river.

By July 25, the furious bombardment on the southeastern corner of San Sebastián seemed to have opened a breach. The mine was detonated at 5am and attackers filed out along the isthmus, nothing more than a diversion from the real assault over the Urumea. In the pre-dawn gloom, the 'folorn hope' of the 1st Regiment of Foot or Royal Scots skidded through the mud, seaweed and ankle-deep water and poured into the breach.

Here General Louis Emmanuel Rey had proven a more than worthy opponent. From the breach to the street level was a 22-foot drop, but Rey had sealed off access to the ramparts above and covered the breach with artillery and snipers. The forlorn hope of the Royal Scots was virtually wiped out, with 600 men falling in a matter of minutes, and the retreating survivors put the battalions advancing behind them to flight. Magnanimously, Rey's garrison - who had lost only 60 men in the assault - scrabbled down to the base of the breach to rescue the British wounded before the tide came in.

Wellington, never slow in making sure to the isthmus and it took three days of heavy shelling and hundreds of casualties for the British to finally secure the structure.

Work could now begin on the batteries across the Urumea, forcing the French to abandon the Cask Redoubt - the next must southernly point in their chain of fortifications. All that remained was the hornwork - so-called because two bastions jutted out like horns - that held the main gate. The western end had been mined when sappers found their way into an old blame was seen to lie elsewhere, immediately pointed the finger at the 5th Division, but his murderous approach to sieges hadn't escaped notice. Major William Gomm, 9th (the East Norfolk) Regiment of Foot, wrote bitterly: "I am afraid our success at Ciudad Rodrigo and Badajoz, owing to the almost miraculous efforts of the troops, has stopped the progress of science among our engineers [...] Our soldiers have on all occasions stood fire so well that our artillery has become as summary in their processes as our engineers. Provided that they have made a hole in the wall, by which we can claw up, they care not about destroying defences."

In any case, San Sebastián's reckoning could wait. The French were on the move.

The Battle of The Pyrenees

Emperor Napoléon I was locked in his tense negotiations with Austria and Russia at Dresden on July 1, 1813 when news of Vitoria struck like a thunderbolt. It was a tonic to the morale of the beleaguered emperors, Francis II of Austria and Alexander I of Russia, and they grew more belligerent in their demands.

The French armies that had been driven from Spain now had the unity of purpose they had lacked during five years of being subject to the competing interests of Napoléon I's prideful marshals, his pretentious and prevaricating sibling, and the diktats of a far-off Emperor. The four surviving formations were reorganised as Marshal Soult's Armée des Pyrénées, and Soult had 73,000 infantry in nine divisions, 7,000 cavalry in two divisions, and 140 cannon.

Supply problems, even this close to France, remained chronic and Soult resolved to strike quickly and decisively to relieve blockaded Pamplona. Wellington, aware that Soult was gathering strength, was convinced that San Sebastián was the more likely target. Both had been crucial to the initial invasion of Spain and ensuring they remained in French hands would leave the Peninsula open to a renewed invasion, as well as check British ambitions to push on into France.

With Wellington certain the French movements were feints, Soult's army advanced over the Bidassoa River in three columns of three infantry divisions apiece. The Battle of Roncesvalles - the first of the series of assaults that make up the Battle of the Pyrenees - began when General Clauzel's divisions advanced into Major General John Byng's screen of light companies at 6 am. Fighting over rugged terrain, Byng's brigade was able to hold off the entire division for three hours before a thick fog descended and the French called a halt.

To Byng's left, Colonel Robert Ross and the 4th Division vanguard faced equally daunting odds as General Honoré Charles Reille's column attempted to force its way onto the commanding Linduz Plateau, with the narrow approach limiting how many men the French could bring to bear, the 4th Division was able to keep them from taking the high ground, until, finally they too were granted respite by the fog.

Shortly after Clauzel and Reille made contact, the third of Soult's columns under General Jean-Baptiste Drouet, Comte d'Erlon faced Major General William Stewart and the 2nd Division at the Battle of Maya. Since his disastrous command at the Battle of Albuera (May 16, 1811), Stewart had rarely been expected to exercise his own initiative and this mindset was vindicated when virtually all his pickets were surprised and slaughtered by the French who advanced under the cover of some dead ground.

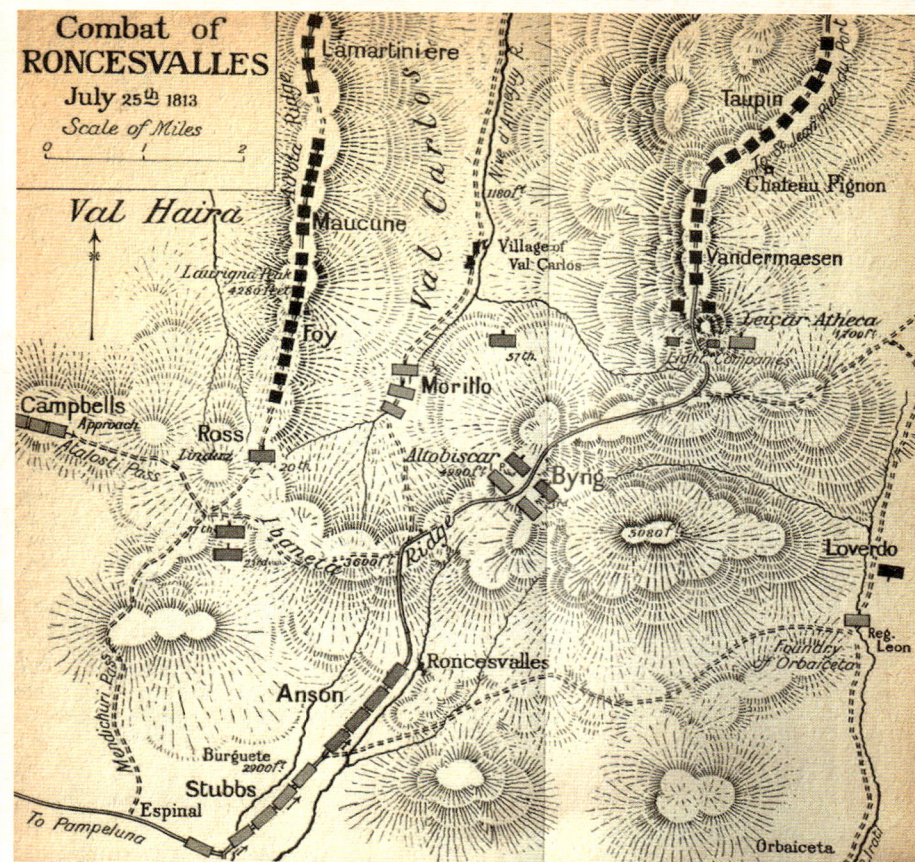

This 1814 painting by John Massey Wright shows brutal close-order combat in the Pyrenees mountain passes.

ABOVE *This map of the Battle of Roncesvalles makes clear the incredible odds faced by Colonel Robert Ross and Major General Thomas Byng in holding off two entire French army columns.*

THE ROAD TO WATERLOO 91

The Road to Waterloo — THE LIBERATION OF SPAIN

The 5th Division's forlorn hope advance through the river at low tide under heavy fire to take the breach, by William Heath, 1836.

The inexperienced Brigadier General William Pringle, temporarily in command of the 7th Division, began flinging battalions forward piecemeal. The 34th (or the Cumberland) Regiment of Foot, 39th (Dorsetshire) Regiment of Foot, and 50th (or the West Kent) Regiment of Foot were cut down as they advanced unsupported into the teeth of the French, and Pringle dutifully led the 92nd (Highland) Regiment of Foot and 28th (or the North Gloucestershire) Regiment of Foot to their doom in person.

By the afternoon, the balance had been redressed somewhat by a series of counter-attacks that inflicted marginally more losses on the French than had been incurred, but there was no disguising that the entire British line along the western end of the Pyrenees was in full retreat.

The Battle of Sorauren

As Wellington made haste to the theatre from San Sebastián, the survivors of Maya and Roncesvalles, and the garrisons around Pamplona - 24,000 men of the 2nd, 3rd, and 4th Divisions - regrouped at the village of Sorauren, which blocked the French progress to Pamplona, for the final engagement of the Battle of the Pyrenees. The army had drawn up on the Heights of Oricain behind the village, and the arrival of Wellington - who rode along the length of the ridge to cheers from the British and Portuguese - roused their flagging spirits considerably.

A third of Soult's force hadn't arrived.

While Generals Clauzel and Reille had successfully moved their troops up following the Battle of Roncevalles, General d'Erlon had dragged his heels, deterred by bad weather and indecisiveness. With the distant chanting of Wellington's name thoroughly unnerving Soult, he opted to wait to see if d'Erlon would arrive, took lunch, and set himself down for a nap causing Clauzel to storm off in frustration. Waking up later that afternoon, Soult begrudgingly authorised a limited attack to probe the enemy's strength, but a sudden, violent storm common to the season saw the whole thing called off.

Soult agreed to attack in the morning of July 28 and sent riders to hurry d'Erlon along. The morning, however, was spent taking up positions with Clauzel and Reille's columns filing out onto the plateau opposite the Heights of Oricain, but the ruggedness of the landscape made an ordeal of manoeuvring the cavalry and artillery, and only four guns were brought onto the field. Time was working against him and Hill's 6th Division was already moving up in the northwest. He sent his men forward, counting on hammering through Wellington's centre by weight of numbers. The Battle of Souraren had begun (July 28 - August 1, 1813).

Dug in at 1,000-feet, the allies responded with what Wellington called "fair bludgeon work." Sergeant William Lawrence of the 40th (or 2nd Somersetshire) Regiment of Foot, wrote: "I never saw a single volley do so much execution in all my campaigning days, almost every man of their first two ranks falling, and then we instantly charged and chased them down the mountain, doing still further and more fearful havoc."

The bold infantry then returned to their positions and repeated the feat over and over. With Soult able to achieve little, other than forcing two isolated Spanish divisions to withdraw, he was close to abandoning the battle entirely - food was running low, as many as 4,000 casualties had already been taken, and it was only a matter of time before Wellington was reinforced - when d'Erlon finally made his approach.

Soult decided to wheel the battle northwards and using d'Erlon as the vanguard, push through Hill's 6th Division and through the foothills of the Pyrenees where he could drop down into San Sebastián instead. On the evening of July 29, Soult began to edge his army to the right and rode off to join d'Erlon, but from Wellington's vantage point the manoeuvre was clumsy and obvious. As dawn rose on the morning of July 30, the allies poured down the heights and into the French positions.

With the marshal no longer in the field and the bulk of the army in transit behind the lines, the rout was near immediate. "Off they danced," recalled Private William Wheeler, 51st (or 2nd Yorkshire West Riding) Light Infantry Regiment, "the Devil take the hindmost, down the hill to our right, the only way they had to escape. We followed them close to their heels."

Pockets of the French continued to fight, particularly in Sorauren itself where they held out for two hours, before being forced to surrender. Those who limped north through thick forests and into the Pyrenees were pursued every step of the way, and the punishing toll for Soult's expedition was 13,000 lost to 7,000 predominantly British and Portuguese.

Once more unto the breach

With the Siege of San Sebastián having been left in Graham's less than capable hands, the situation had gotten less favourable for the allies. The energetic defender, General Rey, had evacuated his wounded, shipped in reinforcements, repaired and reinforced the breaches, and surprised the besiegers with an attack that left 200 killed or injured. Wellington had taken the siege guns with him when he dashed east, and it wasn't until August 26 that they were back in position.

Once again they hammered at the southeastern corner. With Wellington insisting that the previous failure was due to a lack of grit on the part of the 5th Division, they were flung right back over the river with volunteer companies of the Light Division and 1st Division to support them. On the morning of August 31, 1813, the 5th Division ran across the mud and scaled the breach, mines planted by the defenders cutting them to ribbons.

Again they were choked at the breach and riddled with musket fire, and only with the artillery firing over the heads of their own men into the inner defences were the 5th Division able to push on through at enormous cost. With only 1,300 of the defenders left at his side, Rey beat a fighting retreat through the streets to the Castle of La Mota where he planned to make his last stand. It didn't arrive and for three days the British and Portuguese embarked on one of their terrible orgies of violence and looting.

Graham did nothing to thwart the chaos and Wellington wasn't present to stop it if he'd been able to. The city was ablaze - the flames fed by the mob of feral rankers - and a report produced by the civil and ecclesiastical authorities claimed that only 36 homes (and two churches) out of over 600 buildings survived the blaze, that 1,500 were left without food or shelter, and that the sale of stolen goods was done with the complicity of British officers.

Another 3,500 of Wellington's army had been killed or wounded in the second half of the siege, with 2,200 casualties taken in the foolhardy storming of the breach. Rey remained bricked up in his fastness until September 8, when after a week of artillery cascading about his ears, he finally surrendered. Meanwhile, the Spanish-conducted Siege of Pamplona dragged on for substantially longer and the garrison finally capitulated on October 31, 1813. In Catalonia, some French outposts remained defiant until Spring 1814, but that was a campaign for the Spanish to fight.

For the British, the climactic final phase of the war in the Peninsula was finally over. From here on, the Peninsula War would unfold over French soil and end only with the fall of the French Emperor himself.

ABOVE *A piece of contemporary naive art depicting the Storming of San Sebastián on August 31, 1813, from the isthmus.*

LEFT *A map showing the subsequent positions of the 2nd and 7th Division as they flailed against an oncoming French column.*

The Road to Waterloo — THE BAYONNE CAMPAIGN

A Hell of a LICKING

The Bayonne Campaign, October 1813 - May 1814

Despite urging from London to press on into France immediately, Wellington granted Marshal Jean-de-Dieu Soult a stay of execution. He was waiting for news of the negotiations between Emperor Napoléon I and his Austrian and Russian counterparts - if they came to terms, then he had no wish to be caught on the wrong side of the Pyrenees if there was a surge of troops from the east.

Soult did not let this grace period go to waste and set about reinforcing the French positions along the River Bidassoa at the northeastern end of the mountain range. The onset of winter made an advance through the high passes unlikely, while the right of his position where the Bidassoa opened into the Bay of Biscay was 1,000-yards wide, so Soult concentrated his forces over a ten-mile stretch where the river was narrower and the mountains lower.

The high pass near the town of Saint-Jean-Pied-de-Port (meaning, literally "St

94 THE ROAD TO WATERLOO

John at the foot of the pass") was covered by a division under General Maximilien Sébastien Foy, the wide Bidassoa estuary was held by two divisions under General Honoré Charles Reille, and six divisions under General Bertrand, Comte Clauzel and General Jean-Baptiste Drouet, Comte d'Erlon were dug in along the mountains in the centre, hunkered down in a chain of earthworks and redoubts.

"These fellows think themselves invulnerable, but I will beat them out and with great ease," Wellington was recorded to have said. "It appears difficult; but the

RIGHT *"John Bull bringing Boney's nose to the grindstone."* With some help from Tsar Alexander I of Russia, Great Britain applies pressure on Emperor Napoléon I. Cartoon by William Elmes, 1814.

BELOW LEFT *A panoramic painting of the Battle of Orthez by William Heath, with the French holding the high ground.*

BELOW RIGHT *Field Marshal Sir Arthur Wellesley, Marquess of Wellington crossing the Pyrenees. On May 4, 1814 he received the honour of Duke of Wellington, the one he is most commonly known by.*

enemy have not men enough to man the works and lines they occupy. They dare not concentrate a sufficient body to resist the attack I shall make upon them. I can pour a greater force on certain points than they can concentrate to resist me."

The Battle of The Bidassoa

While some of his forces made a series of noisy demonstrations against Clauzel and d'Erlon's positions, 24,000 infantry were to cross the lower Bidassoa, which - as Basque fishermen had explained to him - was no more than four feet deep at low tide and had a number of fords unknown to the French.

On the night of October 6, 1813, the 5th Division moved into positions on the western bank of the Bidassoa - the noise of their arrival startling the weaker of Reille's two divisions, under General Antoine Louis Popon de Maucune. The reports were filtered back to Soult, who dismissed them out of hand. The next morning, the single French battalion on the opposing shore awoke to the sight of vast rows of British, Portuguese and Spanish infantry advancing across the mudflats of the Bidassoa. The numbers were so overwhelming that the French barely offered any resistance before taking flight.

Further along the Bidassoa, the fighting was fiercer. The Light Division - now

"These fellows think themselves invulnerable, but I will beat them out and with great ease," Wellington was recorded to have said. "It appears difficult; but the enemy have not men enough to man the works and lines they occupy."

The Road to Waterloo

THE BAYONNE CAMPAIGN

led by Major General Carl August von Alten of the King's German Legion - supported by several Spanish regiments, made a frontal assault on the French redoubts. With only 6,500 attackers to 4,700 defenders, who were additionally fighting from entrenched positions, the attack should have been futile, but the French were demoralised. Captain Jonathan Leach, 95th Rifles, recalled: "A succession of redoubts and fieldworks were carried by the bayonet, and those who defended them were either shot, bayoneted, or driven off the mountain."

By the time Soult, who had been further east along the line, made it to the scene, Reille's force had been entirely scattered and Clauzel was being driven back at multiple points. The battle clearly lost before he even became aware of it, Soult ordered the men back to a new position along the River Nivelle, where the weary soldiers began digging in.

Wellington declined to pursue, at least until Pamplona had capitulated. He couldn't risk a French toehold in Spain - no matter how small - becoming an entire foot and kick him in his line of retreat. Despite running so low on supplies that they were forced to eat cats, dogs, rats and what turned out to be hemlock, the defenders resisted all Spanish efforts to dislodge them until they finally capitulated on October 31 with the promise that they would be allowed to exit the citadel with their arms and honours.

They would then surrender with dignity and be taken into custody by the British, where they were guaranteed better treatment. Even after years of war between the two nations, the average British soldier found more kinship with his French counterpart than he did his Spanish ally.

Lieutenant Robert Blakeney, 36th (or the Herefordshire) Regiment of Foot, wrote of one encounter with a party of voltigeurs during the Battle of the Bidassoa (October 7, 1813): "They displayed the courtesy of their nation by discharging a general salute; its only result was a shot through my greatcoat and one in my saddle-bow. Having safely run the gauntlet and though in great haste, yet resolving to show the polite nation that we yielded as little in courtesy as in arms, I turned round and taking off my hat bowed low. The firing ceased and they gave me a loud cheer."

The Battle of The Nivelle

By the time Wellington was ready to advance on Soult, the marshal had strung his army out along a 20-mile front that suffered from the same inherent weakness as his line at the Bidassoa: no matter how strong the individual earthworks, he didn't have enough men to defend multiple points in strength. Reille's two battered divisions were stationed on the lower Nivelle, Clauzel's three divisions were entrusted with the centre, including a formidable line of outposts around Sarre, while d'Erlon held the left with his three. Foy's division had come down the mountain, leaving the icy winds to stand sentry in its stead.

Wellington had assembled some 82,000 infantry (again, the cavalry would play little role in this bitter landscape), while Soult had bolstered his ranks with an unimpressive muster of conscripts and garrison troops to bring it up to 62,000. This time Wellington directed feints against the wings, Lieutenant General Sir John Hope's 25,000 on the left (including the 1st and 5th Divisions) and Lieutenant General

ABOVE LEFT *Wellington's forces take the garrison on the opposite bank complete unawares and secure a toehold on French soil at the Battle of Bidassoa.*

ABOVE *Marshal Jean-de-Dieu Soult, 1st Duc de Ragusa, has the distinction of being Wellington's final opponent in the Peninsula War.*

BELOW RIGHT *'The Guards entering France, 7th October 1813.' A depiction of the British army crossing the Bidassoa River by Robert Batty, 1823.*

Sir Rowland Hill's 22,000 on the right (2nd and 6th Divisions), whilst Lieutenant General William Carr Beresford hammered the centre with 35,000 men of the Light Division, and the 3rd, 4th and 6th Divisions.

Lieutenant Blakeney - whose 36th (or the Herefordshire) Regiment of Foot advanced as part of the 6th Division - gushed: "Proceeding rapidly we soon waded the Nivelle immersed above our middle, the men carrying their pouches above their heads, and immediately drove back all the enemy's pickets and outposts on both banks of the river without deigning to fire a shot. Some few we bayoneted who were too obstinate to get out of our way in time. Thus far advanced, the glorious scene became more developed. High up the mountains the blaze from their forts and redoubts was broad and glaring, while the mountainsides presented a brilliant surface of sparkling vivid fire, never ceasing but always ascending as our gallant troops rushed forward; and nearly 200 pieces of artillery angrily roaring forth mutual response, echoed from mountain to mountain, rendering the whole scene truly magnificent."

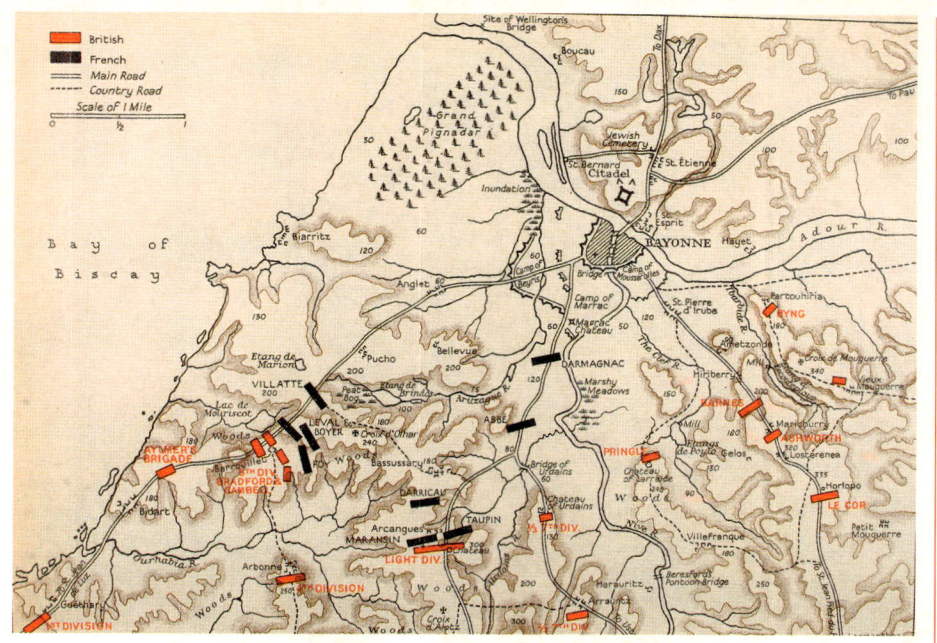

LEFT *The attack on Lieutenant General Sir John Hope's column and the Light Division at Arcangues during the Battle of the Nive. The location of pontoon bridge used by Hope to advance on Bayonne is labelled at the very top of the map, as well as the suburb of St Etienne.*

The Battle of The Nive

Spending the winter wedged between the two rivers was not an option, so Wellington had no choice but to push on towards the new French line on the Nive. The odds were turning towards the enemy, with Wellington's force down to 64,000 due to the loss of most of the Spanish, and Soult having absorbed another round of miserable looking conscripts to bring his army up to 63,000.

Dividing his force into three columns: four divisions under Hope were to take the coastal road to the west of Bayonne, four divisions under Beresford were to march on Ustaritz and either find or construct crossings over the River Nive, while three divisions and two cavalry brigades under Hill were to attempt the same via Cambo. The risk now was Soult cutting them off one-by-one, so the Light Division was tasked with maintaining communication between the three dispersed columns.

At first light on December 9, 1813, they advanced with Hope encountering French forces on the road to Bayonne and driving them swiftly back, before sending out his pickets and setting up camp. Beresford's middle column made it to Ustaritz

Even in leading with an attack on the hard centre of the French lines, the defenders were outnumbered two-to-one and within two hours the Light Division had taken one of the principle earthworks, storming the heights of the Petite Rhune. Without the reserves to mount any sort of defence in depth, the French crumbled again, having lost 4,300 men to the 3,400 casualties suffered by the attackers.

Soult pulled back to a third defensive line, anchored on his right by the fortress of Bayonne and extending east along the River Nive. Again, there was no immediate pursuit as winter whipped down the mountains in earnest, making the roads impassable to large bodies of men.

Wellington's attitude to the French peasants was markedly different from his attitudes to the innocents of Spain who had suffered much from British and Portuguese indiscipline. He deplored the misbehaviour of the Spanish contingent and offloaded most of them - further souring relations still frosty following the Siege of San Sebastián (July 7 – September 8, 1813).

> *"A succession of redoubts and fieldworks were carried by the bayonet, and those who defended them were either shot, bayoneted, or driven off the mountain."*

THE ROAD TO WATERLOO 97

The Road to Waterloo

THE BAYONNE CAMPAIGN

ABOVE *The scheming King Fernando VII of Spain, painted by Francisco Goya in his robes of state, 1815.*

RIGHT *A soldier of the French Garde Nationale, a reserve militia summoned for the territorial defence of France itself. Depicted by the German artist Salomon Pinhas, circa-1813.*

without opposition and immediately began constructing a pontoon over the Nive, while Hill had much the same experience at Cambo, save a brief skirmish with d'Erlon's vanguard. By nightfall, half of Beresford's force and all of Hill's had crossed to the eastern bank.

The situation couldn't be better for Soult. Now it was Wellington who was overextended, while his own defence rested on a single strong point at Bayonne. Under the cover of darkness, he began to bring his men towards Hope's column. Slipping away from their previous positions during the heavy rain, d'Erlon left his distant campfires burning to avoid alerting Hill's sentries to their manoeuvre.

At dawn on December 10, Clauzel's three divisions attempted to overrun the Light Division north of Arcangues, forcing them back to the safety of the village where they hunkered down under a storm of French artillery. Simultaneously, Hope's docile camp was assailed by Reille's two divisions and a brigade of French dragoons, who took scores of prisoners before the remnants of the 5th Division and a Portuguese brigade were able to form up and resist them. Just as the French - bolstered by Foy's division - conspired to overwhelm the entire British left, the 1st Division arrived and managed to drive the exhausted enemy back.

Nonetheless, 1,500 British and Portuguese soldiers had been killed, captured or wounded over the first day. Bafflingly, Beresford had been lulled into a false sense of security by the lack of movement in the early hours of December 11 and when Soult resumed the assault he was again on the back foot, losing 400 troops in under an hour. It's hard to think of a greater measure of a poor tactician than the ability to be surprised in the same location by the same foe for two days in a row.

Whilst Beresford was stunned, Wellington was not, and his reinforcements were already in position. Realising that he had squeezed all that he could from the advantage, Soult decided to transfer the pressure to Hill instead, whose position was significantly weaker with the movement of British divisions towards the west. With three divisions left to hold Bayonne, under the cover of night on December 12, Soult concentrated his entire force in the direction of Hill, whose own column now numbered only 14,000 men.

Hill, easily the most capable of Wellington's corps commanders still in the field, wasn't as easily goosed as Beresford. He had taken up a position south of Saint-Pierre-d'Irube along a chain of three hills, each separated by chasms and anchored by the River Adour on the right and Nive on the left. Though the chasms made communication and reinforcement between the three hills near impossible, it also forced the French to make three narrow frontal assaults that reduced the advantage of their numbers.

As the mist lifted on the morning of December 13, 40,000 French soldiers poured onto the plateau opposite Hill's line, the dragoons pushing on to dislodge the defenders from the hill on the British right. On the centre position, Hill gambled on Wellington racing to his rescue and at the head of his surviving battalions, he led them in a headlong charge down the hill. The first of the advancing French divisions, already battered and smoke-blackened from Hill's artillery, fled down the slope and like a big dog spooked by a belligerent house cat, their comrades followed.

Before Soult could commit to a counter-attack, Wellington vaulted the Nive and into Hill's rear with the weary 3rd and 6th Divisions. Again, Soult realised that the moment had played out and withdrew to Bayonne and a new line over the River Adour. The Battle of the Nive (December 9-13, 1813) was over and Wellington marvelled: "I have often seen the French licked, but I have never seen them get such a hell of a licking as Hill has given them."

The Siege of Bayonne

As the two armies wintered within spitting distance of one another, a long-dormant player in this drama saw 14,000 troops lost to Marshal Soult on nothing more than weasel words. Desperate to buy a peace in the south so he could concentrate on his campaign in the west, Napoléon I proposed to Crown Prince Fernando - languishing in opulent bondage since 1808 - that in exchange for his restoration and the remaining French troops being withdrawn from Catalonia, Spain would end the war with France. Fernando gave an additional guarantee that if the Anglo-Portuguese army continued in their offensive, he would turn over the Spanish army to Napoléon I.

The Treaty of Valençay was signed on behalf of Spain by King Fernando VII and he promptly returned home to a distinct lack of fanfare. The Cortes, the Spanish assembly which was riddled with republicans and liberals, argued noisily that Fernando VII had no authority to negotiate anything on behalf of Spain, and it's doubtful whether Fernando VII himself was sincere in his acquiescence or just saw it as an opportunity to escape home.

Such are the fates of soldiers decided by politicians and Princes, and when the blockade of Bayonne resumed in February 1814, the defence of the city had been reduced to 60,000 men, who were mostly strung out along the River Adour to the east. Soult should surely have stopped expecting the same tactic to reap rewards, having attempted it at the Neville and Bidassoa. As with the latter Wellington attacked the poorly defended Adour estuary, that his foe believed was a barrier enough. First, though, he intended to drive the defenders further east with attacks over the main tributaries, pushing them back across the Bidouse and then the Saison.

On February 23, with another feint to distract the garrison of Bayonne, Hope moved a small party across the wide mouth of the Adour on rafts, where they established a beachhead on the opposite shore. With further operations in the east to keep Soult at bay, on February 24, the Royal Navy moved in to help ferry soldiers and Hope began constructing a boat bridge. Whilst the Bayonne garrison barely lifted a finger to prevent the crossing of the 1st and 5th Divisions, they stubbornly resisted Hope's advance through the suburb of St Etienne.

The Battle of Orthez

Soult's main force, meanwhile, was in full retreat over their fourth waterway of 1814, the River Gave de Pau, and his contact with Bayonne had been severed completely. He resolved to stand and fight rather than relinquish more sacred soil. Soult drew up his force along a ridge, anchored at Orthez where it ran a mile north and three miles west. The Battle of Orthez (February 27, 1814) began with Hill launching a feint at the village from the south bank of the Gave de Pau with the 2nd Division and a Portuguese division, while on the French right the 4th and 7th Divisions under Beresford slipped across the river.

Picton's 'Fighting 3rd' then advanced to their right to pin the French centre, followed by the 6th Division. The overly complex pincer soon fell apart. The 4th Division, who were entrusted with exploiting the flank, were beaten back around the village of Saint-Boès, and Wellington pivoted to the centre. At 11.30 am the 6th and 3rd hammered the centre of the French line, while the 7th Division and elements of the Light Division finally turned the French right at Saint-Boès.

The fierce fighting levelled a toll of 2,200 casualties on the British, a butcher's bill that very nearly included Wellington as a musket ball glanced off his scabbard, bruising his hip but saving him from what might have been a severed artery. Soult lost 4,000 men in the battle and more deserted as he retreated, leaving him with only 35,000 - mostly raw recruits and citizen militia of the Garde Nationale.

With Wellington keen to give his invasion some legitimacy, Beresford marched to the old royalist stronghold of Bordeaux where the mayor, Jean-Baptiste Lynch - grandson of an Irish Jacobite - surrendered the city, hauled down the Tricolore and raised the pre-Revolution flag of the Bourbon dynasty. The First French Empire wasn't just crumbling on its fringes any more, it was beginning to collapse in the heartland too and in the northeast of the country the armies of Russia, Austria and a host of German kingdoms and principalities were bearing down on Paris - a conflict against which Wellington's campaign was a mere sideshow.

The Battle of Toulouse

Bringing some Spanish troops back into the field, Wellington was able to advance towards Soult with 50,000 men, throwing out an 8,000-horse cavalry screen so thick that Soult's scouts were unable to get beyond it and return anything useful on the allies' movements. Soult had spread his army out across the roads to Bordeaux and Toulouse, not yet aware that the former - the so-called 'third city of France' - had thrown open its doors to allies.

Whilst Wellington paused to allow the 4th Division to join them from Bordeaux, Soult realised almost too late that the allies were

'Attack on the road to Bayonne' by William Heath. It's unclear exactly which engagement this depicts, but it may be the action fought by Hope's column on December 9.

The Road to Waterloo — THE BAYONNE CAMPAIGN

ABOVE *A rifleman and an officer of the 95th Rifles in the Peninsula War by the celebrated military artist Richard Simkin, 1902.*

ABOVE RIGHT *'The pursuit of the French near Toulouse' by Denis Dighton, 1814. This might depict the rearguard action at Tarbes that bought Marshal Soult valuable time.*

BELOW RIGHT *The senseless sortie from Bayonne which resulted in nearly a thousand casualties on each side, as well as the capture of Sir John Hope. The last battle of the Peninsula War, as depicted by Thomas Sutherland, 1815.*

advancing south down the Adour Valley, and he drew in his army for a retreat towards Toulouse. He flung two of d'Erlon's divisions in the path of the British advance and began his withdrawal. The Battle of Tarbes (March 20, 1814) was a desperate attempt to cut off the French retreat - the Light Division advancing due south and Hill's corps sweeping south and then east over the river and into Tarbes itself.

The defenders successfully delayed Wellington's army for long enough to give Soult a head start to Toulouse, but the exchange was costly, with perhaps as many as 1,000 French casualties taken to 375 allied fallen. Of note was the valour of three battalions of the 95th Rifles advancing at the head of the Light Division who raced onto the high ground to the north of the village of Orleix. There they found themselves facing an entire enemy division and swiftly drove them from the field.

An eyewitness, Captain John Blakiston, an East India Company adventurer commanding the 17th Portuguese Regiment, wrote admiringly: "They could do the work much better and with infinitely less loss than any other of our best light troops. They possessed an individual boldness, a mutual understanding, and a quickness of eye, in taking advantage of the ground, which, taken all together, I never saw equalled."

Toulouse was a significant regional depot for the French army and as such it was a natural rendezvous point, being filled with both supplies and newly-raised conscripts in abundance. Protected by more than just bastions and walls, the River Garonne and the Royal Canal covered the city on three sides and left open only the southern face. The odds were evening out again, with Soult now able to call on 42,000 troops and his adversary 49,000, surely an ill-omen considering the carnage wrought upon Wellington's ranks by far fewer defenders at Ciudad Rodrigo, Badajoz and San Sebastián.

Like Bordeaux, however, it was a hotbed of lingering Bourbon sympathies and the citizens offered Soult little aid but Wellington's final engagement of the Peninsula War, the Battle of Toulouse (April 10, 1814), would ultimately be a confused and costly one. With his army encircling Toulouse on three sides - leaving the open southern face unguarded - Wellington launched a series of diversionary attacks all around the walls, with the main attack - led by Beresford - concentrated against the eastern face of the citadel. At 5 am on Easter Sunday, the assault began.

Hill, whose 2nd Division assailed the isolated suburb of St Cyprien which clung to the western bank of the Garonne, successfully kept the garrison occupied throughout the battle, sustaining very few casualties. On the northwest, Picton - perhaps confused by not being in the thick of things for once - hurled the 'Fighting 3rd' at the walls with suicidal abandon, but unable to cross the Royal Canal, the consequences were sickening. Around 400 of the division fell in the assault, compared to Hill's 80 wounded.

On the northeast approach, Alten followed his brief with Hanoverian exactitude and the Light Division pinned their opposing numbers down, but even Picton's folly paled before Beresford's main assault. Ordered to attack over the Monte Rave - a row of heights in front of the canal that were crowned with redoubts like molars in the jaw - the preceding rain had been so heavy that they fell behind schedule scrambling through the mud, the artillery falling further back as the wheels skidded and spluttered.

Growing frustrated, Beresford ordered the guns halt and open fire from where they were. Further ahead in the north, a Spanish corps under the gallant General Manuel Alberto Freire de Andrade y Armijo was scheduled to advance once Beresford's 4th and 6th Divisions were in position. Taking the cannon as evidence that the principle assault had begun, Freire charged and scattered the voltigeurs at the northern end of Monte Rave, before heavy fire from the French redoubts forced them into the cover of a sunken lane. The battered Spaniards promptly fled back down the hill.

Having calmed himself after the first assault, Picton watched Freire's Spaniards in full retreat and assumed that Beresford's offensive must be withdrawing. Never one to sit on his hands, he threw the Fighting 3rd forward to draw the French fire and presided over the loss of another 350 of his men to no end.

For the rest of the afternoon, Beresford (having finally managed to bring up his artillery and co-ordinate with Freire) mounted a series of fruitless and bloody offensives up the slopes of Monte Rave, never able to fully secure the high ground in the face of counter-attacks from the redoubts. By 6 pm the battle had run out of steam - with 4,600 allied casualties, and 3,200 French.

The bloody dove of peace

As the sun dipped below the horizon, Marshal Soult - twitchy about spending the night in a broiling cauldron of royalist sentiment - withdrew quietly through the southern gate and made for Carcassonne. The city's great and good wasted no time in throwing open their doors and throwing together a great feast for the allies, that rivalled the reception at Bordeaux for its warmth.

ABOVE *The royalist mayor of Bordeaux greets Lieutenant General William Carr Beresford with a white cockade, the traditional symbol of loyalty to the Bourbon monarchs of France.*

LEFT *A gloriously busy painting of the Battle of Toulouse by William Heath, showing the allied assault on three faces of the citadel.*

Generals on both sides might have briefly pondered the nature of victory and defeat as they counted their dead. The British had taken no ground, it had been given to them, while the French had endured fewer casualties but had limped from their place of safety. The issue of who had actually 'won' the Battle of Toulouse was quickly rendered moot.

News rode a slow horse in 1814 and the tidings from the north came so suddenly as to be almost unbelievable. Paris - the beating heart of the First French Empire - had fallen on March 31 to the armies of Russia, Austria and Prussia. On April I, Tsar Alexander I of Russia addressed the French senate who formally capitulated, stripped Napoléon Bonaparte of his throne, and laid down their arms.

The war had been over before the Battle of Toulouse had even begun. On April 14 the last battle of the Peninsula War was fought when the besieged garrison of General Pierre Thouvenot - enraged by Napoléon I's abdication - mounted a pre-dawn raid on Hope's army, taking them by surprise and even wounding and capturing Hope himself. The Battle of Bayonne left 838 British killed and wounded and 905 French.

The next morning, both sides trooped out numbly to recover their fallen. Lieutenant George Gleig, 85th (Bucks Volunteers) (Light Infantry) Regiment, wrote: "Holes were dug for them in various places, and they were thrown in, not without sorrow and lamentations, but with very little ceremony. In collecting them together, various living men were found, sadly mangled, and hardly distinguishable from their slaughtered comrades [...]

"Many had received bayonet-thrusts in vital parts; one man, I recollect, whose eyes were both torn from the sockets, and hung over his cheeks; whilst several were cut in two by round which had passed through their bellies, and still left them breathing. The hospitals, accordingly, presented sad spectacles, whilst the shrieks and groans of the inmates acted with no more cheering effect upon the sense of hearing, than their disfigured countenances and mangled forms acted upon the sense of sight."

Thouvenot continued to fight until April 27, 1814 when the weary Soult directly ordered him to surrender the fortress.

THE ROAD TO WATERLOO 101

The Road to Waterloo — THE HUNDRED DAYS

All or NOTHING

The Hundred Days, March - July 1815

In April 1814, most of Europe heaved a great sigh of relief as news spread that Emperor Napoléon I had finally been brought to heel by a coalition of foreign powers which included his former allies Tsar Alexander I of Russia and Emperor Francis II of Austria.

Still exhausted and depressed by the devastating failure of his attempt to seize control of Russia (June 24 - December 14, 1812) and his shocking defeat at the Battle of Leipzig (October 16-19, 1813), which had resulted in the deaths of over 35,000 French soldiers, the beleaguered Emperor had retreated to the Renaissance palace of Fontainebleau, where he still hoped to regroup and seize back control of Paris. However, he had swiftly been disabused of this notion when his senior officers, led by the old Iberia hand Marshal Michel Ney mutinied and pressed him to abdicate.

At first Napoléon I attempted to abdicate in favour of his young son, but when this prospect found no favour with his opponents, he instead begrudgingly agreed to fully give up power and unconditionally abdicate the throne on behalf of himself and his heirs. Relieved to have been spared any further fighting, the allied powers were remarkably generous to their fallen foe while putting together the Treaty of Fontainebleau (April 11, 1814), which was intended to officially recognise that Napoléon I's reign was over and his war at an end.

Although many thought that he should be imprisoned and face some justice for his actions, it was decided instead that Napoléon I should be exiled to the tiny island of Elba, which lay 12 miles off the coast of Tuscany and had a population of just 12,000. In a concession to his former status, the allies gave their vanquished foe full sovereignty over the island and even allowed him to retain the title of Emperor, although they demanded the surrender of the royal estates, jewels and other treasures, which would now pass into the hands of the returning Bourbon king, Louis XVIII, who was one of the younger brothers of the guillotined Louis XVI.

Significantly, Robert Stewart, Viscount Castlereagh - Wellington's dedicated patron and the British representative at Fontainebleau - refused to sign the document on the grounds that his nation had never recognised Napoléon as Emperor. They had no wish to confer legitimacy on a man that they had always considered to be a usurper by confirming his title even though they were taking away his power.

At first, Napoléon I had assumed that his wife Marie Louise and their son, who were both ensconced at the royal château

BELOW 'The 28th Regiment at Quatre Bras' by the celebrated Victorian military artist Elizabeth Butler Thompson shows French cavalry assailing a British infantry square, 1875.

I think now my little fellow, you are pretty well clear'd out, and I hope you will never give us the trouble to Prescribe or Proscribe any more.

> "Feeling thoroughly depressed, Napoleon attempted to take his own life with a vial of poison, a mixture of belladonna, opium and hellebore, that he had secreted upon his person but although it made him seriously ill, it failed to work..."

Maurice de Talleyrand-Périgord.

Representing Britain was the Foreign Secretary, Lord Castlereagh before he was replaced by Wellington in February 1815. Although the Great Powers had been superficially united by their need to rid Europe of Napoléon I, they still distrusted each other and without a common enemy to unite them, their own old rivalries and feuds returned to play.

Far away on Elba, Napoléon I watched as his former allies and enemies carved out a new peaceful Europe that would, they hoped, be free of his pernicious presence. Like everyone else, he was all too aware of the hidden tensions that lay beneath the facade of friendliness and knew that it was just a matter of time before serious conflict arose again between the great European powers.

Thanks to his correspondents who kept him fully informed, he also knew that the new Bourbon king, Louis XVIII and his court, who had initially been hailed with much enthusiasm, were already well on their way to becoming as unpopular with the French people as Louis XVI and his court had been in the years before the French Revolution. Most importantly, as far as Napoléon I was concerned, Louis XVIII and his court were especially disliked by the soldiers of Napoléon I's former army, who were now returning in their thousands from outposts all over his empire only to find

LEFT *In this 1814 satire, King George VI of Great Britain holds a peace treaty behind the back of the vomiting Napoléon Bonaparte as all the nations of Europe tumble from the Emperor's mouth.*

themselves being treated with contempt by the new regime.

With their support, Napoléon I knew that he could take advantage of the infighting at the Congress of Vienna and make another grab for power and so he quietly began to plan his escape, spurred on by the knowledge that his enemies at Vienna would almost certainly be discussing either his assassination or removal to an even more distant and obscure spot. Finally, on February 26, 1815, just over nine months after he had first arrived there, Napoléon I escaped from Elba, taking with him

of Rambouillet, would accompany him into exile but he was disappointed when she wrote to inform him that she had been forcibly prevented from joining him by her father. Emperor Francis II of Austria had insisted that she return to Vienna before taking up residence in Parma, the duchy which had been granted to her in the Treaty of Fontainebleau. Feeling thoroughly depressed, Napoléon I attempted to take his own life with a vial of poison, a mixture of belladonna, opium and hellebore, that he had secreted upon his person but although it made him seriously ill, it failed to work, and he would soon afterwards be taken to Elba to begin his exile.

Losing the peace

Meanwhile, the allied leaders prepared for the Congress of Vienna (November 1814 - June 1815), a great meeting that would determine the future balance of power in a Europe that had been ripped apart by 23 years of conflict.

The chief participants of the meeting, which officially convened in November 1814 and featured representatives from virtually every state in Europe, were the so called four Great Powers that had united against Napoléon I: Britain, Austria, Russia and Prussia as well as France itself, represented by the aristocratic veteran politician and wily diplomat Charles

The Road to Waterloo
THE HUNDRED DAYS

ABOVE *Emperor Napoléon I is forced to sign his abdication as stipulated by the Treaty of Fontainebleau, a copy of the 1843 oil by François Bouchot.*

ABOVE *In another satirical print from 1814, Napoléon I and his older brother Joseph-Napoléon, aka King José I of Spain, are led in chains towards exile. Napoléon wears donkey ears and a dunce's hat, while his brother's floppy hat reads "Coward and Thief."*

RIGHT *'The 7th Queen's Own Hussars under Sir Edward Kerrison, charging the French at Quatre Bras. 16th June 1815' in watercolour by Dennis Dighton, 1818.*

the small army of 700 men that he had managed to muster on the island. It was a far cry from the thousands that he had once so proudly commanded, but it was enough and as he made his way across mainland Europe towards Paris, his army continued to swell even further as he was greeted with relief and delight by his former subjects and his former soldiers began to return to him.

In Vienna, the news that Napoléon I had managed to escape Elba was greeted with consternation and alarm as the gathered leaders prepared themselves for the inevitable war. While Louis XVIII hastened to flee from France, the Great Powers declared Napoléon I an outlaw and made their plans, with each pledging 150,000 men to the cause of finally putting an end to his career – a number that the British found difficult to honour, although they made up the shortfall by subsidising the other forces.

Wellington wasted no time before leaving Vienna and making for the Netherlands, where he took command of the Anglo Germany army and their Dutch allies and prepared to defend Brussels while Generalfeldmarschall Gebhard Leberecht von Blücher, who came out of retirement to take on Napoléon I, commanded the Prussian force stationed nearby.

Back in the saddle

By June, both armies were fully ready for mobilisation, well ahead of the Austrians and Russians who had not yet joined them and reported that they would not be ready to take on the French until the start of July. Meanwhile, reports were coming in that Napoléon I's army, which had been extremely modest at the time of his return to Paris had increased to 200,000 men, although they were still scattered enough to give the allied forces an advantage if they consolidated their armies into a single offensive.

However, the longer that the Austrians and Russians delayed, the more time Napoléon I had to pull his scattered forces together and muster more men and ammunition. Swift and devastating lightning strike attacks had always been his forte and as time went on and his force grew stronger, the more likely it became that he would gain the upper hand.

While the coalition prevaricated, Napoléon I was laying his own plans and deliberating between taking a defensive position, which involved waiting for the allies to invade and then decimating them or going on the offensive and pre-emptively taking the war to their territories. He knew that the great allied army was still divided, with the British and Prussian troops isolated in the Netherlands waiting

ABOVE *Generalfeldmarschall Gebhard Leberecht von Blücher, a battlefield commander with a reputation to rival that of Wellington.*

for their allies and decided that his best course of action would be to take them on separately while he still had the chance.

On June 15, the French army, led by Napoléon I and Marshal Ney, crossed the River Sambre into what is now Belgium and then placed themselves between the Prussian and British forces, effectively separating them. The following day, the French army split into two with Napoléon leading 60,800 men against Blücher's Prussian troops, while Ney and a much smaller force of 20,000 soldiers moved to apprehend Wellington and his men and prevent them from assisting their beleaguered Prussian allies. Appraised of the French advance, Blücher and Wellington met that morning to make a defensive plan, riding up to a high point where they could observe the predatory French movements.

As Blücher's right wing was the most exposed, Wellington proposed to advance his own men towards the fray as soon as possible and divert attention by attacking the French left and rear but was instead persuaded, thanks to lack of time, to defend the weak Prussian right wing. Although this was a far riskier undertaking and dependent on his own troops not being engaged by the French before they managed to reach the Prussians, Wellington agreed, only to be thwarted in his aim when he was blocked by Ney's troops at the crossroads of Quatre Bras and thus unable to reach the Prussians. Although the French initially had the upper hand, Wellington's troops put up a good defence and eventually won the day, although at the high cost of just over 4,000 dead and wounded against the 4,800 lost by the French side.

Although the allied troops had prevailed, Wellington was still nonetheless unable to reach his Prussian allies, who were defeated by Napoléon I at the Battle of Ligny (June 16, 1815). To the further dismay of the allies, Blücher, one of the most capable allied military leaders, was seriously injured during the battle and spent several hours trapped beneath his dead horse, during which time he was ridden over by cavalry and was only saved by the quick thinking of his aide-de-camp, who hid him beneath his greatcoat so that the marauding French troops would not realise who he was.

Although Ligny was a disaster for the Prussians, they were still able to efficiently regroup under the direction of Blücher's second in command, taking advantage of Napoléon I's complacent decision not to immediately pursue their scattered retreating forces to try to join the British at a different location. Instead, after spending the night bivouacked on the battlefield and enjoying a leisurely breakfast the following morning, he decided to go after Wellington, who had retreated northwards from Quatre Bras towards an excellent defensive position, a gentle escarpment that he had previously discovered near the village of Waterloo.

Meanwhile, Blücher had sufficiently recovered from his ordeal at Ligny to be able to take command once again and lead his men to join the British at Waterloo. There were some on the Prussian side who believed that Wellington had not honoured his promise to assist them and that they should therefore retreat and leave the British to it, but Blücher nonetheless insisted upon sending two corps ahead to join Wellington while he, exhausted and barely able to stay in the saddle thanks to the injuries sustained at Ligny but defiantly cheerful and optimistic of victory nonetheless, led the rest of his troops on the long march towards Waterloo.

BELOW RIGHT *Blücher narrowly escapes capture after being pinned under his horse at the Battle of Ligny. Watercolour by Charles Tuner Warren, 1818.*

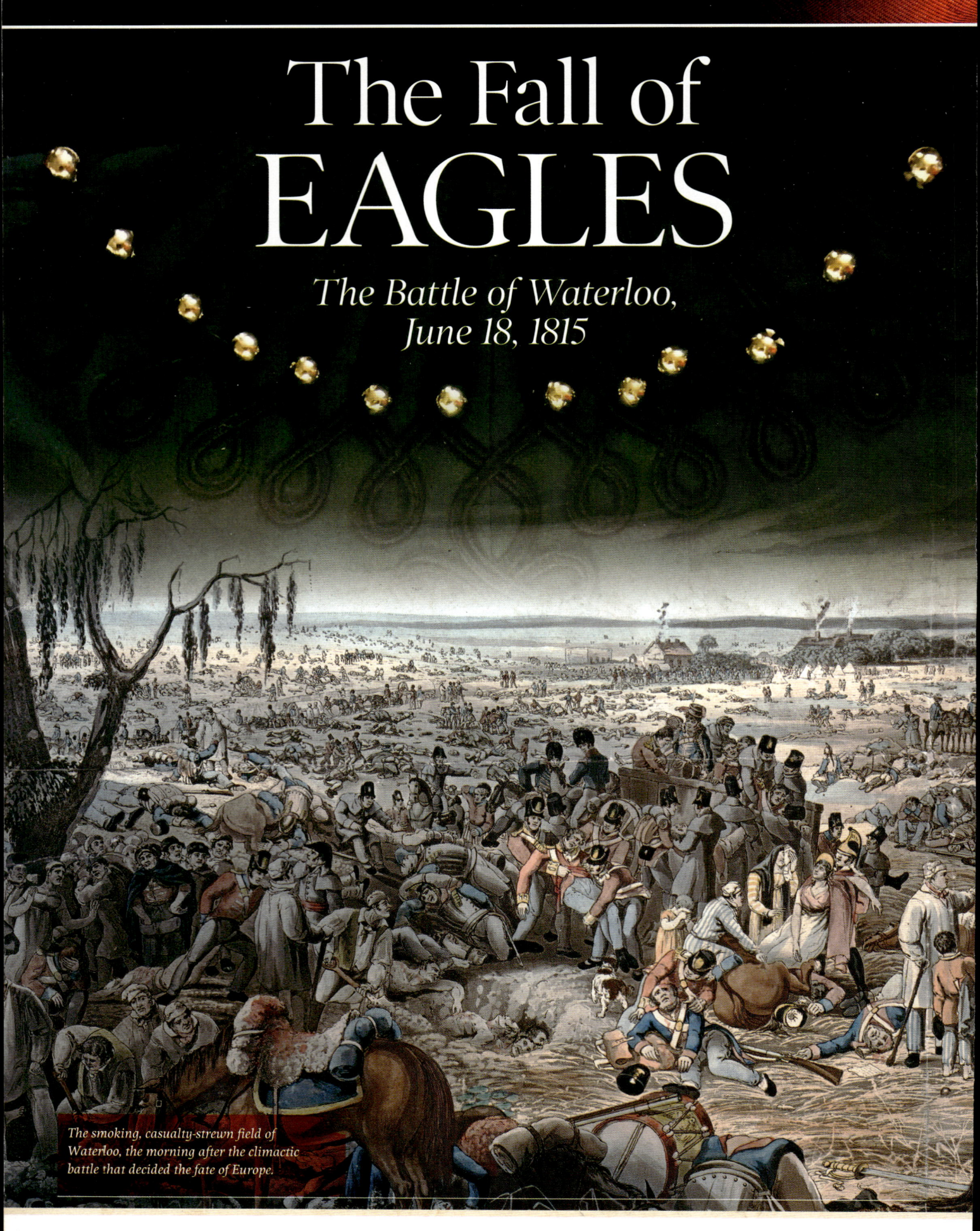

The Road to Waterloo
THE BATTLE OF WATERLOO

The Fall of EAGLES

The Battle of Waterloo, June 18, 1815

The smoking, casualty-strewn field of Waterloo, the morning after the climactic battle that decided the fate of Europe.

106 THE ROAD TO WATERLOO

As the sun rose over Quatre Bras on June 17, 1815, Wellington carefully considered what his next move should be. After the battle, the allies had set up camp on the battlefield, while the French, who were led by Marshal Michel Ney, took up a position to the south.

Based on his previous experience of the bludgeoning Ney, Wellington was braced for attack at any moment but to his surprise, there was no apparent movement other than a false alarm caused by a lost cavalry patrol in the early hours of the morning. He was also concerned about the lack of news from his Prussian counterpart Generalfeldmarschall Gebhard Leberecht von Blücher, who had engaged Emperor Napoléon I at Ligny the previous day.

Forced to conclude that the French had effectively cut off all communication between the two armies, Wellington sent a patrol along the Namur road to gather information - a necessary but hazardous enterprise that involved entering enemy-controlled territory. At 7.30 am, the patrol returned with the news that the Prussians were moving towards Wavre, upon which Wellington decided that it was time to take advantage of the French lack of movement and march north towards Brussels.

During a visit to the Belgian capital the previous year, he had come across the Mont-Saint-Jean escarpment close to the village of Waterloo, a steep slope that would give the British and their allies a distinct advantage over the French. It was therefore Wellington's intention to make for this location as swiftly as possible and take up position before Napoléon I's troops caught up.

To have the best chance of beating the French, Wellington required the assistance of the Prussians, but he was still unable to make contact with them. Despite having given orders for his own troops to move, there was some delay as he continued to wait for news. In the meantime, he gazed out over the quiet French encampment through his telescope, looking for even the smallest clue as to what they were planning to do next.

Ambiguity and advantage

Wellington's plans were finally put into motion when to his relief, a Prussian officer rode into camp with a report about the battle at Ligny and his army's subsequent retreat towards Wavre. Wellington sent the man back with his own update, and a request for two Prussian corps to support his action at Waterloo.

Once this was done, he turned his attention to mobilising his own men as stealthily and carefully as possible to mask their movements from the French camped nearby, who were still unnervingly quiet.

Ney had also been waiting anxiously for news of his master's success at Ligny. His priority was to prevent the two forces linking up and so he had decided in the absence of news to avoid spooking Wellington with an early morning

"To have the best chance of beating the French, Wellington required the assistance of the Prussians, but he was still unable to make contact with them."

The Road to Waterloo

THE BATTLE OF WATERLOO

ABOVE *Marshal Michel Ney, with his shock of red hair, leads a charge later in the battle. From a larger painting by French expressionist Louis Dumoulin.*

BELOW *Lieutenant General Henry Paget, Marquess of Anglesey and Earl of Uxbridge (in red) leads the 7th (Queen's Own) Light Dragoons (Hussars) into French infantry in this watercolour by Charles Turner Warren, 1823.*

offensive, in case he was driven into the arms of Blücher. It was better to wait for news, rather than risk souring a French victory.

In Ney's opinion, the best course of action would be for he and Napoléon I to combine forces as quickly as possible and take Wellington on before the Prussians were able to regroup and come to his aid, however as the hours rolled by, Napoléon I failed to make an appearance and the opportunity was eventually lost. Napoléon I's decision not to immediately pursue the retreating Prussians would turn out to be a huge mistake.

Instead, as the Prussians regrouped at Wavre and Blücher, who had been seriously injured at Ligny, recovered, Napoléon I ordered his men to set up camp and wasted the night and most of the following morning enjoying a late breakfast and then a tour of the previous day's battlefield before he finally turned his attention towards his next move.

Like Ney, he believed that the best policy would be to attack Wellington, but by the time he had made his intentions known to the Marshal, most of the allied troops were slipping away and Ney was forced to send a large force of French cuirassiers to harass the British cavalry that formed the rearguard. The resulting rolling skirmishes were made more difficult and perilous by a terrible thunderstorm and torrential rain.

Meanwhile, Napoléon I was under the impression that the defeated Prussian forces would be making their way towards Namur and Liege and sent the right wing of his army, which was headed by Marshal Emmanuel de Grouchy, Marquis de Grouchy, in pursuit, while reserving the left wing and reserves for his own attack upon Wellington. It was not until late that night that Grouchy realised his error and that the Prussians were in fact on their way north to Wavre, but even then he delayed before sending a despatch to Napoléon I to inform him that he intended to pursue them - by which time it was far too late for him to cut them off.

At the same time, Napoléon I and Ney, seriously hampered by the rain, were still pursuing the British and engaging in skirmishes as they tried to get the upper hand. There was a bitter standoff between the French and Allied cavalry at the town of Genappe, which involved several desperate charges through the narrow main street of the town, including an ultimately unsuccessful one by the British 7th (Queen's Own) Light Dragoons (Hussars), which was repulsed with relative ease by the French, who were then in their turn cut down by the 1st Life Guards during a magnificent charge that filled everyone who saw it with admiration.

Though they belatedly did their best to hamper the movements of the British, the French failed to inflict any severe damage and were unable to prevent them from reaching their goal, the Mont-Saint-Jean escarpment.

The Field of Waterloo

By the end of the June 17, Wellington and his men were safely ensconced in their prime position at Mont-Saint-Jean and busily setting up camp for the night. As he had hoped, they had been able to take up position in a long ridge where he could use the reverse slope to conceal his strength, as he had so many times during the Peninsula War.

As Wellington made his plans, he was heartened by a message sent by Blücher, who was at nearby Wavre with the regrouped Prussian army, assuring him: "I shall not come with two corps only, but with my whole army." This was exactly what Wellington needed to hear. Although he had advantages over the French thanks to their failure to capitalise on Ligny and his characteristic defensive position, the success of his plans relied heavily upon Prussian assistance. He expected the Prussians to take up position on the left of the field as it was closest to Wavre and so moved his own troops into the right and centre, while fortifying the Hougoumont estate on the right and the hamlet of Papelotte on the left to protect their flanks.

The following morning, Wellington was up early to inspect his troops and finalise his plans for the day ahead. He had 68,000 men under his command, predominantly British (including the King's German Legion and the loyal Hanoverians), supported by the Dutch and some of the smaller German states.

The French army, which amounted to 73,000 men, had taken up position on a ridge to the south but lacked line of sight on Wellington's army and knew that the fortifications at Hougoumont and Papelotte made his flanks formidable to turn. Nonetheless, Napoléon I appeared supremely confident that morning as he informed his officers: "Wellington is a bad general, the English are bad troops and this whole affair is nothing more than eating breakfast."

At 6 am, while Wellington was surveying the field at Waterloo, Blücher was at Wavre, overseeing a flank march of his troops, which would be led by the Prussian

LEFT *Wellington and his staff watch from Mont-Saint-Jean as the Battle of Waterloo unfolds around them in a great panorama.*

BELOW *This apocalyptic 1816 print shows the desperate fight for the farm at Hougoumont, which anchored the British right.*

IV Corps. However, thanks to exhaustion, poor weather conditions due to the previous evening's heavy rain and a fire that rendered several streets out of bounds, their progress was slow, and the last men were only able to leave six hours after the mobilisation began.

In the French camp, Napoléon I dismissed the idea that the Prussians would be able to join the battle,

THE ROAD TO WATERLOO 109

The Road to Waterloo

THE BATTLE OF WATERLOO

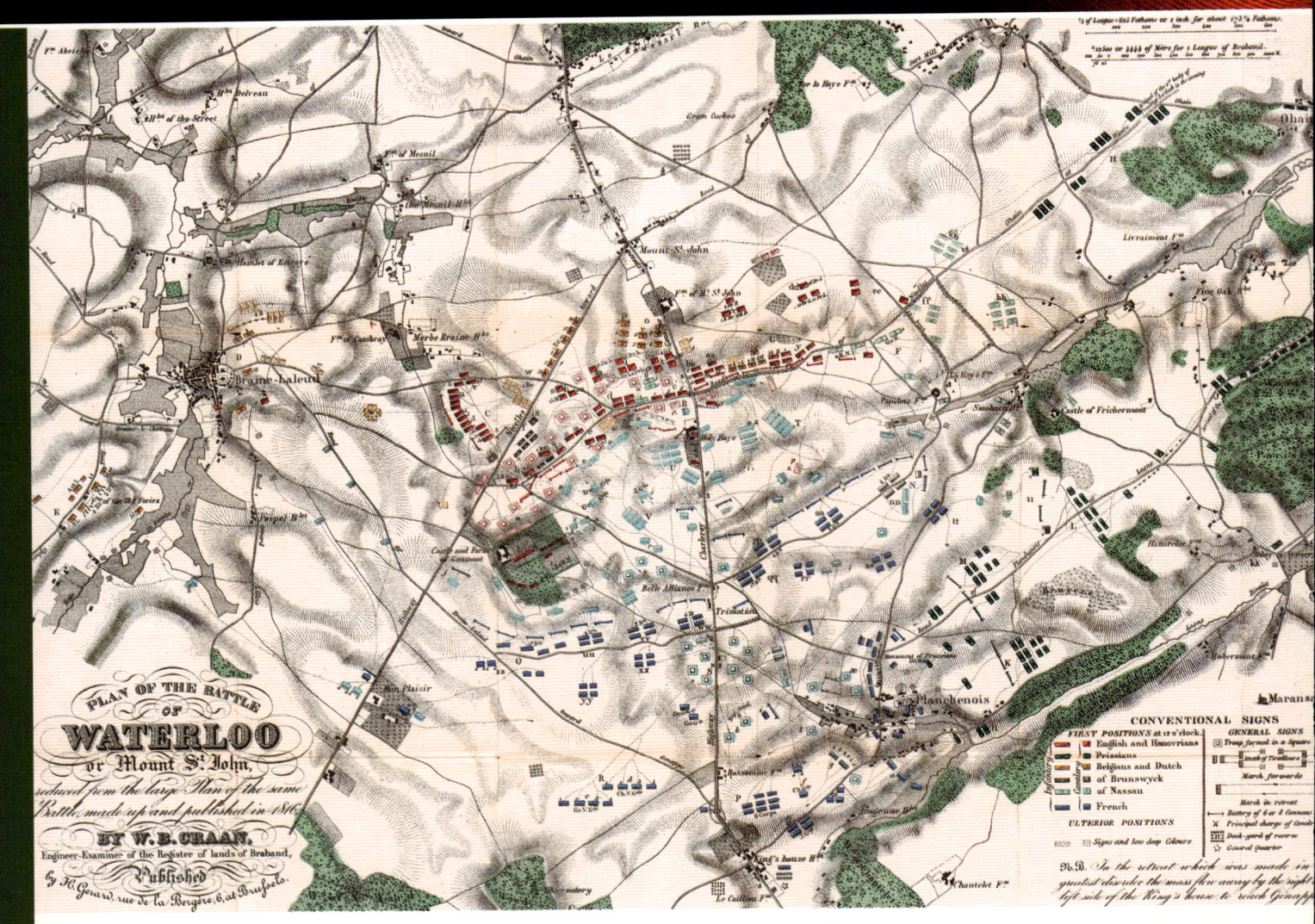

ABOVE *An incredibly detailed 1845 map of the Battle of Waterloo, well worth studying in detail.*

RIGHT *Wounded soldiers of the Principality of Brunswick-Wolfenbüttel, known as 'Black Brunswickers', are carried back through the British lines after their hammering from the Imperial Guard.*

insisting that they would need more time to recover from their ordeal at Ligny and that Grouchy, whom he had ordered to block them at Wavre, would easily be able to deal with them. Determined to follow Napoléon I's orders, Grouchy rejected the advice of his own subordinates who told him that as most of the Prussians were already on the move and it would be better to chase them to Waterloo.

Instead he insisted upon making his way to Wavre with 33,000 men - only to find that three corps were indeed well on their way to the battle, leaving behind the 17,000-strong Prussian III Corps, which had been ordered to linger at Wavre for just such an occasion as this.

The Peninsula veteran Captain Jonathan Leach, 95th Rifles, recalled with the pragmatism of the old soldier: "The two preceding days and nights having been spent in marching, fighting and without sleep, the floods of rain that descended the whole night of the 17th, which we passed on the position lying down by our arms, did not despair our repose. For myself, at least, I can answer, that I never in my whole life slept more soundly, although thoroughly drenched to the skin before I lay down the ground, which was like a snipe-marsh."

The bitter Battle for Hougoumont

Meanwhile, at Waterloo, the rain had stopped but as the ground was still sodden, Napoléon I decided to delay the onset of

ABOVE *A British Army-issue flintlock taken from the battlefield by an officer in a Dutch cavalry regiment as a trophy. It has the royal crest 'GR' and the words 'Tower', which denotes the arsenal at the Tower of London.*

the battle as long as possible as he was relying on his cavalry to deliver the killing blow. Finally, after several hours of tense waiting on both sides, he began his offensive with an attack on the fortified British post at Hougoumont, which was initially repulsed by heavy artillery fire before the French managed to gain some ground.

The fighting at Hougoumont was bitter and would last for several hours with the French managing to get past the defence to attack the troops massed on the British right. Although it has been suggested that Napoléon I used his relentless attack upon Hougoumont as a means of diverting Wellington's attention away from other areas of the field, it's clear that both Wellington and Napoléon I believed that holding Hougoumont was key to mastery of the field and so the area was hotly contested.

Meanwhile, while the two sides fought to gain the upper hand at Hougoumont, Napoléon I ordered that the 80 fearsome cannon that made up his Grande Batterie should be drawn up in the centre of the field and begin their relentless bombardment of the enemy - although with limited success thanks to Wellington's canny positioning of his men on the far side of the slope.

It was at one in the afternoon, shortly after the cannons began their bombardment that Napoléon I, who was surveying the battlefield from the farmhouse at Rossomme where he had established his base, noticed the arrival of increasingly large numbers of Prussian soldiers - Blücher's three corps who had marched from Wavre to reinforce the British. Chagrined by this unwelcome spectacle, he fired off a message to Grouchy, demanding that he leave Wavre and instead bring his men to Waterloo to cut down the Prussians as they arrived. Grouchy didn't receive this missive until that night, by which time he had already decided to attack the Prussian corps that had been left behind at Wavre. A pyrrhic victory as they easily defeated the Prussians, but their numbers could have easily made the difference at Waterloo, especially once Blücher's 50,000 Prussians arrived.

Hot on the heels of the cannon bombardment, Napoléon I's infantry made their first attack, advancing forward in a large columns. Although the fighting was initially very equal, the French, thanks in part to their superior numbers soon gained the upper hand and pushed the British troops before them, breaking their lines and scattering them.

Within an hour, it very much looked as though Napoléon I was winning the battle and Wellington's situation had become extremely perilous unless the promised Prussian troops made an appearance. Blücher's men had been arriving at Waterloo in a steady stream since midday, but by 3pm they still didn't make up enough force to turn the tide.

Desperate to regain the upper hand, Wellington's dashing cavalry commander Lieutenant General Henry Paget, Earl of Uxbridge - who had served in Sir John Moore's campaign in Portugal, presiding over the Battle of Sahagún (December 21, 1808) - brought the Household Brigade and the Union Brigade out of their concealment behind the ridge and sent them into the fray to assist their beleaguered infantry colleagues.

The Household Brigade charged down the embankment and swept through the enemy, scattering the French cuirassiers who were defending their left flank

BELOW *Lord Paget leads the Household Brigade into the French cuirassiers, by the Victorian military artist Orlando Norie, 1870.*

THE ROAD TO WATERLOO

The Road to Waterloo

THE BATTLE OF WATERLOO

and then crashing through the French infantry. However, they went too far into the field and found themselves in trouble until the Union Brigade, so named because it comprised cavalry regiments from England, Wales, Scotland and Ireland, came to their rescue.

In the ensuing fighting, the 2nd or Royal North British Dragoons - known as the 'Scots Greys' - behaved with particular heroism and captured the treasured eagle of the 45th Ligne, one of the leading French regiments, while the 1st (Royal) Dragoons captured that of the 105th. Although the British cavalry regiments were rightly considered to be amongst the finest in Europe, they suffered from a significant lack of discipline and were notoriously difficult to call back once their blood was up and they were in the thick of battle, which could lead to serious problems if they exhausted their horses before they made it back to their own lines. This had happened to the Household Brigade earlier and would now happen to the intrepid Union Brigade, who found themselves in the midst of the enemy and with little clear idea what to do next.

In the vicious fighting that ensued the gallant Scots Greys were virtually wiped out and the rest of the British cavalry suffered heavy losses. However, they had succeeded in their objective, which was to give the infantry some breathing space and decimate the French lines, which resulted in 3,000 enemy deaths and the capture of 2,000 prisoners.

The scythe of Napoléon

While the cavalry slashed their way through the French infantry lines,

ABOVE *A highland regiment forms a square and braces itself for the oncoming French cuirassiers and lancers by William Heath, 1836.*

RIGHT *Towards the end of the day Paget was hit by a cannonball, exclaiming to the nearby Wellington "By God, sir, I've lost my leg!" He was forced to have it amputated and replaced with a prosthesis made from willow and leather.* SCIENCE MUSEUM, LONDON CC BY 4.0

Wellington ordered that the casualties should be moved behind the lines so that they were out of the line of fire. Observing this movement from his own vantage point on the other side of the field, Ney interpreted it as a general retreat and decided to take advantage by pressing home with another attack. However, as most of the remaining French infantry were either caught up in the abortive attack on Hougoumont or had been scattered by the devastating charges of the British cavalry, he had few troops at his disposal and so was forced instead to resort to a retaliatory cavalry charge - much to Napoléon I's annoyance as he was planning to bring them into play much later in the day.

The first charge, which involved 4,800 cuirassiers and a light cavalry division of the Imperial Guard, was easily repulsed by Wellington's infantry, which responded by forming dense squares, four ranks deep, which stood their ground behind a thick hedge of bayonets. The artillery took refuge within the squares as the French cavalry attacked and then hastened to their cannons to fire upon them with deadly accuracy as they retreated. Even more devastating were the actions of one artillery captain who refused to take shelter but instead insisted upon firing his battery of six 9-pounders at the French cavalry as they charged, later describing the effects of his relentless and perfectly timed assaults as "a fall of men and horses like that of grass before the mower's scythe."

When the first charges failed to make an impression and resulted in tremendous loss of both men and horses, Ney sent in an even bigger assault of around 9,000 men with additions from the heavy cavalry corps. His cavalry commander General François Christophe de Kellermann quickly realised that the enterprise was doomed to failure and so did his best to keep his most elite regiments from the field, only to be overruled by Ney, who insisted that they should join the fray.

For the British, the advance of the French cavalry was a terrifying spectacle, with Captain Rees Howell Gronow, 1st Regiment of Foot Guards, later recalling that "not a man present who survived could have forgotten in after life the awful grandeur of that charge [...] On they came until they got near enough, whilst the very earth seemed to vibrate beneath the thundering tramp of the mounted host [...] In an almost incredibly short period they were within 20 yards of us, shouting 'Vive l'Empereur!'"

However, although the French cavalry was an indisputably impressive sight, it failed to make much impression upon the Anglo allied infantry who stood firm against their repeated attack. If the French infantry had been able to support them then they may have had more success, but they were initially unable to get close enough to the action to be of much use until Ney ordered another full infantry attack combined with more cavalry charges and a heavy artillery bombardment.

At the same time as Ney's triple-pronged attack on the British infantry, General Jean-Baptiste Drouet, Comte d'Erlon's troops were attacking La Haye Sainte, a walled farm house in a crucial position at the bottom of the escarpment. It had been heavily fortified and garrisoned by 400 German and British troops. The French had already made several attempts to seize La Haye Sainte, which would be a valuable asset as it would make it easier for them to penetrate Wellington's centre.

At around 4 pm, the defenders ran out of ammunition and when the French seized control shortly afterwards, they used it to move men and horse artillery within 60 yards of Wellington's now worryingly exposed centre, which they proceeded to bombard at short range with canister, causing heavy losses. Captain Leach of the 95th Rifles, recalled: "For several hours afterwards they kept up a dreadful fire from the loop-holes and windows in the upper part of it, whereby they raked the hillock so as to render it untenable by our battalion."

While the French artillery pulverised the British centre, multitudes of tirailleurs poured into La Haye Sainte and began to fire upon the square formations of infantry, causing even more havoc. They even fired at Wellington and his command when they rode to close to the farmhouse, causing them to flee through a nearby hedgerow. The British situation was now looking hopeless - they were unable to take back La Haye Sainte, their cavalry was spent and the incessant bombardment of the French artillery and swarming of the French cavalry meant that the infantry was unable to break free and defend themselves.

For Wellington, who had taken refuge in the centre of an infantry square while several of his staff were killed, it had become more imperative than ever that the Prussians make their promised move. "The time they occupied in approaching seemed interminable," he wrote later. "Both they and my watch seemed to have stuck fast."

The Prussians to Plancenoit

Wellington and Blücher had agreed earlier that if the British centre was under attack then the Prussian should attack Plancenoit, which was ideally placed to act as a conduit to the French rear. General Georges Mouton, Comte de Lobau was sent to intercept the Prussian forces before they reached Plancenoit, but his troops were forced out of the way by a lethal bayonet charge before being pounded by artillery fire, which sent them into a wild retreat.

Although the Prussians were briefly able to seize their prize, they were quickly driven out again by the reserves sent by Napoléon I, who was determined not to let it fall from his clutches. Meanwhile, the Prussian I Corps, led by General Hans Ernst Karl, Graf von Zieten had arrived on the battlefield to support Wellington's left, much to the dismay of the French who had hoped to see Grouchy rather than his Prussian prey.

The arrival of the long expected and much longed for Prussians had an incredible effect on British morale and enabled them to push back against the French advances. However, Wellington's centre was still dangerously exposed and at 7.30 pm, Napoléon I decided that

BELOW *The 2nd or Royal North British Dragoons - better known as the Scots Greys - make their decisive charge in this watercolour by Orlando Norie, 1880.*

The Road to Waterloo

THE BATTLE OF WATERLOO

A melodramatic German depiction of Napoleon leaving the battlefield as his army fights on, making his way through the rear echelons of wounded and prisoners.

"Those amongst us who had witnessed in the Peninsula many well-contested actions," wrote Captain Leach, 95th Rifles, "were agreed on one point, that we had never before seen such determination displayed by the French as on this day."

it was time to deploy the Imperial Guard, which had never been defeated in combat and which he hoped would definitively crush Wellington's centre and sweep his troops as far from the Prussians as possible. Although Napoléon I himself oversaw their deployment, it was Ney who led them into battle against the weakened centre.

The Imperial Guard nearly punched a hole in the British line until they were thrown back by Dutch forces led by Lieutenant General David Hendrik Chassé at which point other regiments moved in for the kill, eventually forcing the French to retreat. A moment of gentle irony, following the annexation of the Netherlands to the French Empire, Chassé had fought under d'Erlon at the Battle of Vitoria (June 21, 1813) and the Battle of the Pyrenees (July 25, 1813). What a difference two years can make, although Wellington was still wary of the mercurial Dutchman.

When the news spread through the French ranks that the great Imperial Guard, the pride of their army, had been forced to retreat there was a tremendous uproar as shouts of "The Guard is retreating! Every man for himself!" rang through the air, only to be swiftly cut off as Wellington, triumphantly raised himself on his stirrups, waved his hat in the air and ordered a general advance of the entire army on the confused and fleeing French.

The moment was made all the sweeter by the fact that after hours of intense fighting, the Prussians had just managed to storm and seize Plancenoit and gain access to the French rear. Although Napoléon I had been confident of victory, he had nonetheless stationed two battalions of the Old Guard nearby to either act as a last-ditch reserve or, in the case of defeat, act as his protection during a retreat.

Seeing the battle turn into a confusing and shambolic melee, he now made a final attempt to rally his army behind these two élite battalions but to no avail as his left, right and centre were all smashed beyond repair and his armies were in an irretrievable mess and so they too were forced to retreat, surrounded by the straggling, shell-shocked and devastated survivors.

That evening, as darkness fell upon the torn and ravaged battlefield, which was littered with thousands of dead and dying, Wellington and Blücher met for the first time that day and saluted each other. Their victory over the French was complete but had come at a high cost to both sides with a total of 24,000 men on the allied side killed, injured or missing in action while the French lost 41,000, including the 6,000 men who were captured during the retreat.

"Those amongst us who had witnessed in the Peninsula many well-contested actions," wrote Captain Leach, 95th Rifles, "were agreed on one point, that we had never before seen such determination displayed by the French as on this day. Fighting under the eye of Napoléon, and feeling what a great and important stake they contested for, will account for their extraordinary perseverance and valour, and for the vast efforts which they made for victory."

Napoléon I's last stand had ended.